PROGRESSION AND PRO
IN PHYSICAL EDUCATIO

CW00925317

How well do I take account of the needs of different classes and individual learners to facilitate and enhance progress? Do I plan for progress based on where learners are currently at? Does the curriculum facilitate and enhance progress?

Exploring these questions and more, this book examines what progress in physical education looks like and conditions for facilitating and enhancing the progress of individual learners across different domains of learning.

Progression and Progress in Physical Education contains 12 units, each of which highlights an aspect of progression or progress in physical education. Throughout, the book emphasises that it is individual learners that make progress therefore highlighting the importance of catering for the holistic, individual learner. Grouped into four sections, units cover:

- What is meant by progression, progress and learning?
- The holistic nature of individual learners
- The Physical, Cognitive and Affective Domains of learning
- Teaching to facilitate and enhance progress
- Recognising and charting progress
- The role of the curriculum in facilitating and enhancing progress
- The broader context in which physical education teachers work

Filled throughout with examples of existing good practice and useful tips, this text will support all primary and secondary physical education teachers in facilitating and enhancing learner progress in physical education.

Susan Capel is a Professor Emerita at Brunel University, London.

Margaret Whitehead is currently a Visiting Professor at the University of Bedfordshire and an Adjunct Professor at the University of Canberra.

Julia Lawrence is Assistant Professor at Northumbria University and Secondary Lead Mentor for Scarborough Teaching Alliance.

PROGRESSION AND PROGRESS IN PHYSICAL EDUCATION

Susan Capel, Margaret Whitehead and Julia Lawrence

Routledge
Taylor & Francis Group

LONDON AND NEW YORK

Designed cover image: © Getty Images

First edition published 2025
by Routledge
4 Park Square, Milton Park, Abingdon, Oxon, OX14 4RN

and by Routledge
605 Third Avenue, New York, NY 10158

Routledge is an imprint of the Taylor & Francis Group, an informa business

© 2025 Susan Capel, Margaret Whitehead and Julia Lawrence

British Library Cataloguing-in-Publication Data
A catalogue record for this book is available from the British Library

ISBN: 978-1-032-00118-0 (hbk)
ISBN: 978-1-032-00120-3 (pbk)
ISBN: 978-1-003-17282-6 (ebk)

DOI: 10.4324/9781003172826

Typeset in Interstate
by Newgen Publishing UK

CONTENTS

FIGURES

TABLES

SCENARIOS

ANNEXES

Introduction

The core mission of education is to ensure that all learners learn. Thus, the notion of progress in learning by each and every learner lies at the heart of schooling. It follows that the responsibility of all teachers, including physical education teachers, is to facilitate and enhance the progress of individual learners. This book aims to support that endeavour.

The title of this book is *Progression and Progress in Physical Education*. The words progression and progress are both nouns which relate to the process of moving (improving or developing) from one state or stage to another over a period of time. However, in this book, progression refers to the conditions which need to be in place to enable the process of moving from one state or stage to another to occur. It includes constituents of teaching that contribute to facilitating and enhancing learner progress. On the other hand, progress refers to actually moving from one state or stage to another, i.e. the learning which is taking place. Generally, where the word progress is used in the book, it subsumes the word learning. Where we refer to facilitating and enhancing the progress of all learners this includes establishing the right conditions to enable progress to occur. The words progression and progress are used either in combination or individually in this book, depending on the specific focus of the point being made.

This purpose of this book

Demos (2005, p.4) highlighted "What happens in school should enhance students' capacities to learn and their motivation to learn." Facilitating and enhancing the progress of each and every learner is complex and challenging. It requires all teachers to ask the question 'How will this impact on learning?' in relation to everything they do.

This includes having a progressive curriculum which is translated into relevant learning activities and teaching approaches that facilitate and enhance the progress of each and every learner. However, as each learner is different and unique, they need to be treated as individuals who have different needs and progress at different rates. Hence, the curriculum, learning activities and teaching approaches need to be differentiated/adapted appropriately to meet the needs of individual learners.

As each learner is a unique individual, so is each teacher. They have their own personality and attributes from which they create their own unique teaching style. There is no one right way to teach, to provide the right conditions to facilitate and enhance progress; different

DOI: 10.4324/9781003172826-1

learning activities and different teaching approaches are needed by different classes and different learners at different times and in different contexts.

It is a daunting, but worthwhile, challenge for a teacher to provide the right conditions to facilitate and enhance the progress of each and every learner they teach. This book is designed to challenge and support teachers in this endeavour. It aims to highlight the importance of focusing on progression and progress in physical education and enable teachers to identify constituents of their teaching which they can develop, adapt and refine to effectively create the conditions to facilitate and enhance the progress of all learners in their own specific context.

There is a great deal to consider for a teacher to be able to develop, adapt and refine teaching to effectively create the conditions to facilitate and enhance the progress of all learners in their own specific context. For example, they need:

- Knowledge about learning
- Knowledge about individual learners
- Knowledge of the curriculum to be taught
- A wide repertoire of learning activities and teaching approaches on which to draw and well developed professional judgement to decide which activity(ies) and approach(es) they may use to facilitate and enhance the progress of individual learners at a specific moment in time in a specific context
- To be clear about and reflect on their beliefs, values and attitudes about the subject, about teaching, about learning and about learners themselves and reflect on how these impact on their commitment to, as well as their actual practice in, facilitating and enhancing the progress of all learners
- To reflect critically on an on-going basis, on the progress of individual learners, as well as the conditions to facilitate and enhance progress and the impact of their own teaching and of the curriculum on learner progress
- Identify areas for their own learning and development as a teacher in relation to better creating the conditions for facilitating and enhancing the progress of each and every learner.

About us

In writing this book we have inevitably drawn on our own experiences over many years of involvement in physical education. These experiences have influenced our beliefs, values and attitudes, our views of, and priorities for, physical education. In turn these influence the book, including the selection and presentation of content.

This book reflects our belief in the importance of prioritising progression and the progress of all learners. It is an honest attempt to encourage all teachers to put learner progress at the centre of all work in the subject. Although we hope teachers agree with the importance of prioritising progression and the progress of each and every learner, and have a commitment to making this the focus of their work, we recognise that teachers may not agree with everything (or indeed anything) we have written in the book. In either case, we would be delighted if they take this work as a starting point and develop it further.

About teachers

We recognise that teachers have different beliefs, values and attitudes about physical education and its purpose, as well as about teaching, learning and learners. We also recognise that they have different amounts and types of experience in physical education and are working with different learners in different contexts.

In light of the above, whatever a teacher's beliefs, values, attitudes and experience we want them to reflect on, constructively critique and actively engage with the content of the book to consider, for example:

- Their beliefs, values and attitudes and why they hold these
- Whether or not they agree with what we are advocating (and more specifically what we have written) in this book
- Why they do or do not agree with what we are advocating (and have written) about facilitating and enhancing the progress of individual learners, including the impact of their beliefs, values, attitudes and experience
- How the content in this book can be developed and used to put progression and progress at the heart of physical education for each and every learner who experiences the subject, wherever they are and whatever the context.

We also recognise that teachers are busy. There are many things which command their attention on a day-to-day basis. They therefore have to juggle myriad things. However, in our view, what can be more important than the progress of all learners they teach? Further, focusing on the conditions for facilitating and enhancing learner progress may not take up more of a teacher's valuable time – rather, it may be that they use the same time in a different way.

About the book

The book includes 12 Units of varying length. Each Unit focuses on a specific element of progression and progress in physical education. Each Unit is designed to stand alone. Thus, if you only read one Unit, there is enough information so that you do not have to keep referring to other Units in the book. However, there is inevitably overlap of content between Units. As a result, some content is deliberately included in more than one Unit, albeit generally considered from a different perspective.

The Units are grouped into four sections.

Section 1 Progression, progress and the individual learner

Section 1 contains three Units. The first Unit concentrates on the importance of focusing on progression and progress in physical education in order to explain the raison d'etre for this book.

Unit 2 looks at what is meant by progression and progress. Within this Unit, the concept of learning is also considered, which, as highlighted above, is essential for progress to be made. It is individual learners that learn; hence Unit 3 focuses on the nature of the individual learner – being both holistic and unique.

Section 2 Progress in the Physical, Cognitive and Affective Domains of learning

Section 2 builds from section 1 to concentrate on the three domains of the holistic nature of learning we view as integral to progress in physical education; progress in the Physical Domain, the Cognitive Domain and the Affective Domain. These Units represent the core of the book.

Unit 4 introduces the domains and how these are considered within the book. It also explains the Aspects, Foci and Ladders of Progress which are integral to Units 5, 6 and 7.

Units 5, 6 and 7 consider, respectively, the Physical, Cognitive and Affective Domains of learning in physical education, each being subject to clarification and explanation and proposals for recognising progress in Aspects and Foci of learning in the domain through Ladders of Progress.

In Units 5, 6 and 7 the three domains are considered separately. However, as learners are holistic, the three domains are in fact significantly interdependent. Learner progress depends on the capabilities within these domains working together, in concert. For example, progress in the Physical Domain is facilitated by declarative knowledge as well as interest, motivation and positive experiences in the subject. Likewise, declarative knowledge is enhanced by its application in practice (procedural knowledge). In addition, progress in the Physical and Cognitive Domains is enhanced where learners are motivated, confident, apply themselves and persist in their learning.

Unit 8 brings the domains together and looks at how they interact in physical education, based on the premise that effective learning requires a blend of doing, thinking and feeling.

Section 3 The conditions for progression in physical education

In section 3 attention turns to the conditions to facilitate and enhance the progress of all learners in physical education, i.e. it focuses on progression. A book such as this can only support teachers in facilitating and enhancing learner progress by identifying what we view as some significant constituents of the teaching enterprise on which they can reflect and/or incorporate into their practice.

There are three Units in this section. These are: Unit 9, *Teaching to facilitate and enhance progress*. This Unit includes teaching holistic, individual and unique learners, using the Ladders of Progress identified in Units 5, 6 and 7. It also highlights some constituents of teaching which underpin each of the principles for facilitating and enhancing progress (see Units 2 and 3) so that individual learners are more likely to progress.

It is no good facilitating and enhancing progress if it is not recognised and used to inform further progress. Hence, Unit 10 focuses on *Recognising and charting progress*. It includes sections on observation *for* learning, assessment *for* learning, feedback *for* learning and charting progress *for* learning. We include observation in this Unit because we believe it is a key skill which teachers need to facilitate and enhance learner progress in physical education, but in our view is a skill which can be overlooked and underdeveloped.

Unit 11 focuses on *the Curriculum* and its role as a condition for progress to occur; as a broad framework to guide teaching to make progress in physical education possible, rather than a series of units of work or lessons that should be strictly adhered to.

Section 4 The broader context

Physical education teachers cannot maximise the impact of progression on the progress of individual learners by working independently, however effective an individual teacher is. Each teacher is part of a broader context. This broader context is the subject of section 4. In this section there is one Unit. This Unit (Unit 12) considers three parts of *the broader context*; the importance of the team working together and pulling in the same direction to create a coherent experience for all learners, the wider school and the external context.

Although the content is divided into sections and Units; as stated above, there is some content which is deliberately included in a number of Units. Where content is included in a number of Units, it is generally considered from a different perspective; designed to reinforce that in other Units.

Throughout the book, we deliberately do not focus on constituents of teaching and components of learning in physical education which we perceive are covered in the wealth of material, readily available in text and on-line. These include books and guidance written in various formats on, for example, teaching skills, teaching strategies or approaches, creating curricula and units of work, planning individual lessons, the analyses of Movement Patterns that are needed to engage in a range of different Movement Activities and learning Movement Activities. It is beyond the remit of this book to do justice to all this work. However, as a teacher focuses on their own practice to create the conditions to facilitate and enhance progress, where they perceive that some constituents of teaching need further development, for example, teaching skills or knowledge of constituents of teaching and components of learning, they are recommended to seek out more information from a range of other sources.

How you might use this book

To reiterate, this book is designed to put progression and the progress of individual learners at the heart of physical education. To achieve this, it provides guidance designed to support teachers in focusing their attention on ensuring the conditions are right for progress to occur and prioritising and improving their ability to facilitate and enhance the progress of individual learners in physical education. It is also designed to support teachers to recognise whether or not individual learners are making progress and, as a result, on how they can better create conditions to facilitate and enhance learner progress. We hope the book inspires teachers to prioritise this in their work.

Overall, the book is designed so that Units taken together build up a picture of progression and learner progress. But how you choose to use this book depends on many factors, including your beliefs, values and attitudes, your experiences and current practice in relation to facilitating and enhancing the progress of individual learners in your own context.

First, you can, of course, read the book from cover to cover (indeed, we would like to think of it as a book you find you become so engrossed in that you cannot put it down!!). If, for example, you are interested in progression and facilitating and enhancing the progress of individual learners but have limited knowledge about progression and progress in the subject or want to refresh your memory or to see how we view this important topic, you might choose to read the book from cover to cover. Following a first read you may select the Units most relevant for your particular needs.

However, we are realistic – not only about the book being so engrossing you cannot put it down (it is, after all, a textbook), but also about the limited amount of time most of you have to read and/or think about and reflect on your daily practice generally as well as a specific component of that practice. Thus, rather than read it from cover to cover, you might dip in and out of the book. Indeed, depending on your reason for reading the book, the book is designed so that you can select the content most appropriate, pertinent and/or of interest to you in your context and concentrate on that. For example, you may be interested in a particular element of progression and/or progress, or you may identify a particular issue in your practice in relation to the progress of individual learners and be interested in reading about that to support you in developing your practice. For example, if you are interested in:

- What is meant by progression and progress in physical education and why this should be the priority in lessons, you might start with Unit 2, which starts by defining progression, progress and learning
- The progress of individual learners, you might start with Unit 3 to help understand learners as being holistic and unique
- What progress looks like in the Physical, Cognitive and Affective Domains – separately and/or together, you might start with Units 4 to 8 which highlight some levels of progress in specific Aspects and Foci within the specific domain
- What a teacher might do to effect progression in order to facilitate and enhance the progress of individual learners, you might start with Unit 9 – teaching
- How progress can be recognised, you might start with Unit 10 – recognising and charting progress, which looks at observation, assessment, feedback and charting progress
- Understanding the role and importance of the curriculum in providing an optimal context and broad guidelines for progression and hence progress, you might start with Unit 11 – the curriculum
- The broader context, including the importance of working with others to facilitate and enhance progress for each learner in the school, above and beyond what an individual teacher can do alone, you might start with Unit 12 – the broader context. This broader context involves working together as a department and working with others both within the school (particularly the headteacher and governors) and in the external environment in which physical education operates (such as agencies and organisations outside the school).

In order to decide where to start reading, you might reflect on how you respond to the brief descriptions of the sections and Units in the book (above). Does any one section or Unit of the book prompt you to say, for example, 'I would like to learn more about that;' or 'I don't focus on that;' or 'I would like to consider what I do in relation to that and how I could do it better with' If so, that might be a good place to start. If you are a teacher, you might also ask yourself some questions, such as for example:

- How well do I take account of the needs of different classes and individual learners in order for all learners to progress?

- Do I plan for progress based on where learners are currently at?
- Does the curriculum facilitate and enhance progress?

Thus, put simply, we encourage you to use the book in the most appropriate way for you. However you use the book and whatever your starting point, we hope this leads you onto other elements of progression and progress within the book to enable you to appreciate the importance of progression and progress in physical education and, if you are a teacher, develop, adapt and refine your teaching in order to facilitate and enhance the progress of each and every learner in your lessons. We hope also it encourages you to refer to other resources to support you in facilitating and enhancing progress, readily available in text or on-line.

We consider reflection essential in developing the conditions to effectively facilitate and enhance progress and encourage teachers to engage in the reflective process as they engage with this book; to think about and reflect on their current approaches to/practice in relation to progression and progress, to consider what they currently do and how this might change/develop as a result of reading and engaging with the contents of this book.

Essential themes throughout the book

There are a number of recurring themes which permeate the whole book.

In order for learners to progress, it follows that they need to be involved in learning activities that are self-fulfilling and meaningful. To achieve this, we believe that learners

- Should be at the heart of all teaching
- Should be respected as holistic
- Should be appreciated as unique
- Should be engaged in learning that facilitates and enhances progress

These four essential themes permeate the structure and writing of this book, such that in ensuring the conditions to allow for progress to be made, it is recommended that, for example:

- The design of learning activities prioritises progression and the progress of individual learners
- All components of learning enable learners to make progress towards an aim
- The lesson focus is the learners rather than the content and/or the lesson plan
- Individual learners are treated holistically in that their physical, cognitive and affective potentials are recognised
- The individual learner is catered for as a priority, with inclusion and differentiated/adapted teaching used as appropriate
- All judgements on progress relate solely to the individual; the progress of an individual learner should not be compared to that of others
- The identification of learner progress guides future progress.

Other resources

Whilst this book is written to stand-alone, the book will not suffice alone. Although we have not attempted to provide guidance to further resources in the book, the references in each

Unit should provide a starting point to enable other sources in relation to specific parts of the content of the Unit to be identified and explored in greater depth in order to increase knowledge and understanding of progression and progress as considered in this book. There is also considerable relevant material readily available in text and on-line to which you can refer.

And so ...

We sincerely hope you find this practical workbook useful in considering how to facilitate and enhance the progress of all classes and each individual learner. We also sincerely hope that the book provides a starting point from which work on progression and progress can be developed further for the benefit of all learners who experience the subject.

We wish you well in both endeavours and look forward to seeing the fruits of your work in future years.

Susan Capel
Margaret Whitehead
Julia Lawrence
May 2024

Unit 1 The Importance of Progression and Progress in Physical Education

1.1 Introduction

The core mission of all education is to ensure that all learners learn. Thus, the notion of progress by each and every learner lies at the heart of schooling. Schooling here refers to the education that takes place in the years during which learners are required to be at school; a journey from the age of 4/5 years to the age of 16/19 years. Throughout this journey, a key intention of schooling is to facilitate and enhance the progress of every learner across the whole curriculum towards one or more aims. Therefore, everything teachers do, including planning and translating the curriculum into practice, the learning activities and teaching approaches used, should facilitate and enhance the progress of all learners.

In respect of schooling as a whole, aims frequently include preparedness for the world of work, initiation into the culture of the parent community, the development of confident independence and sensitive interpersonal skills. For example, the general requirements of the current National Curriculum in England are that it is balanced and broadly based and

(a) Promotes the spiritual, moral, cultural, mental and physical development of pupils at the school and of society, and
(b) Prepares pupils at the school for the opportunities, responsibilities and experiences of later life (Department for Education (DfE), 2014, p. 5).

It follows that facilitating and enhancing learner progress is an important issue for all teachers and subject areas, not least physical education. It is the responsibility of all teachers (age/phase and subject specific) to focus on progress in order to allow each individual learner the opportunity to work towards achieving the aims of both the school curriculum as a whole and the subject curriculum across the years during which learners are required to attend school and to take part in a subject.

It is therefore pertinent to pose the question 'How good are teachers of physical education at ensuring the conditions are in place to facilitate and enhance progress and then facilitating and enhancing progress in their teaching?' We are somewhat concerned and would have to answer that progression and progress do not always seem to have a high priority for some physical education teachers at some times. Although all teachers know

DOI: 10.4324/9781003172826-2

that progression and the progress of all learners in physical education should be prioritised and the focus of all their work, unfortunately, sometimes, a range of other priorities may take precedence. For example, the Association Internationale des Écoles Supérieures d'Éducation Physique (International Association for Physical Education in Higher Education, AIESEP), 2020, p. 7) states that

> Learning should be the goal of physical education, as it is of all education. Physical education is not about playing games or sport, nor is it about simply building fitness or accumulating a minimum amount of physical activity during lessons; the focus should be on purposeful learning.

Further, the Office for Standards in Education, Children's Services and Skills (Ofsted (2023a) highlighted the focus on progress when it stated

> it is important to consider whether PE in schools is nurturing pupils' physical development and teaching them the important knowledge they need to participate in sport and physical activity and make informed decisions about how to live a healthy, active life.

Thus the focus of this book is on progression and on the progress of all learners in physical education (please refer to the Glossary, Unit 2 for definitions, including knowledge, learning, progress, progression).

1.2 Why it is important to focus on progression and progress?

We have suggested that some teachers at some times, do not prioritise progression and progress. As a result, lessons may not specifically focus on the learning taking place and respond to the progress or otherwise of individual learners.

In addition to some teachers not prioritising progression and the progress of individual learners at some times, it seems to us that progression and progress are also frequently overlooked or, at best, seen as implicit, within much current literature. To us, it seems there is a sense that learning is automatically occurring in physical education and this does not need to be questioned. In light of what we perceive to be the lack of priority being given to progression and progress, we have identified the need to focus on what is a very (perhaps the most) important consideration in physical education; progression and progress.

As a result of our perception that progression and learner progress does not seem to have a high priority for some teachers of physical education at some times or to have a high profile in literature on physical education, the incentive to focus on this aspect of physical education is fourfold. That is to:

1. Highlight the importance of focusing on progression and progress in physical education
2. Advocate for putting learners and their progress at the heart of physical education
3. Provide guidance and support to focus attention on planning and teaching for progression, to recognise whether learners are making progress or not and, as a result, on how to better facilitate and enhance the progress of individual learners
4. Provide a starting point for work on progression and progress to be taken forward in a practical way to benefit all learners.

We are somewhat disappointed to have identified what we perceive is a need to focus on progression and progress. To us, it is perplexing that learner progress is not the top priority for all teachers of physical education at all times as it seems that the whole rationale behind physical education, being to facilitate and enhance each individual learner's progress in developing physical competence, is being lost. One of the consequences of this is that learners are being, in some way, 'neglected.' This does not mean that learners are disregarded. Learners are generally engaged in a variety of tasks in which they are active and safe, what Placek (1983) called 'busy, happy and good.' However, they may not be making progress.

This lack of attention to progression, what has been learnt and what progress has been made, can have one or more consequences, including that the needs of individual learners may well be being overlooked, such that:

- Some learners may be expected to work on tasks that are too challenging and thus get disillusioned, while
- Other learners may be set tasks that are not challenging enough or that they have worked on before and thus get bored.

In both scenarios, learners are unlikely to make progress. As will be seen in later units in this book, learners are unique individuals with different needs and, in order to progress, these needs should be catered for; it is essential that appropriate challenges and support are given to individual learners in order for them to progress.

It is suggested that there could be at least four possible reasons for a lack of focus on progression and learner progress. These relate to:

1. A lack of consensus as to the core purpose and aims of the subject
2. Reliance on national or school curricula, schemes and units of work and/or lesson plans
3. Teachers being expected to do too many things
4. An attitude that, historically this is what has always been done, so why fix it if it's not broken.

These are considered briefly in turn.

1. In order for learners to progress, it is important that learning is directed towards an aim. All subjects in the curriculum are expected to have clear long-term aims and a well-articulated process to reach these. In respect of physical education, there has traditionally been no clear consensus as to the aims of the subject, nor are aims consistently presented or justified. Indeed, a cursory investigation would highlight a variety of aims that have taken centre stage over the last 50 years. For example, at times the chief focus has been on health and fitness, while at other times it has been on talent identification. Again at times enjoyment has been seen as key, while at other times personal and social skills have been paramount (see Whitehead 2021a) for further information about different aims for physical education). This is further complicated by aims held by individual physical education teachers (implicit or explicit) and/or any organisations involved in teaching physical education in a specific school which may not be the same as those specified in that specific school curriculum.

Without clear and consistent aims (both for physical education as a whole and within an individual school), it is very difficult to facilitate and enhance progress. Consequently, the subject may appear to lack direction, purpose and serious intent. As a result, not having clear aims can sometimes result in the subject not being taken seriously by learners, parents/carers and other members of staff.

2. Some teachers may presume that following a published curriculum, along with associated schemes and units of work, and maybe even lesson plans, will automatically build in progression and facilitate and enhance learner progress. However, in order to facilitate and enhance progress, the curriculum must be designed intentionally and incrementally such that the important knowledge learners need to progress is sequenced and coherent and they are given enough time for learning to be secure before they move on to new learning. This includes the curriculum in a secondary school building on that in the primary schools from which learners transfer. A curriculum designed around a range of Movement Patterns and Movement Activities will not achieve this unless their selection is based on what learners need to learn through those Movement Patterns and Movement Activities at a specific time, in order to progress.

    Where a set curriculum is followed, to a degree individual learners may become 'lost' in the process of adhering to set curricula, schemes and units of work and/or lesson plans. In this book we suggest that a curriculum should be viewed as a broad framework to guide teaching. A curriculum, schemes and units of work and set lesson plans should not be strictly adhered to. As will become clear, decisions about facilitating and enhancing progress should be made based on what learners need at a specific time. Learners need to be at the heart of all decisions about the curriculum, schemes and units of work and lessons. Hence, schemes and units of work as well as lessons need to be differentiated/adapted to the needs of different classes, groups of learners and individual learners.

3. Teachers have many expectations placed on them, resulting in them, at times, becoming overburdened. Such are the pressures on teachers to ensure the safe management and organisation of lessons at the same time as providing engaging learning activities, as well as undertaking a wide range of other responsibilities, that they may have little time, space or energy to fully focus on facilitating and enhancing learner progress. As a result, some teachers may at some times resort to short cuts such as teaching pre-planned lessons from within a set scheme or unit of work (see also point 2 above) or perhaps repeating lessons taught to another class in the same year or in previous years. Both of these may involve teaching the same content in the same way to different classes in one year and/or from one year to the next without thinking about how this is impacting on the progress of individual learners. In this context there is a danger that little regard is paid to the nature of any progress achieved by a particular class, group of learners and/or individual learner.

4. There may be an attitude that historically this is what has always been done, so if it's not broken, why fix it? One reason for this might be that the content and teaching approaches adopted have become normalised and it is taken for granted that teaching something at a specific time in a specific way (for example, teaching a particular invasion game in a particular term or teaching a swimming stroke in a particular way) is the best – or only, way of teaching it. On the other hand, some teachers may refer back

to what and how they were taught and because something 'worked for them', they assume it 'works for others.' However, while it might work for some able learners, it might not work for others or indeed for any learners. It is not enough to claim vaguely that something worked for me, or it works here, so it's unquestionably a good practice. Alternatively, if current content and teaching approaches are not perceived to be broken, teachers with many things to do may put their time and energy into things they do perceive as needing to be changed or 'fixed.' Whatever the reason, the result is that some teachers may not question what and how the subject is taught. They do not question whether this is appropriate for all learners in schools today. Further, they may not be open to other ideas, for example, from other teachers in the department or brought in by new teachers (either newly qualified or moving from another school) to the school. As a result it is difficult for new ideas which may facilitate and enhance progress to become embedded.

1.3 The complexity and challenge of the topic

Like teaching, facilitating and enhancing progress is complex and challenging. One major complexity and challenge is the scope of the aims and possible content that could be included in the subject; physical education can cover a wide area and work towards a range of aims (see also lack of consensus on aims above). Thus, in a book such as this, choices have to be made. These choices are, inevitably, based on experience.

In order to provide a clear overview and message about progression and learner progress in physical education, we have drawn on our extensive experience and selected what we believe are some pertinent elements of progression and progress and related theory/ evidence relevant to physical education. We do not cover the whole complexity of the subject and the content we have chosen is by no means comprehensive, nor does it form a coherent whole. As a result, the book cannot be used as a blueprint to plan and teach to facilitate and enhance the progress of all learners.

Teachers (and other readers) may not agree with our selection of, views on or interpretation of, the content, or the content we have selected to highlight what progression and progress can look like in the subject may not be priorities in the specific context in which they are working. This may be for a number of reasons, for example:

* A teacher (or other reader) has strong personal views of, for example, the aims of the subject, teaching, learners and their progress in physical education that prioritise other content or do not mirror all (or indeed any of) our views in interpreting that content
* Priorities in physical education in a specific context are different to those prioritised in this book, or
* Other theories and/or evidence are considered more appropriate.

Thus, teachers might prioritise other content for progression and progress not addressed in the book or interpret the content we have included in a different way. Additionally teachers may identify other ways of addressing progression and learner progress in their context. Therefore, we also hope that this book will stir teachers to take this work further and, where appropriate, to come up with alternative foci relevant to their own context. We also hope that it will encourage teachers to consider how they can develop, adapt and refine their practice to better ensure that learner progress is facilitated and enhanced at all times.

Whatever teachers views, beliefs, values and attitudes or the context in which they are working, this book is designed to provide guidance and support to enable them to focus (either by re-energising or starting) their efforts in thinking about, and taking action in relation to this crucial area of their work. We hope that this book encourages, and even persuades, teachers to prioritise this key area of their work at all times. We also hope that the information included is of value, and provides support, to help teachers to better understand the nature of progression and learner progress they identify as most apposite to physical education in their context.

Thus, to stress, what is written in this book is just a start in this important area. Our aim is to challenge teachers to build on and take this work forward, develop and improve it, so that there is clarity about what progression and learner progress mean in physical education in their specific context. Indeed, we would be delighted if the book is read critically, generates greater awareness in this key area, encourages teachers to (re)focus their efforts both on ensuring the curriculum and its respective schemes and units of work and lessons are progressive to underpin this work and on facilitating and enhancing the progress of all learners they teach. Indeed, we would be delighted if this book becomes a springboard from which progression and learner progress become the heart of every physical education teacher's work and from which they develop and extend the work in this book further.

It is important to highlight that there is little new in this book; rather, what we are writing is, at least partially, reiterating what has already been written in different places. For example, a number of different agencies, organisations and schools have identified progression in aspects of physical education, many of which are available on the web. Some of these descriptions focus on what learners should have learned and the progress they should have made at different ages or stages (for example, what learners at grade X or key stage Y should be able to do), either explicitly or implicitly.

Further, principles of instruction (related to our principles for facilitating and enhancing progress (see Units 2, 3 and 9)) have been identified by others. For example, Rosenshine's (2012) Principles of Instruction are used by many teachers. These include:

- Present new content in small steps with learners practising after each step
- Limit the amount of content learners receive at one time
- Give clear and detailed instructions and explanations
- Ask a large number of questions and check for understanding.

What may be different in this book includes, for example, the range of content and/or our interpretation of the content or the specific focus on physical education.

1.4 The aim of physical education against which progression and learner progress are recognised and charted in this book

As stated above, learner progress is made towards an aim. However, as previously explained, in respect of physical education there has traditionally been no clear consensus as to the purpose and aims of the subject. Additionally, it is recognised that, in any one context, there is likely to be a range of aims towards which learners are working; both those stated within the curriculum but also those identified, implicitly or explicitly by teachers themselves. However in a book on progression and learner progress, it is imperative that a clear aim is identified against which progression can be planned and taught and progress can be measured. This raises the question of what is the aim of physical education towards which progress is being made in respect of this book?

With current concerns relating to a serious lack of participation in physical activity by individuals of all ages, with subsequent impact on physical and mental health (see, for example, Public Health England, 2022; Sport England, 2022a, 2022b), we propose that a valid aim for physical education is for learners to choose to adopt a physically active lifestyle, both whilst at school and throughout their life. (Note: different terms are used by different people, for example, healthy active lives; active lifestyles/lives/living; lifelong participation in physical activity. In this book, these are all embraced within the term physically active lifestyle.) Thus, in this book, where we refer to a single aim for physical education, it is in relation to learners adopting a physically active lifestyle.

To us, this is important because, as Ofsted (2023a) remind us, curriculum physical education lessons "might be the only opportunity for some pupils to learn the knowledge they need to make informed decisions about participating in physical activity and sport and leading a healthy, active life."

Indeed, adopting a physically active lifestyle is one common aim of physical education in many contexts. For example one of the aims of the current National Curriculum for Physical Education (NCPE) in England (DfE, 2013) refers "to lead[ing] healthy active lives." In Scotland, reference is made to "a programme of activities that aims to provide children and young people with learning experiences that enable them to develop the knowledge, motivation and ability to lead a physically active life" (Education Scotland, 2017) and in Singapore "The purpose of Physical Education is to enable students to demonstrate individually and with others, the physical skills, practices and values to enjoy a lifetime of active, healthy living" (Ministry of Education, 2016, p. 1).

Physical education is well placed to facilitate and enhance progress towards this aim. This was stressed by the Declaration of Berlin 2013, made at the United Nations Educational, Scientific and Cultural Organisation (UNESCO) World Sports Ministers Conference (MINEPS V) in the statement that "Physical Education in school and in all other educational institutions is the most effective means of providing all children and youth with the skills, attitudes, values, knowledge and understanding for lifelong participation in society" (UNESCO, 2013, p. 3). It was also highlighted by the International Council of Sport Science and Physical Education (ICCSPE) (2010) who stated that

> Physical education in school is the most effective and inclusive means of providing all children, whatever their ability/disability, sex, age, race/ethnicity, cultural, religious or social background, with the skills, attitudes, values, knowledge and understanding for lifelong participation in physical activity and sport.

Further, it was stressed by Ofsted (2023a) when they said

> For many pupils, physical education (PE) will be the first and only place where they are taught safe, efficient and intelligent movement. In PE, pupils are also taught important health-related knowledge to help them make informed decisions about how to live a healthy, active life.

This aim of adopting a physically active lifestyle is relevant to learners in both primary and secondary school. For example, Duggan (2022, p.132) said that "teachers of primary PE can lay the foundations for lifelong engagement in physically active lifestyles, 'providing' they facilitate enjoyable, inclusive learning experiences that enable all pupils to achieve positive outcomes." Likewise, if they are going to engage in a physically active lifestyle, learners should start to learn about, for example, the short- and long-term benefits of physical activity, local opportunities to be physically active and participate and taking responsibility for their own learning and engagement in physical activity, whilst they are in primary school and progress this learning in secondary school (see, for example, Bowler and Salmon, 2020; Quennerstedt, 2019).

This aim would also seem to be in line with other current strategies that work towards increasing participation in physical activity to enhance the quality of life, physical and mental well-being. These include, for example, various campaigns by Sport England to increase participation, such as 'This Girl Can' (Sport England, 2015), 'We are Undefeatable' (Sport England, 2019); 'Join the Movement' (Sport England, 2020), and governmental policy through the 'School Sport and Activity Action Plan' (DfE, 2023d).

We firmly believe that learners adopting a physically active lifestyle as one aim of physical education is highly pertinent and, where achieved, will have significant benefits for every individual learner not only whilst in school but throughout their life. This is similar to Lawson (2018) who said "Active, healthy lifestyles established during childhood are life-enriching and, if they continue, they are life-extending and perhaps life-saving" (p.xii). Thus, it is this aim which is the focus of progression and learner progress throughout this book.

In order to achieve this (and other) aims, there need to be clear, shared expectations both about exactly what is important to teach and when to teach it.

We recognise there are other aims towards which learners are working. However, for reasons of clarity, progress towards other aims are not explicitly addressed in this book. We would, however, encourage teachers to consider progression and learner progress towards other aims relevant to their context. We hope that our work on progress towards an aim of a physically active lifestyle will help teachers to achieve this.

1.5 Summary and key points

To conclude, it is a privilege to be a teacher of young people, but it also carries with it major responsibilities; in particular, to ensure the progress of each and every learner in physical education towards the aims of the curriculum.

It is worth highlighting that, if progression and learner progress are not at the heart of every physical education teacher's work, then it is less likely that each individual learner will progress. It is also not without value to mention briefly that there are wider implications of the absence of a well-managed progressive pattern of learning in physical education. From a learner's perspective these are likely to include not having a positive attitude to the subject, through, for example, lack of, or too much, challenge, through repeating work and becoming bored or uninterested in learning or lacking motivation. This may result in learners not wanting to engage in lessons or to engage in physical activity outside lessons, outside school or after they leave school.

In light of this, we stress the importance of focusing on progression and the progress of each and every learner in every lesson.

It may seem that being able to cater for individual learners is idealistic and/or intimidating, when one secondary physical education teacher is teaching a class of 30+ learners and perhaps 25 or so different classes per week and hence may not know individual learners very well. Although a generalist primary teacher will know the learners in the class very well, they might have limited knowledge about, and very little time to develop knowledge and/or plan for, physical education.

However, if catering for the needs of every learner is considered to be no more than adapting content and teaching as appropriate for different classes and individual learners, this is something that all teachers should be doing all the time. Adapting teaching to meet the needs of individual learners may involve changing one (or more) aspect of the content being learned, how the content is learned (the process), or what the learners produce and how they show their learning (the product). All of these do not need to be changed at the same time.

Even if teachers cannot (immediately) facilitate and enhance the progress of each and every learner in every class in every lesson, it is certainly good to aim for the ideal. Teachers may start by, for example, grouping learners according to their current progress and consider what changes are needed in the content, process and/or product of learning. Perhaps, if at first you don't succeed try, try and try again is pertinent here. As with all constituents of teaching, and as many teachers will be aware, this becomes easier over time because, for example, teachers both get to know learners as individuals and develop a bank of knowledge about what might better facilitate and enhance the progress of individual learners. This is the challenge we set. Are you up for the challenge? If so, read on.

Unit 2   Progression, Progress and Learning

2.1 Introduction

As stated in Unit 1, the notion of progress by each and every learner lies at the heart of schooling and responsibility lies with teachers to facilitate and enhance progress within the subject, in our case physical education. In order for learners to progress, the main focus of all teaching should therefore be learning.

The purpose of this Unit is to clarify what is meant by progression, progress and learning. It considers the concepts generally but also in relation to physical education. This Unit underpins the rest of the units of the book, which focus on progression, progress and learning in different ways.

The Unit starts by considering what is meant by progression, progress and learning in physical education. This includes considering briefly theories of learning which provide different views of the way in which learning takes place. Finally, the Unit identifies some principles for facilitating and enhancing progress we perceive to be particularly relevant in physical education.

2.2 Progression and progress

Progression has been defined as "the process of developing gradually from one stage or state to another" (The Oxford Advanced Learners dictionary, n.d.) or "the process of changing or developing towards an improved situation or state" (The Cambridge Advanced Learners Dictionary and Thesaurus, n.d.).

Progress has been defined as "the process of improving or developing, or of getting nearer to achieving or completing something" or "to improve or develop over a period of time" (The Oxford Advanced Learners dictionary, n.d.) or "movement to an improved or more developed state, or to a forward position" or "to improve or develop in skills, knowledge, etc." (The Cambridge Advanced Learners Dictionary and Thesaurus, n.d.).

Thus, progression and progress both relate to the process of moving (improving or developing) from one state or stage to another over a period of time. In this book we use the word progression to refer to the conditions which need to be in place to enable the process of moving from one state or stage to another to occur, i.e., to make progress possible. On the other hand, we use the word progress to refer to actually moving from one stage

DOI: 10.4324/9781003172826-3

to another, i.e., the learning which is taking place. Generally, where the word progress is used in the book, it subsumes the word learning. Where reference is made to facilitating and enhancing the progress of all learners this includes establishing the right conditions to enable progress to occur. We use the words progression and progress either in combination or individually in this book, depending on the specific point being made. Progression and progress are explained below.

2.2.1 Progression and progress in education

In schools generally, and physical education specifically, progression is planned and progress occurs in different timescales, i.e., in the short, medium and long term, for example:

- A section within one lesson
- A whole lesson
- A unit of work
- A scheme of work
- A school year
- A key stage
- A phase of schooling (for example, primary/secondary)
- The whole of compulsory schooling (i.e., ages 5-16 years).

Note: progress also occurs across the whole lifespan, but this is not the focus of this book.

In this book, the short term is used to refer to a lesson, the medium term is used to refer to a unit of work and the long term is used to refer to a scheme of work or curriculum.

2.2.2 Progression in physical education

As far as we are aware, there are few definitions of the word progression in relation to physical education. In England the word is not used in the current National Curriculum for Physical Education (NCPE) (Department for Education (DfE, 2013). However, in the first NCPE, progression was defined as "the sequence built into children's learning through curriculum policies and schemes of work so that later learning builds on knowledge, skills, understandings and attitudes learned previously" (Department of Education and Science and the Welsh Office (DES/WO), 1990, p. 13). In this book we use this definition as a basis for considering progression in physical education.

On initial reading, the definition may seem to be straightforward. However, it does require some interpretation and clarification in order for it to usefully underpin progression in the subject. Firstly, the definition refers to the curriculum, i.e., "the sequence built into children's learning through curriculum policies and schemes of work." Secondly, it refers to learning, i.e., "later learning builds on knowledge, skills, understandings and attitudes learned previously" (DES/WO, 1990, p.13). The sequence of learning in the curriculum and building new learning on previous learning through the learning activities and teaching approaches developed are both conditions to make learner progress possible, i.e., to facilitate and enhance learner progress.

Although the word progression is not used in the current National Curriculum for Physical Education in England, the Association for Physical Education (AfPE, 2018a) provides guidance around what progression in the curriculum looks likes. Table 2.1 shows an adapted version of this guidance (using the language we use in this book).

Note: in this book physical activity is defined as "bodily movement produced by skeletal muscles that results in energy expenditure above basal metabolic rate" (Marshall and Welk, 2008; Youth Sport Trust (YST) (2023b). Sport is generally defined as competitive, physically vigorous, institutionalised activity, although it can be defined more broadly to include more informal and recreational 'lifestyle activities' or 'lifestyle sport,' at least some of which are more informal recreational and less or non-competitive. In this book we include these activities under the umbrella of sport. Physical activity is a broader term which includes sport and where we use the term physical activity in this book, we take this as including sport.

Table 2.1 An (adapted) simple guide to progression in the National Curriculum for Physical Education in England

---

Early Learning (Nursery and Reception Years; 3–5 years old)
Learners developing normally will:
• Develop General Movement Patterns

Be able to
• Negotiate space and obstacles safely, with consideration for themselves and others
• Demonstrate strength, balance and coordination when playing
• Move energetically in general Movement Patterns such as climbing, dancing, hopping, jumping, running and skipping

Key Stage One (years 1 and 2; 5–7 years old)
Learners should continue to develop general Movement Patterns, becoming increasingly competent and confident. They should access a broad range of opportunities to extend their agility, balance and co-ordination, individually and with others. They should be able to engage in competitive (both against themselves and against others) and co-operative activities in the Physical Domain, in a range of increasingly challenging situations.

Key Stage Two (Years 3 to 6; 7–11 years old)
Learners should continue to develop and apply a broader range of Movement Patterns, learning how to use them in different ways and how to link them to make Movement Phrases. They should enjoy communicating, collaborating and competing with each other. They should develop an understanding of how to improve in different Movement Activities and learn how to evaluate and recognise their own progress.

Key Stage Three (Years 7 to 9; 11–14 years old)
Learners should build on and embed the Movement Patterns learnt in Key Stages 1 and 2, becoming more accurate, competent, confident, consistent, efficient and secure in these, and be able to adapt/differentiate them to apply them across different Movement Activities. They should understand what makes learning effective and how to apply these principles to their own and others' work. They should understand the long term benefits of participating in physical activity and have the confidence, interest and motivation to get involved in physical activity out of school and in later life.

Key Stage Four (Years 10 to 11; 14–16 years old)
Learners should tackle complex and demanding Movement Activities and should get involved in a range of Movement Activities as part of a physically active lifestyle.

Source: Adapted from AfPE, 2018a.

Progression in physical education might include, for example, moving from:

- General Movement Patterns to refined and specific Movement Patterns
- Being able to combine Movement Patterns into Movement Phrases to being able to engage in a range of Movement Activities (generally building up from simplified/modified versions of the activity to the full recognised version of the activity)
- Applying learning in one Movement Activity to being able to transfer learning across Movement Activities in the same Movement Form
- Dependence to independence in learning, for example, learning activities designed by the teacher to learners designing their own learning activities
- Learning being recognised by the teacher to learners using criteria given to them to recognise their own (and others') learning.

In this book we argue that establishing the conditions to make learner progress possible through the sequence of learning in the curriculum and building new learning on previous learning through the learning activities and teaching approaches are not enough in themselves. They cannot be relied on totally to ensure that each individual learner is making progress. In other words, they do not replace the need for learning activities and teaching approaches to be appropriate for individual learners at a specific time or the need to monitor and respond to learner progress in a specific context at a specific time. The needs of the individual learner must always supersede a pre-planned sequence of learning in the curriculum, learning activities and teaching approaches. Thus, in this book we view the sequence of learning in the curriculum, learning activities and teaching approaches as providing a broad framework to facilitate and enhance progress, but that they are flexible and can be differentiated/adapted to meet the needs of the learners; a specific class, group of learners and individual learners. Progress is considered next. The curriculum is considered further in Unit 11.

Before continuing to look at the importance of progression and progress, it is important to explain the use of the word knowledge as used in this book. DES/WO (1990) (see above) referred to knowledge, skills, understandings. This is quite common in education. However, in this book we use the word knowledge on its own; this incorporating the words skill and understanding. Bloom et al (1956) identify four different types of knowledge, i.e., Factual, Conceptual, Procedural and Metacognitive. To further refine the terminology Anderson (1976; 1993; 1995) was instrumental in developing two descriptions of knowledge: declarative (facts and information about a topic or knowing what) and procedural (knowledge about how to do something or knowing how). This wording is used in recent work by Office for Standards in Education, Children's Services and Skills (Ofsted) (2022) and others. In this book whilst we refer to Bloom et al's (1956) taxonomy in Unit 6 (the Cognitive Domain), we adapt this slightly by collapsing two of his types of knowledge; factual and conceptual, into declarative knowledge (knowing what). Because metacognition is learning to learn, which is knowing how, we also collapse procedural and metacognitive. We call this procedural knowledge – the application of declarative knowledge to practice (knowing how) (this is explained further in Unit 6). Therefore, when we use the word knowledge in this book we are referring to declarative and procedural knowledge – unless otherwise stated. Relating this back to the words knowledge, skills, understandings, 'knowing what' includes understanding and 'knowing how' includes skills.

Whatever terminology is used in physical education, progress in the Physical Domain is the raison d'être of the subject. However, this requires learners to have some declarative knowledge to underpin procedural knowledge; knowing what is important to progress in knowing how and knowing how begins as knowing what (see, for example, Anderson, 2007; Chatzipanteli et al., 2016). For example, a learner must know what a Movement Pattern (for example, a handstand) looks like and how they can retain their balance before they learn how to do a handstand. Likewise, before learners can apply conventions of a Movement Activity in practice they must know what these conventions are. Further, as stressed by Wright et al. (2005) and Ennis (2015), learners need to be explicitly taught the links between knowing what and knowing how. Also, in our view, whilst both knowing what and knowing how are important in physical education, progress in knowing what should be to underpin progress in knowing how, rather than developed in its own right.

In this book we focus on procedural knowledge (knowing how) first – in Unit 5 (the Physical Domain). Progress in procedural knowledge (knowing how) is described in relation to two Aspects: Aspect 1 – Movement Patterns; and Aspect 2 – Movement Activities (see Unit 5; the Physical Domain)). In Unit 6 (the Cognitive Domain) progress in declarative knowledge (knowing what) is described in relation to two Aspects: Aspect 1 – Constituents and principles of movement and Aspect 2 – Adopting a physically active lifestyle.

2.2.3 *Progress in physical education*

As stated above, it is individual learners who progress. So what does learner progress look like in physical education? In physical education, progress can be evidenced in a number of ways. For example, where progress is being made, individual learners would be more able to, inter alia:

* Use a specific Movement Pattern to engage in a specific Movement Activity, for example, a serve in volleyball or a leap in a dance sequence
* Increase the difficulty, complexity or quality of an existing Movement Pattern, under-pinning this learning by increased declarative knowledge, for example, increase precision in executing a turn in swimming by understanding drag and propulsion
* Modify and adapt a Movement Pattern appropriate to the context, for example, execute a somersault in diving as well as in trampolining
* Combine a number of different Movement Patterns into Movement Phrases, for example, create a sequence of three Movement Patterns in gymnastics or use principles of composition in dance
* Engage in a range of Movement Activities in different Movement Forms, for example, participate with interest in dance as well as a competitive game
* Transfer learning from one Movement Activity to a new or different Movement Activity in the same Movement Form, for example, apply the principles of using space to effect in tennis to squash
* Work in a different or unpredictable environment or in a different relationship with people, for example, a different route in orienteering or accommodate others in executing a tactic in a game situation

- Act independently, for example, plan own learning activity to improve an aspect of fitness
- Reflect on and evaluate own Movement Patterns and/or ability to engage in Movement Activities, for example, analyse where improvement is needed in a handstand or in a tactic in a game.

The next section looks briefly at learning.

2.3 Learning

Learning is a complex concept, as demonstrated by the fact that it is difficult to define the word precisely. One reason for this is that the word is used in different ways. As a result, there is no one answer to the question, 'What is learning?' and no one definition of the word. For example:

> Ambrose, et al. (2010) describe learning as a *process* that leads to *change* and increases the potential of improved performance and future learning
> For Gagné (1985, p. 2), learning is "a change in human disposition or capacity that persists over a period of time and is not simply ascribable to processes of growth"
> For Heritage (2008, p. 4), learning is envisioned as the "development of progressive sophistication in understanding and skills within a domain."

As with the words progression and progress, the word learning requires some interpretation and clarification. A couple of points are made below in this regard.

Firstly, the many definitions of learning are saying something similar, albeit in different ways (after all, they all focus on learning), i.e., that there is a change, development, general improvement or progress in a human capacity not due to growth, that lasts over a period of time.

However, there are also some differences in focus. For example, Ambrose et al. focus on learning as a process, i.e., the means by which a learner makes sense of learning to acquire new knowledge. On the other hand, in Gagné's definition, learning is viewed as an increase in knowledge which is the outcome or the product of learning (for example, a learner is able to perform a standing dive rather than a sitting dive). Hence, learning can be recognised or seen. Thus, the process and product of learning might be conceived as knowing *how* and knowing *that*. The process of learning is considered further in Unit 9.

However learning is described or defined, it is important to note that none of the descriptions or definitions of learning contains any reference to age, school year or phase of schooling. As learning is undertaken by individual learners and each learner is unique, they progress at different rates and individual learners are likely to be at different stages at the same age. Thus, learning is age related, not age dependent.

Although descriptions or definitions of learning aim to explain what learning is, they do not explain the way in which learning occurs. Rather, there are a number of different theories of learning which provide different views of the way in which learning occurs, for example, how individuals learn and what facilitates and enhances progress. Theories of learning are considered briefly next.

2.3.1 Theories of learning

Theories of learning provide frameworks to allow us to understand how people learn. Theories of learning are worthy of in-depth investigation in considering how best to facilitate and enhance the progress of individual learners. There are many different theories of learning, with new theories emerging at different times. Theories are generally grouped into categories. However, the categories are somewhat arbitrary for a number of reasons. For example, because learning theories draw from each other they overlap, the same theory might be included in different categories (for example, social theories can be grouped separately or under cognitive and constructivist theories). Recognising the complexity of categorising theories and recognising that there are other categories and theories which could be identified, Table 2.2 is designed to briefly introduce a number of categories of theory, i.e., Behavioural, Cognitive, Humanistic, Social/Situational and Constructivist theories of learning.

In this Unit we only highlight and summarise some categories of theory and do not attempt to look at any one category or theory in depth. A teacher will need to decide which category(ies) and specific theory(ies) are appropriate in their context and explore these in depth. There are many resources providing further information to which reference can be made.

Although there are some similarities between some theories, as can be seen from Table 2.2, these categories of theory involve contrasting ideas as to the purpose of learning, the process of learning, the focus of learning and the role of teachers in facilitating and enhancing progress.

A category and/or specific theory of learning may be popular at a certain time, but its popularity may fade and it may become obsolete. At the present time, constructivist and social constructivist theories of learning are popular in education and we believe they have much to offer in facilitating and enhancing progress in physical education. For example, Vygotsky's (1978) concepts of the zone of proximal development and more knowledgeable other (teacher, other adult in the learning situation or more competent peer) and Bruner's (1966) concept of scaffolding are important in active learning (by which we mean learners are actively engaged in constructing their own learning) which we argue is key to learning in physical education.

According to Harris (2019, p. 312)

> Active learning occurs when a learner takes some responsibility for the development of the activity, emphasising that a sense of ownership and personal involvement is the key to successful learning. ... Active learning can also be defined as purposeful interaction with ideas, concepts and phenomena ... Simply, it is learning by doing, by contrast with being told.

It is important to stress that although physical education is a subject in which learners are engaged in doing in lessons, 'just doing' in physical education is not necessarily active learning. For example, if learners are doing something without thinking (for example, passing a ball back and forth to each other in what Mosston and Ashworth (2002) called a command or practice style without thinking about what they are doing), they are not engaged in active learning.

Rather, active learning involves learners engaging with what they are doing, for example, they need to think about the passes they are making back and forth to each other or which type of pass to use in a specific situation in Netball and then execute that pass. They then need to consider either how effective the pass was and how they are going to adjust the pass in future attempts or how effective the pass was in the situation and either what different pass they would use or how they would execute the pass differently in future. Active learning therefore also involves thinking. It helps promote higher order thinking such as application of knowledge, analysis and synthesis (see Bloom et al., 1956; Krathwohl, 2002; also Unit 6), which enable learners to engage more deeply with the learning in order to apply and transfer knowledge better (for example, applying learning about balance to doing a handstand or dive). To reiterate, just being physically active in physical education, but doing activities that involve copying and repeating and do not require thinking, is NOT active learning.

Returning to Vygotsky's (1978) zone of proximal development; proximal refers to something the learner is near to mastering, therefore the zone of proximal development is the difference between what a learner can do without help and what they can achieve or master with guidance and encouragement from a more knowledgeable other. A more knowledgeable other might be the teacher, a classroom assistant or a more competent peer. One way in which guidance and encouragement can be provided is through the concept of scaffolding. Wood et al. (1976, p. 90) defined scaffolding as a process that enables a learner "to solve a task or achieve a goal that would be beyond his unassisted efforts." Thus, learners progress by being supported to complete a learning activity within their zone of proximal development. This support can be provided in different ways, for example, directly from the teacher or other person or the design of the learning activity. Support is tapered off and eventually withdrawn when it is no longer needed, that is when the learner is able to complete the task on their own. A task may be returned to later – adding, for example, more difficulty, complexity or challenge.

Although constructivist and social constructivist theories of learning are popular in education at the present time and we believe they have much to offer in facilitating and enhancing progress in physical education, as Rink (2009, p. 162) stated "there is no single theory of learning that explains learning or lack of it in all situations." Each theory provides a piece of a complex phenomenon.

Thus, other theories of learning are used in physical education. For example, behaviourist theories which underpin the reproductive command and practice styles of teaching (on the continuum of teaching styles of Mosston and Ashworth, 2002 (Mosston and Ashworth are covered further in Unit 9)), seem to be predominant in much teaching in physical education. In these styles, learners are set a learning activity, following a demonstration, for example repeating a specific stroke in tennis. For such an activity to be 'active' to facilitate and enhance progress, learners need to be encouraged to think about how they are completing the stroke and what they can do to improve the quality and accuracy of the stroke. Thus, learners need feedback on how they are completing the stroke which they can review, reflect on, identify steps to improve the stroke and put these steps into practice.

Table 2.2 Some key points about categories of learning theory

	Category of Theory				
	Behavioural theories	Cognitive theories	Humanistic theories	Social/situational theories	Constructivist theories
Examples of theorists	Pavlov, Skinner, Thorndike, Watson	Ausubel, Gagné, Koffka, Kohler, Lewin, Piaget, Sweller	Maslow, Rogers	Bandura, Rotter, Lave and Wenger	Bruner, Dewey, Vygotsky
Purpose is to:	Produce behavioural change in desired direction	Develop capacity and skills to learn better	Develop self-actualisation and autonomy	Learn new roles and behaviours	Build knowledge
The learning process involves:	Passive learning through stimulus-response. A change in behaviour as a result of interaction with the environment	Constructing knowledge through internal mental process such as attention, perception and memory	A personal act, with freedom of choice, in order to fulfil potential for growth, involving the affective and subjective as well as the cognitive	Observing other people in a social setting and modelling behaviour	an active process to construct knowledge and create meaning from experience
The focus of learning is on:	Stimuli in the external environment as opposed to internal events like thinking and emotion	Internal cognitive structuring	Affective and cognitive needs, including, for example, underlying emotions, peer pressure and a desire to fit in	Learning as an interaction or relationship between people and environment Communities of practice	Knowledge is personal and actively constructed; Building new knowledge from previous learning; Incorporating new knowledge into existing Schema. In social constructivist theories: An interactive process by groups of learners to socially construct knowledge; Observation underpinning a conscious decision to imitate behaviour

The teacher's role includes:	Setting achievable, observable objectives/learning outcomes with success criteria; Arranging the learning environment to bring out the desired response; Rewarding and positively reinforcing appropriate behaviour to motivate the learner by associating current response and reward	Planning learning so that new knowledge is assimilated into existing knowledge, and enabling learners to make appropriate modifications to their existing intellectual framework to accommodate that knowledge	Facilitating and enhancing: The development of the whole person; The ability to self-direct own learning	Arranging groups in class to facilitate progress; Modelling and facilitating new roles and behaviours	Arranging the learning environment to allow experiential/active learning opportunities for learners to actively construct knowledge

Thus, although constructivist and social constructivist theories are highlighted in this Unit, and in other Units in the book, aspects of other theories are also relevant in designing learning activities to facilitate and enhance progress in physical education.

Although theories of learning provide frameworks to allow us to understand how people learn, they do not give specific information to enable learners to progress. Thus, we have identified nine principles for facilitating and enhancing progress we perceive to be particularly relevant in enabling informed decisions to be made about operationalising learning effectively so that individual learners are more likely to progress in physical education in the short, medium and long term. These are listed and described in the next section of the Unit. We call these principles for facilitating and enhancing progress.

2.3.2 *Principles for facilitating and enhancing progress*

Below, we have identified nine principles as particularly relevant in relation to establishing conditions to facilitate and enhance progress in physical education. These are:

1. Each learner is holistic; the Physical, Cognitive and Affective Domains are all inter-related, therefore all need to be considered
2. Each learner is unique, therefore needs to be treated as such
3. Learning is purposive, towards achieving an aim
4. Learning is an ongoing process that takes time, practice, application and effort
5. Learning attempts to move the learner on; new learning builds from where the learner is in respect of current learning
6. Learning is coherent, with a logical order, going step by step
7. Learning is presented in such a way that it motivates the learner to apply themself
8. Learning accommodates opportunities for feedback to the learner
9. Learning provides opportunities for the learner to take responsibility for their learning.

The first two principles above (learners are holistic and unique) are addressed in more detail in Unit 3, so are not considered further below. Some aspects of the remaining seven principles for facilitating and enhancing progress are highlighted below. Although these seven principles are considered separately in this Unit, they are interconnected, so they also have to be considered together. For example, learners need to be given time to build their knowledge so that it is secure, before moving on to more complex content or applying their knowledge to a specific situation. However, it is important that the time for practice is used effectively and purposefully. This requires that teachers, for example:

• Build learning on what learners already know and can do, so that they can be successful in the practice
• Have high expectations of all learners to participate in a lesson fully and to make the effort required to learn – and for learners to do so
• Model expectations clearly both verbally and physically, highlighting the key points for learning and the success criteria and providing clear feedback for learners to improve the quality of their learning

- Give learners additional, more complex tasks or adapt/differentiate the task, provide structured scaffolding and/or more time to practice, as appropriate
- Identify the most important knowledge to be learned, giving verbal or visual cues as appropriate for learners to focus and ensure there are no misconceptions. This allows learners to maximise the use of the time to practice.

Hence, in the descriptions below, there is some implicit reference to other principles, as appropriate. Also, where appropriate, aspects of constructivist and social constructivist theories are highlighted.

These principles for facilitating and enhancing progress are followed up in other Units (for example, in Unit 3, there is a focus on application of the principles for facilitating and enhancing progress so that individual learners are more likely to progress, whilst in Unit 9, a third column is added to the table to highlight some constituents of teaching which underpin each of the principles so that individual learners are more likely to progress).

2.3.3 *Learning is purposive - towards achieving an aim*

An aim gives learning direction. Thus, all learning involves purposeful activity towards achieving that aim. In this book, we use the term aim as the long term goals of a curriculum or scheme of work; the term, objective, is used for the medium term goals of a unit of work; and the term, learning outcome, is used for the short term goals of an individual lesson. Long term aims are too far away to inform learning on a day-to-day basis; hence, medium term objectives and short term learning outcomes provide the building blocks to enable progress to be made towards the long term aims; they describe what learners are expected to achieve along the way to achieving the aims. As indicated in Unit 1, we focus on learner progress towards adopting a physically active lifestyle. However, there are other aims towards which learners might be working, frequently in addition to (or instead of) adopting a physically active lifestyle. If the aims towards which learners are working are not clear, it is not possible to either plan a curriculum and learning to enable the aims to be achieved or to know whether or not a learner has acheived the aims.

2.3.4 *Learning is an ongoing process that takes time, practice, application and effort*

Learning is an ongoing process so the learner has to be actively involved; being engaged in purposeful activity towards achieving an aim takes time, practice, application and effort. Learning is not a series of discrete events or independent chunks of content that have to be mastered in a given timeframe. Time, practice, application and effort are now each considered briefly in turn.

Firstly, learning takes time. Progress cannot be fostered by, for example, learners learning a new Movement Pattern or participating in a Movement Activity in an isolated lesson or unit of work, at a specific age or in one year, key stage or phase of schooling and then moving onto something else in the next lesson or unit of work. A learner might be able to demonstrate basic 'achievement' of a learning outcome at the end of a lesson or unit of work (for example, they might be able to demonstrate a volley in tennis or a short sequence in dance). However, they are unlikely to be able to do a volley consistently or in different situations or repeat the dance sequence with precision on future occasions because they do not retain that learning without further time to practise and consolidate that learning. Opportunities for practice can be built into the lesson or across a series of lessons to allow learners to retrieve prior learning and build on it. Thus, for example, a learner cannot learn how to throw a discus in one lesson, shot putt in the next and javelin in the third lesson. In addition, some learning outcomes are complex and require practice over a period of time (for example, choreographing a dance or a tactic in a game). Whatever they are learning, learners need to practise over a period of time, developing and building as appropriate.

Secondly, the nature and quality of the practice is as important as the amount of time spent in practice. Some practices are unlikely to facilitate and enhance progress, for example, practices which require learners to copy and repeat without thinking; practices in which learners repeat exactly what they were required to do previously in exactly the same way (i.e., throwing and catching a ball facing a partner) and hence are not challenging; or practices without feedback being given, and acted upon. Rather, learning needs to be active (see above). Further, in order to progress, practices need to provide challenges that reinforce or build on existing knowledge. Such challenges might involve, for example:

- Changing the context (for example, a gymnastics routine with a partner rather than alone or from a floor routine to using apparatus)
- Increasing the accuracy, difficulty or complexity of a Movement Pattern or Movement Activity (for example, better coordination of breathing and arms in front crawl or a more complex sequence in dance)
- Focusing on different learning points to stress a different aspect of a Movement Pattern of engagement in a Movement Activity (for example, stressing the importance of the length of the lever in throwing a javelin or reading a map in orienteering)
- Learners striving for greater consistency in a Movement Pattern or engagement in a Movement Activity (for example, being able to repeat a pattern for a tactic in a game).

In addition, learners should not just go through the motions of learning. Rather, they need to apply themselves and put effort into the learning. Progress is not just about repetition of, say, a Movement Pattern without thinking. It requires learners to be engaged in the learning. This is helped by use of feedback to support a learner to reflect on the Movement Pattern and any changes that might need to be made to improve it. Learners then need time to take action based on that feedback.

Further, in order for learners to apply themselves and put in effort, the learning activities and teaching approaches need to be appropriate. For example, the level of challenge of a learning activity needs to be appropriate for the capabilities of an individual learner. If the challenge is too low, for example, if accuracy in a Movement Pattern is not required or a learner has developed competence in that Movement Pattern, that learner may be content with a loose interpretation of the Movement Pattern or may be bored or unmotivated and not apply themself and put in effort. On the other hand, if the learning is out of reach because the level of challenge is felt to be above a learner's current level of learning, for example, a learner is being asked to try a standing dive from the side of the pool but is not confident in entering the water and has not learned to do a sitting dive, the learner may not apply themself or put in effort, because they perceive they cannot meet the challenge. Thus, some learners need new and different challenges to keep them engaged, whilst other learners need the level of challenge to be reduced (so it is within their zone of proximal development, Vygotsky, 1978), with building blocks, or scaffolding (Bruner, 1966), put in place to move learning forward.

Learners are more likely to apply themselves and put in effort when the conditions for progress are in place. This includes applying the principles for facilitating and enhancing progress being discussed here. For example, learners can see clearly how the learning fits into the long term aims, new learning builds on previous learning, the learning is challenging (but not too challenging) for the individual, they are motivated, they are required to think, plan, reflect, evaluate what they are doing, or they receive feedback which they have time to act upon.

2.3.5 Learning attempts to move the learner on, building from where the learner is in respect of current learning

Any one component of learning does not occur in isolation. Rather, learning in the short, medium and longer term is interconnected, i.e., learning outcomes and objectives should enable a learner to progress towards achieving the long term aims (see also principle 3). In attempting to move learners on – for learners to progress, new learning towards achieving a long term aim should build on existing learning; that is on what learners already know. For example, the general Movement Pattern of an overarm throw is a prerequisite to throwing for distance, accuracy or speed. In turn, this is a prerequisite for refined and specialised Movement Patterns in which the overarm throw is applied in different contexts such as a serve in tennis, putting a shot, a long throw from the boundary in cricket or a throw in water polo. If a learner has not learned how to do an overarm throw effectively, they will not be able to refine this in order to achieve distance, accuracy or speed. Likewise, if a learner has not learned how to refine the throw, they will not be able to learn the specialised Movement Patterns. Building on current learning requires, for example:

- Identifying and correcting any misconceptions from previous learning experiences, before the new, or correct, learning takes place; and
- Establishing current gaps in knowledge before new learning takes place.

Current learning should also prepare learners for what comes next. It is therefore important that clear connections are made between what has come before, current learning and what is to come after; between what has already been learned and whether progress has been made. Indeed, Ausubel (1968, p.vi) stressed the importance of this when he said "The most important single factor influencing learning is what the learner already knows. Ascertain this and teach him [or her] accordingly."

2.3.6 *Learning is coherent, with a logical order, going step-by-step*

In order to facilitate and enhance progress, there needs to be coherence, that is all parts of the learning should fit together. This refers both to the holistic nature of learning as well as learning typically occurring or progressing in the short, medium and longer term in a logical order, following an expected path or sequence.

Certain components of learning are prerequisites for later learning so the preceding steps in the learning need to have been learned and embedded as a basis for next learning. For example, the general Movement Patterns of jumping for distance and height can be built on to develop refined and specific jumping, e.g. jumping in gymnastics and dance or jumping to receive a pass or shoot a goal in a game, long jump, triple jump, high jump. Likewise, steps in developing a dance motif might include first copying the motif, then following instructions, then developing a motif with guidance and then working alone/in a pair/group to combine a motif in a creative way.

Thus, in order to progress, learning should be developed step-by-step; the steps forming building blocks or scaffolds for learning (Bruner, 1966).

The steps in learning can be progressed faster along a continuum if a learner has already achieved prior learning. However, where a learner has not achieved prior learning, building blocks are missing or because things already learned are not secure or have not been learned correctly, progress in learning may be slower, or indeed result in backward steps needing to be taken along the continuum. Thus, knowledge of the steps or the continuum of how learning should occur should allow an appropriate match to be made between the learners' needs and learning experiences.

2.3.7 *Learning is presented in such a way that motivates learners to apply themselves*

Learners generally strive to learn more, and that learning is strengthened, if learning is a positive or satisfying experience that motivates them to apply themselves to learning. Conversely, learning is weakened when the experience is unpleasant or unsatisfying and hence results in a negative attitude or does not motivate a learner to learn. Learning therefore needs to be presented in such a way that motivates learners to apply themselves and to make an effort in learning (Unit 7 also considers motivation).

Presenting learning in a way that motives learners includes factors which are:

- Directly related to the learning, that is both what is to be learned and how it is presented; and
- Indirectly related to the learning itself, for example, clothing to be worn, the time of the learning/lesson, the learning environment.

In relation to what and how learning is presented, learners are more likely to be motivated if they understand the value of what they are learning and the learning is interesting, relevant and meaningful to them. What is of value, interesting, relevant, and meaningful will change over time as learners get older; it will also be different for individual learners.

Although meaningful learning experiences have been described in different ways, meaningful experiences are taken here as purposeful – directed towards an aim (see also principle 3, above), engaging, relevant, challenging and rewarding. Application of the principles for facilitating and enhancing progress listed in this Unit should support learning to be of value, interesting, relevant, and meaningful.

Indirect factors also influence motivation to learn. For example, clean, warm changing rooms in which learners have some privacy when changing, clothing that is comfortable, warm and appropriate for the activity are more likely to result in learners being motivated and applying themselves to the learning in the lesson. Further, in relation to how learning is presented, motivation is likely to be affected by the learning environment. Learning in physical education can be readily viewed by others, a learner is likely to be more motivated where there is a safe, secure, positive learning environment (for example, in which a learner is not laughed at, humiliated, embarrassed or in which they don't like being watched) with consistency of teacher expectations. How this is experienced by each learner can impact on how the learner sees themselves in relation to others, impacting either positively or negatively on their motivation. For example, if learners are required to perform a sequence to one other group or to the whole class, this can impact their motivation positively or negatively.

However learning is presented, both directly and indirectly, there are also personal factors which impact on the motivation of individual learners, in the short, medium or long term. These include, for example, the learners' physical, mental and emotional readiness to learn as a result of factors such as learners' physical and mental health, anxiety/worry/tension, their level of fatigue at the time of learning, the amount and quality of the food and drink they have consumed (both immediately and over a period of time). Maslow's (1943) hierarchy of needs is relevant here as it focuses on the importance of lower levels of need being met in order for learners to be motivated to learn. Thus, it is important to know individual learners and factors which impact on their own motivation to learn as well as how learning is presented. This is a highly complex area. Motivation to learn is considered as part of Unit 7; the Affective Domain. Further, there is a considerable amount written about motivation to learn to which reference can be made.

2.3.8 *Learning accommodates opportunities for feedback*

Feedback, or knowledge of results, is an essential component of learning; hence, learners need regular and frequent constructive feedback. The ultimate aim is for an individual learner to be able to obtain feedback for themselves (for example, from video observation or from within (kinaesthetic feedback)) (see taking responsibility for own learning below and in Unit 9); however, feedback is more commonly given by another person (either a teacher or peer).

Feedback can be in relation to, for example, a specific Movement Pattern, aspect of engagement in a Movement Activity or progress towards a longer term aim. It provides knowledge about current learning, understanding and commitment and hence what progress a learner is making. It also provides information to move the learner forward. Effective feedback needs to be positive, with information about, for example, what has been learned or mastered (fully or in part), what still needs to be learned or mastered, how mistakes or misunderstandings can be corrected, what new challenges are needed to move learning forward. It should therefore build from a learners current level of learning/mastery and identify how further progress can be made. This will enable new learning to build on current learning. However, to be effective, feedback requires follow-up action, i.e., a learner needs to put the feedback into practice. For example, feedback might be given on a particular aspect of how well a tumble turn in swimming is executed. Based on this feedback, the learner makes changes to how they execute the tumble turn and is given time for additional practice. Feedback is given on progress made in light of the first feedback. Feedback is considered further in Unit 9.

2.3.9 *Learning provides opportunities for learners to take responsibility for their learning*

Much of the time the focus in learning in physical education is on the product of learning; what a learner can do differently after the learning than they could before. However, the process of learning is also important; even though that is less easily measured than the product of learning (see Unit 9 for more on the process of learning).

For Demos (2005, p.5) if, in addition to progress in a component of learning, a learner can develop their learning skills, resulting in a more general ability to progress in different contexts, they will become more effective learners and be better served by their education. The process of learning includes learning how to learn. Indeed, for Nixon et al. (1996, p. 128), "the most effective process of learning is learning how to learn." There is confusion around the concept of learning how to learn. Various writers have used different words to mean the same thing or, alternatively, the same word to mean different things. Hence, it is very difficult to define the concept or identify exactly what it might comprise. For Aynsley, Brown and Sebba (2012) learning how to learn includes, for example: understanding how to learn; understanding the need to, and how to, manage own learning throughout life; learning to think; exploring and reaching an understanding of own creative talents and how to make best use of them; learning to enjoy and love learning for its own sake and as part of understanding self. Thus part of the process of learning is learners taking responsibility for their own learning. Taking more responsibility for learning is considered further in Unit 9.

The ultimate goal of learning how to learn and taking responsibility for their own learning is for a learner to become a lifelong learner who is able to make choices about what to learn, at what pace and how to assess their own learning. There is a view that now knowledge is readily available, taking responsibility for own learning – and the process of learning how to learn, is as, if not more, important than the outcome (product) of learning (Education Endowment Foundation, 2018b). The process of learning and taking responsibility for own learning are equally important in progress in Movement Patterns and participating in Movement Activities as they are in increasing knowledge and making decisions about participating in physical activity outside lessons and outside school, both now and in the future. Therefore, taking responsibility for own learning fits an aim of physical education identified in this book – adopting a physically active lifestyle. To adopt a physically active lifestyle, learners need to make decisions and take responsibility for their engagement in physical activity.

Learners taking responsibility for their own learning enables them to identify their own strengths and areas for development and develop a learning plan to focus on certain components of their learning which need most development. It also involves developing a group of personal skills, knowledge, attitudes and values that involve learners thinking for themselves and taking responsibility for their actions in order to work out for themselves what to do. This requires active learning (active learning is covered above).

However, although taking responsibility for own learning is perhaps easier to define than learning how to learn, there is no definitive list of what this entails. However, most lists would probably include a learner being increasingly more able to, for example:

- Have the will to learn and engage in deep rather than surface learning
- Understand what it means to engage in the learning process and reflect on how they learn
- Value, and work collaboratively with others to support learning
- Build learning from the knowledge and attitudes brought into the classroom, i.e., what is already known
- Assume an active role in, and take ownership of, managing and regulating own learning
- Take the initiative, self-direct and lead their own learning rather than all learning being led by the teacher, but also know when to seek help
- Experiment with ideas and take risks, in the knowledge that mistakes are an inherent part of learning and provide a learning opportunity
- Independently solve learning problems rather than rely on the teacher
- Identify how best to use learning cues
- Plan and organise own learning (for example, pay attention; establish goals; determine and manage essential information; find patterns and chunk information; plan, manage and prioritise time)
- Set own clear and challenging aims, objectives and learning outcomes towards which to work
- Have the capacity to persist in learning challenges in striving for progress, being able to deal with success and failure or frustration
- Identify, explore and correct misconceptions
- Self-assess own progress in order to identify possible barriers to and improve own learning
- Use feedback constructively
- Identify new goals and be creative and flexible in working towards them.

Learners do not just absorb skills to take responsibility for their own learning, learn how to learn and become a lifelong learner; they need to learn these skills by gradually taking increasing responsibility for their own learning. Although all subjects in the school curriculum have a responsibility for this, physical education should contribute to this learning and development as learners work individually, in small or larger groups or teams in making progress and solving movement challenges in physical education.

Taking responsibility for own learning is considered further in Unit 9: Teaching to facilitate and enhance progress. Further, Autonomy is considered in Unit 7: The Affective Domain.

These principles for facilitating and enhancing progress are considered further in Unit 3 where they are considered in relation to individual learners being more likely to progress and again in Unit 9 in relation to some constituents of teaching which underpin each of the principles so that individual learners are more likely to progress.

2.4 Summary and key points

This Unit has focused on progression, progress and learning. Progression and progress both relate to the process of moving (improving or developing) from one state or stage to another, over a period of time. In this book the word progression refers to the conditions which need to be in place to enable the process of moving from one state or stage to another to occur, i.e., to make progress possible. On the other hand, progress refers to actually moving from one stage to another, i.e., the learning which is taking place.

Progress involves learning – a process which results in an increase in knowledge. Progression, progress and learning are complex concepts. We have only been able to give a brief introduction to these concepts in this Unit to provide a foundation for focusing on learner progress in physical education. There is a considerable body of literature available which provides further information on these concepts to which reference can be made.

To support the concepts of progression, progress and learning we have sought to identify learning theories that we feel support effective teaching in physical education to facilitate and enhance progress, and in doing so identified the role of active learning and the learner taking responsibility for their own learning in the learning process.

Taking responsibility for their own learning is one of nine principles for facilitating and enhancing progress in physical education which we have identified in this Unit. However, it is individual learners who learn and progress (or not), hence these principles for facilitating and enhancing progress must be applied to individual learners. The individual learner is considered further in Unit 3. At the end of Unit 3 we return to the principles for facilitating and enhancing progress and add a second column in which each principle is considered so that individual learners are more likely to progress.

Unit 3   The Learner

3.1 Introduction

In this book, the focus is on the progress of individual learners as the key consideration in physical education. Unit 2 considered progression, progress and learning. It stressed that progress involves effective learning, i.e. a learner can do something they could not do before. These concepts were considered in general in Unit 2. However, it is individual learners that learn and make progress. Thus, with respect to progress, there is little doubt that the learner should be centre stage. Thus, in this Unit the individual learner becomes the centre of attention.

In this Unit we propose that there are two learner characteristics that need to be taken into account in facilitating and enhancing progress. The first characteristic is concerned with the holistic nature of the learner endowed with a range of capabilities and the second addresses the wide range of differences between learners which are a result of their own endowment, potential and individual biographies. While different, these two characteristics are closely related. These are considered below. However, in a book of this nature the explanation is necessarily brief. Further information can be found elsewhere, including in relation to the concept of physical literacy. Learners as holistic and unique are integral to the concept of physical literacy (Whitehead, 2010) (a good place to start for further information on physical literacy is the website of the International Physical Literacy Association (https://physical-literacy.org.uk)).

In lessons, it appears that there are common expectations of individuals as learners that are 'managed' by the teacher. For example, a learner should be intent on taking part in learning activities that are incrementally challenging and enable them to work towards an aim. The learner is required to be mindful of the feedback being given and put the feedback into practice. In addition the learner is expected to demonstrate motivation, concentration and persistence, apply themselves, make an effort and gradually take responsibility for their learning. This might sound easy, but it is far from it. Indeed, this is far from the end of the story as each learner brings to any learning their own attributes, expectations, perceptions, hopes and fears which need to be taken into account.

The Unit starts by considering the holistic and individual nature of learners. It then considers how the principles for facilitating and enhancing progress, first introduced in Unit 2, can be applied as appropriate, so that individual learners are more likely to progress.

DOI: 10.4324/9781003172826-4

3.2 The holistic nature of the learner endowed with a range of capabilities

This book is based on the belief that individuals are a whole. The notion that humans are just some sort of partnership between the mind and the body, referred to as Dualism (see, for example, Descartes, 1970; Whitehead, 2010), is rejected. The learner is not just some sort of animated machine. Current views describe humans as being comprised of a range of inter-related and inter-dependent potentials or capabilities (see, for example, Nussbaum (2000) who has championed the concept of human capabilities). These capabilities include, for example, the physical, cognitive and affective. This view is known as Monism. Maiese and Johnson have written extensively on Monism (see, for example, Hanna and Maiese, 2009; Johnson, 1987; Maiese, 2015; Maiese and Hanna, 2020). The upshot of this view is that learners engage a spectrum of capabilities to address whatever is asked of them. In all that humans do they characteristically draw on a range of capabilities, with each challenge presented to individuals requiring an interaction between a range of these capabilities.

To take an example from physical education, when serving in tennis the decision on what type of serve to execute is based on the success of previous serves against this opponent. For the serve to be successful the learner must draw on their physical ability to serve. Patience and creativity may be important if, for example, weather conditions change. In this enterprise the learner draws on a wide range of capabilities in relation to the task at hand. This combined enactment of various capabilities does not usually require conscious thought, rather it is drawn on as needed.

Thus learning in physical education draws on a range of capabilities. It is suggested that the physical, the cognitive and the affective capabilities of a learner are of particular importance (see, for example, Bloom et al, 1956; Krathwohl, Bloom and Masia, 1964, Simpson, 1972). These three capabilities, or domains, of learning are introduced in Unit 4, considered in detail in Units 5, 6 and 7 respectively and drawn together in Unit 8. However, they are introduced briefly here in order to demonstrate the holistic nature of learners.

Developing human capabilities of movement are the bedrock of learning in physical education as they enable every learner to develop physical competence in a range of Movement Patterns appropriate for participating in a wide variety of Movement Activities (for definitions of Movement Patterns and Movement Activities, see Glossary and Unit 5). This area of capabilities is referred to as the 'Physical Domain.'

Cognitive capabilities are essential partners in developing physical competence as any movement involves both doing and thinking. Cognitive capabilities facilitate thinking about, declarative knowledge of and ability to reflect on, for example, the underpinning nature of movement, the nature and purpose of different Movement Activities and the value and benefits of adopting a physically active lifestyle. This area of capabilities is referred to as the 'Cognitive Domain.'

Affective capabilities include feelings, emotions and attitudes which can be seen as the drivers of all human action. These include, for example, motivation, confidence, sensitivity and autonomy. These capabilities provide an interest in and a springboard for the development of physical competence and knowledge concerning physical activity. This area of capabilities is referred to as the 'Affective Domain.' Work in the Physical and Cognitive Domains relies heavily on capabilities in the Affective Domain.

The holistic nature of the individual has important implications for learning in physical education. Physical, cognitive and affective capabilities are interrelated and all are interrelated with progress in the subject. All learning will be perceived by the learner as involving interest and cognition as well as adept physicality. In any learning situation in physical education the physical, the cognitive and the affective aspects of being human need to be considered and planned. We believe that there is a case to be made that the aim of adopting a physically active lifestyle can be curtailed where learners have not been appreciated 'in the round.'

3.3 Learners as unique individuals

The second belief that permeates all the work in this book is that each individual is unique. On the face of it this statement is unremarkable. However it is often the case that in a school context the statement frequently seems to have resonance only in respect of those individual learners who have significant needs. This could relate to, for example, exceptional athleticism or to a very challenging endowment (see glossary). When viewed in this way the notion of uniqueness may be seen as referring to a minority of learners. As a result, a large number of learners are likely to be 'lost' in the mass and not have their individual needs catered for.

Further, we want to highlight the fact that each and every learner is different with a unique endowment, potential and biography as a result of different life experiences. As was made clear in Unit 2, each learner will thrive best if expectations, learning activities and challenges are 'in tune' with their needs. To achieve this, learning should be differentiated/ adapted such that all learners can access and engage in the learning process with the intention that they progress in their own learning journey. For this reason it is advised that in all deliberations about planning, teaching and recognition of progress, the learner should be at the heart of the decision making. We are, in fact, advocating learner-centred teaching. Learner-centred refers to a learning environment which recognises that learners are not empty vessels which need to be filled; rather, each learner brings something to the learning. A bridge is built between a learner and their learning. New learning is built from the knowledge, cultural practices, interests, attitudes and beliefs that learners bring to the learning, that is what each learner knows, cares about and wants to do. This requires a teacher to know about individual learners and their learning. We strongly advocate that supporting learners and facilitating and enhancing their progress should take priority, rather than, for example, introducing and honing Movement Patterns – without consideration for individual learners.

It is important to have knowledge of the range of different interacting factors which impact progress in general terms as well as how they relate to individuals. One of these factors in relation to individual learners is their individual growth and development. The next section briefly considers growth and development in general as well as how it might impact on an individual learner. However, this brief overview hardly does this huge and complex area justice. It is therefore necessary to supplement this information with more detailed information from other sources. Although there are a range of sources to which readers might refer, in our view Donnelly, Mueller and Gallahue (2016) is a good place to start.

3.3.1 Growth and development

The brief summary of growth and development below is based on the use of the two terms as generally applied in physical education as follows:

- Growth refers to changes or increases in the size and shape of the body as a person ages and is therefore largely applied to the Physical Domain
- Development refers to progressive change which can be applied to the Cognitive and Affective Domains as well as the Physical.

Growth and development is generally divided into five significant stages, that is:

1. Infancy (neonate up to one year old)
2. Toddler (one to five years of age)
3. Childhood (three to eleven years of age) – divided into early childhood (three to eight years of age) and middle childhood (nine to eleven years of age)
4. Adolescence or teenager (from 12 to 18 years of age)
5. Adulthood.

There are many factors which impact growth and development. For example, genetic factors influence height. Nutrition is also important, as are environmental factors (for example, children in families with higher socio-economic status and/or educational qualifications are generally taller than their peers in families with lower socio-economic status and/or lower educational qualifications (see, for example, Balasundaram and Avulakunta, 2022)). These various factors also impact on education. For example, it is recognised in education that deprivation has an impact on learning. In light of this, for example, the pupil premium grant in England provides funding to state schools to improve educational outcomes for disadvantaged pupils (see Department for Education (DfE), 2023a, 2023b). We do not explore the impact of deprivation further here. However, there is a body of literature which explores factors, including deprivation, which impact both growth and development and progress in depth. A good place to start in relation to deprivation might be the Sutton Trust, an educational charity which aims to improve social mobility and address educational disadvantage (see https://suttontrust.com).

General differences in growth and development can be seen across the different domains (Physical, Cognitive, Affective) in learners of different ages. In addition, growth and development does not occur at the same rate; at times growth and development is rapid and at others much slower. For example, the Department of Education and Science and the Welsh Office (DES/WO, 1991, p. 26) said that

> Throughout the key stages [of the National Curriculum in England], pupils' progress will follow their natural development. Physical growth and changes in physical ability in children are at their greatest in key stages 1 [ages 5–7 years] and 2 [ages 7–11 years]. They reduce and decelerate a little as the child enters the pre-puberty phase. Marked

changes occur during adolescence when the growth spurt experienced by some pupils can result in a temporary decline in physical energy and skill. At this time learners become more aware of their body shape and size and may need to be helped to adopt positive attitudes [brackets added].

Much of the description below in relation to growth and development (adapted from DES/WO (1991, p. 26)), highlights that children and young people/adolescents are not mini adults. It also highlights differences in learners of different ages. For example, five-year-old learners differ in very many ways from 14-year-old learners. Further, it is important to remember that there is a gradual transition from one stage of development to the next (see stages of development above), rather than an abrupt change. As a result, at times a learner may be exhibiting elements of development from different stages. This has some important implications for education in general and physical education in particular, as highlighted below.

First, the physical appearance of young children is quite different to that of adults. Their arms and legs are rounded and are short in proportion to the rest of their bodies. Their muscles are relatively weak. This affects the way they move. As they grow, older children's limbs become longer in relation to the rest of their body. As a result, the length of their levers increases. This helps them to generate greater strength and speed. As their muscle strength increases, the ratio of body weight to strength becomes more favourable for some Movement Activities. This generally reaches a peak between about ages 7 and 11 years. Girls usually enter puberty before boys. During adolescence most learners experience a decline in body strength in relation to body weight. A better balance is normally restored from about aged 14 onwards, although it can be more challenging for some girls to balance strength and body weight. Natural flexibility decreases with age.

When they start school children find it difficult to attend to more than one thing at once. They also have difficulty in judging the direction and speed of movement of both people and objects. This means that, for example, they have difficulty catching, find it easier to hit a stationary ball than one that is moving and are rarely aware of what other children are doing while they are working in a space. As they grow older, physiological changes, along with increased experience, mean that children become more able to judge both speed and direction. Once they have become competent in basic actions children are able to carry them out whilst concentrating on how they apply them. As children become more experienced, they are able to make quicker judgements and offer more sophisticated responses.

By the time they start school – and provided they have been given sufficient opportunities and have the capability, most children have experienced, and have an extensive repertoire of, general Movement Patterns such as climbing, jumping and running. At this stage, these general Movement Patterns often lack refinement. As they grow and develop physically and cognitively, these general Movement Patterns are able to be adapted and developed into refined and then specific Movement Patterns that can be used in Movement Activities. Movement Patterns and participating in Movement Activities in each stage forms the basis for new learning to be brought into operation at the next stage.

What has been written above refers to growth and development generally. However, it is important to consider the growth and development of each individual learner in physical education because, for example:

- Although there are general changes expected in growth and development as children get older; for example, they follow a normative sequence of developmental milestones, go through stages of development in the same order and do not miss out any stage, different children grow and develop at different rates.
- So, children of the same age might be at different stages of growth and development (it only takes one look at any class of any age to see marked differences in their growth and development). Developmental age is not necessarily linked to chronological age and milestones cannot be linked to a specific age.
- As a result, children learn to do different things at different times; it is not possible to specify when an individual child will be ready to learn something.
- Thus, although it is useful to consider age loosely as a guideline in considering progress in physical education throughout the years of schooling, it is the developmental age of each individual learner that is key to the progress of each learner. Thus, learning is age-related not age-dependent.
- As a child grows and develops and as they learn more, they can do more things and there are extended opportunities for learning.
- Further, "progress is not the same in all areas of activity, nor at a consistent pace within an area" (DES/WO, 1991, p. 26).
- Thus, as Murdoch (2004, p. 287) stressed, "Any proposed estimate of attainment for all pupils can only be given as a benchmark. Pupils do not conform to a norm ... Equally, it is not possible to be confident about the actual progression rates of any individual pupil. Pupils tend to follow a similar pattern in their learning progression but it is unlikely that they all follow it *at the same rate*" [italics in original]. For some learners progress against suggested levels and stages is steady, whereas for others progress is uneven, e.g. there may be periods of apparent delay or acceleration at different stages.

As the above demonstrates, individuals grow and develop at different rates and it is important to take this into account in facilitating and enhancing the progress of each individual learner in physical education. However, growth and development are not the only factors which impact on learners that need to be taken into account.

3.3.2 Other factors which impact on learners

In addition to growth and development, each learner's particular biography makes them unique. This biography includes, for example, a person's endowment, potential, special educational needs, gender, ethnicity, religion, social class, their background and life experiences.

There is a considerable body of work considering ways that individuals develop many of their characteristics more on account of their life experiences than as a result of their genes/inheritance (known as the nature/nurture debate). For example, behaviourists such as Skinner (1953) emphasise the role of the environment in learning and social constructivists such as Vygotsky (1978) emphasise the importance of social and cultural practices in learning. For example, Wilson (2014, p. 21) argues that we are not individuals who "interact with our environment on a purely biological basis;" rather, we engage and interact with our environment based on the mediation of other people and the context of which we live. Briefly and simply put, it is suggested that each person creates him or herself as each lives through a particular variety of experiences. As a result, not only does each person develop a specific set of capabilities and evidence particular strengths and areas for development in some or all three domains which are the focus of this book (i.e. the Physical, Cognitive and Affective Domains), but each will have a different perception of the world.

Background and life experiences contribute to learners 'capital.' For example, for some learners physical education is only one area in which they learn in the physical context. These learners may, for example, attend extra-curricular activities and also have access to participation in physical activity outside school. This may be for a number of reasons, for example, because their parents/carers are able to finance participation, have a positive attitude towards participation in physical activity and are supportive. The learner may enjoy the opportunities, have developed a social group who also participate and have learned a considerable amount. On the other hand, for other learners, physical education lessons are the only opportunity they have to learn in the physical context. There may be a number of reasons for this. For example, parents/carers are unable to finance participation, have a negative attitude towards participation in physical activity and/or are not supportive of their children participating in physical activity outside compulsory physical education lessons. The learner may not enjoy the opportunities and/or have a negative attitude towards participation. This may 'spill over' into curriculum physical education in that the learner will not bring much prior learning to the subject. Hence, some learners bring more capital to physical education than others. Therefore, it is important to take into account, as far as possible, the unique background and life experiences of each learner in physical education lessons.

We do not explore these various factors further in this book. However, there is an extensive literature on various factors which impact on progress in physical education to which reference should be made for further information. As a start, reference could be made to Evans and Davies (2006). In reading this further information it is important to bear in mind that these factors may be considered separately in the literature, whereas in reality they interrelate. Further, the author(s) do not always consider the factor(s) in relation to an individual learner. It is therefore important that these factors are considered as interacting both in relation to one another and in relation to each and every learner individually. The different combination of these factors for each learner in general and specifically in relation to physical education highlights the need to cater for each learner as an individual.

Catering for each learner as an individual is highlighted further below in considering the principles for facilitating and enhancing progress in relation to their application so that individual learners are more likely to progress.

3.4 Principles for facilitating and enhancing the progress of every learner

We now return to the principles for facilitating and enhancing progress that were introduced in Unit 2. However, in this Unit we highlight some factors in relation to each principle so that individual learners are more likely to progress. Principles 1 and 2 have been added to the table; each learner is holistic and each learner is unique. As each learner is unique, each learner is likely to need something different in relation to each of the principles. The principles, plus some examples of how they may be interpreted so that individual learners are more likely to progress are shown in Table 3.1.

Table 3.1 Considering principles for facilitating and enhancing progress so that individual learners are more likely to progress

Principles for facilitating and enhancing progress	Individual learners are more likely to progress if, for example, ...:
1. Each learner is holistic, with Physical, Cognitive and Affective Domains all inter-related	• They are recognised as a whole with physical, cognitive and affective capabilities operating in concert • Learning in the Physical Domain is underpinned by relevant declarative knowledge, thinking is promoted and affective responses are monitored, as appropriate for the individual learner
2. Each learner is unique, therefore needs to be treated as such	• Their uniqueness (endowment, potential and biography) is recognised and catered for • Learning activities and challenges are appropriate for their personal strengths and needs (in both the Physical and Cognitive Domains) and take account of the Affective Domain • Learning activities and challenges support the development of confidence and motivation to make it more likely that they will adopt a physically active lifestyle
3. Learning is purposive – towards achieving an aim	• They are clear about the learning outcomes and related success criteria, objectives and aims towards which they are working as well as the steps they are going to take to get there • They engage in purposeful learning activities that enable them to work towards achieving the success criteria of learning outcomes which are used to guide learning towards medium term objectives and the long term aims
4. Learning is an ongoing process that takes time, practice, application and effort	• The speed at which each learner is able to progress through the steps in learning is considered and planned. If a learner has learned the prerequisite for next learning they are able to progress, whereas if prerequisite learning has not been achieved they will need to spend time learning the prerequisite(s) and progress more slowly • They are given an appropriate amount of time to practice in order to learn, consolidate and embed learning • Learning activities are challenging and stretching within each learner's capability so that learning is not out of reach or is not too easy • They are actively engaged in learning, apply themself fully and put effort into learning rather than just going through the motions of learning

Table 3.1 (Continued)

Principles for facilitating and enhancing progress	Individual learners are more likely to progress if, for example, …..:
5. Learning attempts to move the learner on; new learning builds from where the learner is in respect of current learning	• Evidence of prior learning is used as the basis for judgements about whether or not they are ready to move on to future challenges • New learning builds on their current learning – what they already know and can do • Clear connections are made for each learner to previous learning • Current learning leads into future learning; hence it is important that each learner knows what they are going to move onto and can make connections between past, current and future learning
6. Learning is coherent, with a logical order, going step by step	• They have learned the steps that form the underpinning foundations or pre-requisites before they progress to the next step in the learning. If a learner has not learned one step, they will not be ready to progress to the next. Where an individual learner has not learned the previous steps in the sequence they may need more time on the same or different practices or may need to take a backward step along the continuum • Careful consideration is given to the speed at which each learner progresses through the sequence of clear, coherent, continuous steps, each of which builds from the previous one • The scaffolding needed for each learner is carefully considered and planned
7. Learning is presented in such a way that motivates learners to apply themselves	• The learning environment is considered and planned such that each learner has a positive, satisfying learning experience in a secure learning environment • Learning is perceived by an individual learner as of value, interesting, relevant and meaningful • Personal factors which impact an individual learner's motivation are considered and action taken to increase motivation • A learners basic needs are met in order for them to be motivated to learn
8. Learning accommodates opportunities for feedback to the learner	• Each learner receives specific information, given constructively, about their current learning so that they know what they are doing well (in whole or in part) and what they need to work on further in order to progress their learning • They take action on the feedback in order to learn from it and progress • It is recognised that a learner may not like public feedback and hence, unless it is general feedback to the whole class, feedback is given privately to an individual learner • In addition to feedback from others (a teacher or peer), each learner develops their ability to receive feedback from themself, e.g. through video recording or kinaesthetic feedback.
9. Learning provides opportunities for learners to take responsibility for their learning, thus enhancing their learning	• Each learner gradually develops a set of skills that enables them to take responsibility for their own learning (e.g. they learn how to learn and how to plan and evaluate their own learning) so that they develop into a lifelong learner who is able to make choices to enable them to adopt a physically active lifestyle

The points raised in column 2 of Table 3.1 reinforce the point that facilitating and enhancing progress is complex. If each learner is to progress, specific consideration in relation to the different principles is needed, as appropriate for that learner. However, as the principles both overlap and interact it will not always be possible to consider them in isolation. Hence when planning, it is necessary to consider and plan for the range of principles both individually and together.

3.5 Summary and key points

This Unit has focused on each learner being holistic and unique and some implications of this for their progress in physical education.

As learners are holistic, if each learner is to progress, it is important that the Physical, Cognitive and Affective Domains are all taken into consideration. As learners are unique, if each learner is to progress, it is important that factors which impact on their learning in relation to each of these three domains are also taken into consideration.

There are a number of factors which impact on a learner. A learner's stage of growth and development needs to be considered. Although a learner's level of physical maturity is particularly important in a subject with significant practical content; development in the Cognitive and Affective Domains is also important. Facilitating and enhancing progress for each learner therefore needs to consider the interaction of these three domains in relation to the growth and development of a particular learner. However, there are other factors which impact on learners, all of which make up their individual biography (e.g. endowment, potential, special educational needs, gender, ethnicity, religion, social class, background and life experiences). Thus, each learner needs learning opportunities and activities that enable them to progress. For example, the focus of learning at any one time for any one learner may need to be on the physical, for another learner it may need to be on the cognitive and for another it may need to be on an aspect of the affective. To facilitate and enhance the progress of each learner is therefore complex.

We appreciate that it is a significant challenge for teachers to cater for the individual needs of each and every learner in every lesson in physical education. However there are clear grounds for this to be an aspiration if the progress of each learner is going to be facilitated and enhanced.

Steps that teachers can take include, for example, viewing the curriculum, schemes and units of work not as concrete documents but rather, as organic documents to be revised as needed. In addition lesson plans need to be organic, written to take account of the needs of a particular class, groups of learners and individual learners at a particular time and differentiated/adapted in light of the progress of each learner in each lesson. This does not mean to say that an individual lesson plan needs to be written for each learner – that would be impossible. Rather, consideration needs to be given to planning a range of learning activities which, through the lesson and series of lessons, support each learner in making progress. Thus, assessment for learning is important. If this reveals (both within and at the end of a lesson) that a learner has not made progress, this needs to be addressed both within a lesson and in the next and future lessons. This might mean, for example, spending more time practising on the same or a different practice or maybe explaining in a different way and/or taking a different approach. It might also mean other learners supporting a learner who has not progressed. How to achieve this is considered further in the Units in Section 3 (Units 9, 10 and 11).

Any steps that engage more learners will undoubtedly be valuable, not least in respect of the aim of physical education as identified in this book; adopting a physically active lifestyle.

Attention in the next Units (Units 4 to 8) now turns to the Physical, Cognitive and Affective Domains.

Unit 4 Domains of Learning in Physical Education
An Introduction

4.1 Introduction

So far in this book we have considered the importance of focusing on progression and progress in physical education (Unit 1), explained what is meant by progression, progress and learning (Unit 2) and highlighted the importance of taking account of the holistic and individual nature of each learner (Unit 3). We have also identified some principles for facilitating and enhancing progress (Unit 2), along with some suggestions as to how these might be applied so that individual learners are more likely to progress (Unit 3). In Unit 9 in Table 9.2, a third column has been added which identifies some constituents of teaching in relation to each of the nine principles so that individual learners are more likely to progress.

As was explained in Unit 3, because humans are holistic, an individual learner is endowed with a range of capabilities in different domains. The domains operate in concert to enable an individual to essentially function as an integrated whole. Life is lived as a complex web of inter-relationships of human potential, with different domains working in concert. All perceptions and actions arise from the totality of previous experiences and provide the context for future perceptions and actions. The different capabilities of each individual are enriched by each other in their unavoidably inseparable nature. It is as true in physical education as it is in other aspects of life that human activity involves the whole person.

In this Unit we introduce the three domains of learning which are generally recognised as important in education (see, for example, Bloom et al, 1956; Gagné, 1985); the Physical (sometimes called psychomotor), the Cognitive and the Affective Domains. We perceive these to be particularly relevant in physical education and therefore these form the subject of analysis of progress in this book.

Despite the inaccuracy, or indeed impossibility, of referring to discrete human behaviours to describe the highly complex nature of human functioning in general and in learning in particular, to attempt to consider the different domains together in a holistic way in relation to progress in physical education is overly complex in this short book. In this highly complex context we have decided the best approach to take in this book is to consider the three domains separately, one at a time – with frequent reminders that, in fact, they are interacting and never function alone. The aim of covering the Physical, Cognitive and Affective Domains in three separate units is to break down a very complex area into manageable sections, showing what progress in the three domains looks like.

DOI: 10.4324/9781003172826-5

We accept that there is something of a conflict between the approach we are taking and the perspective that at all times a learner should be perceived as a whole; as a doing, thinking and feeling human being. At any one time an individual is experiencing all three modes of being simultaneously. However, we believe the approach we are taking aids clarity because each domain draws on a different facet of being, is distinctive and is accessed in different ways. We hope that this approach makes the exercise of recognising progress as clear as possible.

This Unit provides an introduction to the three domains and underpins Units 5 to 7, which each focus on progress in one domain; the Physical (Unit 5), the Cognitive (Unit 6) and the Affective Domain (Unit 7), respectively. Unit 8 draws the three domains together and highlights the complexity of learning in a holistic way.

The Unit starts by justifying the selection of the three domains of learning in physical education. It introduces each domain before considering how progress is addressed in the domains. This includes introducing the Aspects, Foci and Ladders of Progress which are used in each of the domains to describe progress. Consideration is also given to how the Ladders of Progress might be used.

4.2 Justification for the selection of the three domains of learning in physical education

It is generally accepted that in education three distinctive, but functionally integrated aspects of human potential, or domains of learning, are the Physical, Cognitive and Affective Domains (see, for example, Bloom et al,1956; Gagné, 1985). These highlight physicality, thinking and feeling, respectively. We perceive these are particularly pertinent to physical education and in any learning situation in subject these three aspects of being human need to be considered. This is supported by, for example, the Association for Physical Education (AfPE, 2018b) referring to Head (thinking), Hands (doing), Heart (behavioural change) and the Youth Sport Trust (YST, 2024) referring to physical, thinking, social. The Physical, Cognitive and Affective Domains are therefore the subject of analysis of progress in this book.

It is accepted that there are a range of other domains that could, usefully, have been analysed, including for example, the social domain and the aesthetic domain. The Association Internationale des Écoles Supérieures d'Éducation Physique (International Association for Physical Education in Higher Education, AIESEP) (2020, p. 7) highlighted that,

> Depending on the cultural and regional context, this learning [in physical education] includes objectives in the psychomotor, cognitive, social and affective domains. These objectives can be reached through various content offerings, for example sport and games, dance, fitness, and/or outdoor pursuits; or a combination thereof
>
> [bracket added]

Our choice of the Physical, Cognitive and Affective Domains does not pre-judge the value of other domains. However, the need for accessibility, clarity and manageability of the material did not make it possible to examine domains other than the three considered particularly pertinent in learning in the subject. This might be considered a criticism of this book. However, we hope that the information in this book on progress in the Physical, Cognitive and Affective Domains will provide a framework to enable progress to be identified in other domains which are important in the context in which a teacher is working.

Our justification for these three domains rests firstly on the acknowledgement that progress in the Physical Domain lies at the heart of learning in physical education. Indeed, the bedrock of progress in physical education is the physical. In this book we describe progress in the Physical Domain in terms of Movement Patterns and Movement Activities in a range of Movement Forms (see Glossary and Unit 5 for further explanation).

Secondly, the decision reflects our belief that progress in the Physical Domain cannot occur in isolation. Learning procedural knowledge requires thinking and declarative knowledge which underlies, and which can be applied to, learning in the physical (see Glossary, Unit 2 and Unit 6). Effective movement involves thinking as well as doing. The Physical Domain focuses on the human capability of movement and the Cognitive Domain actively works alongside this in involving the acquisition of thinking skills and underpinning declarative knowledge about, for example, the constituents and principles of movement, the nature and purpose of Movement Activities and an appreciation of the value of adopting a physically active lifestyle throughout life which can be applied to the Physical Domain. In addition, this knowledge provides a rationale for the learning and is drawn on by the learner in thinking about and reflecting on components of learning in the Physical Domain and also fosters informed motivation to progress. Thus, the Cognitive Domain is an essential partner in learning in the Physical Domain and as a result is included in this book.

It is our view that effective progress in the Physical and Cognitive Domains in physical education is unlikely to become a reality unless learners have a positive attitude to the subject. Analysis of learning supports this view in the frequent mention of motivation as essential in achieving intended learning. Capabilities such as confidence, motivation, sensitivity, feelings and emotions, which can be seen as the drivers of all human action, provide an interest in and a springboard for learning in the Physical and Cognitive Domains. This area of capabilities is referred to as the Affective Domain. Krathwohl, Bloom and Masia (1964) referred to this as the way in which things are dealt with, including appreciation, attitudes, enthusiasms, feelings, motivations and values. Thus, progress in the Physical and Cognitive Domains relies heavily on the Affective Domain. As a result, the Affective Domain is also included.

Because the various capabilities in the different domains do not function in isolation – just as the Cognitive Domain is an essential partner of the Physical Domain in physical education, the Affective Domain is an essential partner to both the Physical and Cognitive Domains. Progress in the Physical Domain cannot be developed without consideration of capabilities in the Cognitive and Affective Domains. Cognitive capabilities are engaged, for example, to remember and apply information to the Physical Domain. Also, the Affective Domain is important in relation to, for example, a learner having the motivation and confidence to persevere with the task at hand, for example, how a Movement Pattern can be developed further or which Movement Pattern to use in a specific situation (e.g. how the arm can be better used as a lever in swimming the front crawl or which type of pass is best in a specific situation in a game of basketball).

4.3 Analysis of the three domains

In order to be able to facilitate, enhance and recognise the progress of each learner in each of these three domains, there is a need to clarify, identify and describe how progress will manifest itself. Thus, one question that needs to be asked is, 'What behaviours need to be in evidence in each of the three domains to indicate that progress has been made towards realising the learning outcomes, the objectives and ultimately the aims towards which learners are working?'

To facilitate, enhance and recognise progress, in the next three Units each domain is analysed in detail through a number of descriptions which become gradually more detailed. These are Aspects, Foci and Ladders of Progress. The first process of analysis in each domain identifies specific Aspects of learning. An Aspect is a key component of learning in each of the domains of learning. It is the highest level of analysis. Where appropriate, an Aspect of learning has been broken down into specific Foci. Foci identify different components of learning in an Aspect in a domain. They represent a more detailed level of analysis than Aspect. In turn, Foci lead into Ladders of Progress. A Ladder of Progress is an instrument designed to identify what progress might look like in the key components of learning (in Aspects and Foci) (there is further information on Aspects, Foci and Ladders of Progress in each of the three domains below).

The Aspects and Foci in the three domains were identified as pertinent to physical education, based on our own experience, and based on learners working towards an aim of adopting a physically active lifestyle. It is important to stress that the Aspects and Foci identified in each of the three domains are not comprehensive nor do they form a coherent whole. This is because, for example, these Aspects and Foci do not consider progress in physical education more broadly, i.e. in relation to other aims towards which learners are working. In a book such as this it is not possible, and indeed, it would be overwhelming if we tried to consider Aspects and Foci for all learning in the subject. As a result, there may be other Aspects and Foci which could be identified which are relevant to achieving other aims and/or to a particular context. Because they only highlight what progress can look like in the subject, these Aspects and Foci cannot be used as a blue print to plan, teach and recognise all progress in the subject. As a result, we hope our work in this book will help to identify progress in other Aspects and Foci. In light of this, the Ladders of Progress can also be used to help inform the development of other Ladders of Progress to facilitate and enhance progress in other Aspects and Foci the subject.

The Aspects and Foci in each domain are listed below. These are:

4.3.1 *Physical Domain*

4.3.1.1 *Aspect 1: Movement Patterns*

The three foci in this Aspect are:

Focus 1: Learning an individual Movement Pattern
Focus 2: Developing a repertoire of Movement Patterns and Movement Phrases
Focus 3: Adapting Movement Patterns for different contexts

4.3.1.2 Aspect 2: Movement Activities

The three foci in this Aspect are:

Focus 1: Applying the conventions of a Movement Activity
Focus 2: Enacting roles alongside other learners in the working space
Focus 3: Participating effectively in a range of Movement Activities in different
Movement Forms.

4.3.2 Cognitive Domain

4.3.2.1 Aspect 1: Constituents and principles of movement

The two foci in this Aspect are:

Focus 1: Knowing how to move efficiently and effectively
Focus 2: Recognising the effects of physical activity

4.3.2.2 Aspect 2: Adopting a physically active lifestyle

The three foci in this Aspect are:

Focus 1: Knowing the nature and purpose of Movement Activities
Focus 2: Knowing the importance and benefits of participating in physical activity
Focus 3: Planning for participation in physical activity

4.3.3 Affective Domain

Aspect 1: Motivation
Aspect 2: Confidence
Aspect 3: Autonomy

As a reminder, as learners are holistic, the Aspects and Foci are interrelated. They do not stand alone. Identifying Aspects and Foci for all three domains of learning reminds us that all three domains need to be explicitly considered in relation to progress. There should not be an implicit assumption that progress is being made in the Cognitive and Affective Domains as well as the Physical Domain.

4.4 Using the Aspects and Foci to recognise progress

Progress should be made by all learners throughout their time in compulsory schooling. It might be argued that the recognition of progress in the longer term is explicit in some of the Aspects and Foci (see, for example, Physical Domain Aspect 1, Focus 3 - *participating effect-ively in a range of Movement Activities in different Movement Forms*; Cognitive Domain Aspect 2, Foci 2 and 3 - *Knowing the importance and benefits of participating in phys-ical activity and Planning for participation in physical activity*; and all three Aspects in the Affective Domain - *Motivation, Confidence and Autonomy*). Whilst in others, (e.g. Physical

Domain, Aspect 1, Focus 1 *Acquiring an individual Movement Pattern* and Aspect 2, Focus 1 *Applying conventions of a Movement Activity*), this is less evident.

However, in order for learners to progress it is important that all Aspects and Foci are viewed in the longer term. This is because progress is continuous. As an example, a Movement Pattern cannot be learned once and 'forgotten about.' Rather, it needs to be revisited, and developed, at different times. For example, a learner needs to practise a Movement Pattern in different contexts. They may also need to learn (declarative) and apply (procedural) knowledge in the physical. Further, learners are learning new Movement Patterns throughout schooling as they progress from general to refined to specific Movement Patterns which they apply in different Movement Activities.

A further reason for viewing these Aspects and Foci in the longer term is that Aspects and Foci are interrelated, therefore as learners make progress in one Aspect and Foci, it impacts on their learning in others. For example, as learners improve their Movement Patterns, their ability to participate in a Movement Activity improves. Likewise, learners are able to apply conventions of a Movement Activity in more advanced ways. In addition, some Aspects and Foci rely on progress having been made on other Aspects and Foci (e.g. in the Physical Domain, in order to progress on Aspect 1 Focus 3 *Adapting Movement Patterns for different contexts*, learners must first have learned the Movement Pattern (Physical Domain Aspect 1 Focus 1).

As a result, learning and the curriculum needs to be spiral and learners need to return to different Aspects and Foci during their schooling (see Unit 11). This approach is also in line with the principles for facilitating and enhancing progress (see Units 2, 3 and 9) (particularly, principles 6, 7 and 8, respectively, i.e. learning is an ongoing process that takes time, practice, application and effort; learning attempts to move the learner on; new learning builds from where the learner is in respect of current learning; and learning is coherent, with a logical order, going step by step).

However, in relation to recognising progress, the Aspects and Foci are not specific enough. In order to facilitate, enhance and recognise progress we have identified a Ladder of Progress for each Aspect and Focus. Ladders of Progress are considered below.

4.5 The Ladders of Progress

The Ladders of Progress are an instrument designed to identify what progress looks like in the key components of learning, i.e. in the Aspects and Foci, in each of the three domains. They provide a description of what learners should be able to do as they progress in each Aspect and Focus.

Each Ladder of Progress is divided into four levels, set out in four columns. These four columns are called, respectively, baseline, growing, establishing and consolidating. These terms were selected to 'paint a picture' of progress made by a learner in the particular Aspect and Focus in the domain.

It is difficult to provide a simple explanation of each of these terms in light of the differences in Aspects and Foci (as will be seen in the Ladders of Progress in Units 5, 6 and 7). However, to illustrate how progress might be made, a brief description of the meaning of each of the terms is given in Table 4.1 with an example from the Physical, Cognitive and Affective Domains.

Table 4.1 Illustration of the levels in the Ladders of Progress

Baseline	Growing	Establishing	Consolidating
Is beginning to be able to … For example:	Is developing the ability to … For example:	Demonstrates clear evidence of ability to … For example:	Is secure in ability to … For example:
A learner is in the Cognitive stage of learning a Movement Pattern, therefore it requires conscious thought	A learner is in the Associative stage of learning a Movement Pattern, exhibiting a mixture of automatic and conscious control	A learner is moving into the Autonomous stage of learning a Movement Pattern, becoming able to enact a Movement Pattern largely without conscious attention	A learner is in the Autonomous stage of learning a Movement Pattern, requiring no cognitive activity
A learner is able to describe why regular physical activity is important and beneficial in the short term, e.g. feel good/ alert, gives them energy	A learner can articulate the importance and benefits of participating in physical activity in the short term and is beginning to recognise the longer-term benefits, e.g. strengthening bones, muscles, heart and lungs	A learner recognises and applies their knowledge of the importance and benefits of participating in physical activity to their own participation in physical activity outside lessons and outside school	A learner uses their knowledge of the importance and benefits of participating in physical activity in the short and long-term to underpin decisions about their participation in physical activity outside lessons and outside school
A learner fears failure and shies away from challenging tasks. Focuses on what they cannot do rather than what they can do. Easily loses faith in own abilities	A learner is receptive to failure, and is developing the ability to persist with an activity. There is some realisation that where effort is expended, progress can be made, and this can enhance self-image and self esteem	A learner does not fear failure, rather uses this to resolve to apply self whole-heartedly	A learner views challenges as something to be mastered rather than threats to be avoided. Recovers quickly from failure and is more likely to attribute failure to a lack of effort

Whilst progress in the Ladders of Progress in the Physical and Cognitive Domains and in Autonomy in the Affective Domain should normally be incremental (moving from baseline to growing to establishing to consolidating) at some points there might be regression in progress. This might be due to, for example, a learner adding a new feature to a Movement Pattern (e.g. adding a spin to a discus throw rather than a standing throw) or applying a Movement Pattern in a new context (e.g. learning a triple jump rather than a long jump) or where there has been serious illness or injury, an accident or other major event disrupting learning.

However, progress in Motivation and Confidence may not necessarily move consistently from baseline to consolidating; rather, learners may move in the other direction for a number of reasons. These reasons might include, for example, their growing bodies, social comparison and expectations (see, for example, Youth Sport Trust (YST, 2023a). A learner who has low motivation and/or low confidence has to be remotivated or to regain confidence to continue to progress in the Physical and Cognitive Domains and in developing Autonomy as a learner and taking responsibility for their own learning.

Further, it should also be noted that these four levels are not necessarily discrete. A learner working in any one level may largely be displaying features of progress as described in that level. However, the learner may also display features of progress in the previous or following level. Thus, when using the Ladders of Progress they should be viewed as a best fit for the learning being displayed by an individual learner.

However, Ladders of Progress cannot be used to make decisions about what learners are going to learn. Once decisions have been made about the Aspect and Focus of learning for a class, group of learners and for individual learners, the relevant Ladders of Progress can be used as a framework to facilitate, enhance and recognise progress in those Aspects and Foci. Thus, decisions about what is to be learned at a particular time should be made first and then the Ladders of Progress used to facilitate and enhance progress.

To achieve this, the Ladders of Progress can be used in a number of ways, in light of learners working towards specific learning outcomes. For example, they may help to:

- Identify what progress might look like in specific Aspects and Focus of learning
- Identify at which 'level/step' an individual learner is located at any one time on any one Aspect and Focus as well as how they have progressed over time
- Identify where attention should be directed to facilitate and enhance the next 'level/step' towards which a learner might strive in order to progress
- Create a plan for improvement to enable a learner to work towards achieving the success criteria for the learning outcomes of the lesson, the objectives of the unit of work and the aims of the curriculum.

Thus, the Ladders of Progress are best viewed as a broad guide to facilitate and enhance progress in specific Aspects and Foci of learning.

4.6 Summary and key points

The purpose of this Unit has been to give a brief introduction to Units 5, 6 and 7 (the Physical Domain; Cognitive Domain and Affective Domain, respectively). It has provided a justification for the selection of the three domains of learning, explained the Aspects and Foci we have selected within each domain as well as the Ladders of Progress for each Aspect and Focus. It has also reemphasised the imperative of focusing on the holistic nature of learning.

Identifying the Aspects, Foci and Ladders of Progress in each of the three domains highlights the diverse nature of progress in the subject. After reading the above, you might think 'this is all very complex.' We would agree. Learning and progress in physical education are complex. As a result, facilitating and enhancing progress in a range of Aspects and Foci in all three domains could seem overwhelming. However, it is important to make it manageable. Because learners cannot progress in everything at once, learning needs to be 'packaged.' In order for learners to progress, at any one time the Aspect and Foci selected should reflect the needs of a class, groups of learners and individual learners in relation to the content and focus of learning at that particular time.

It is important to stress that providing a short, simplified description of a range of Aspects and Foci and a Ladder of Progress for each Aspect and Focus in each domain cannot do justice to the complex nature of progress in physical education. However, it is hoped that the explanation of what progress might look like, as outlined in the Ladders of Progress, is sufficiently descriptive to provide some guidance to facilitate, enhance and recognise the progress of individual learners in each Aspect and Focus in each domain.

It is important to remember that we are not making definitive proposals with these Aspects, Foci and Ladders of Progress; rather, they should be understood and used as appropriate in a specific context; as an aide-memoir which should be referred to regularly. However they are used, they should help progress to be recognised and, where appropriate, to develop additional Aspects, Foci and Ladders of Progress for specific classes, groups of learners and individual learners.

In Units 5, 6 and 7 (the Physical Domain, the Cognitive Domain and the Affective Domain, respectively), the nature of each Aspect and Focus in each of the domains is described briefly before progress in each Aspect and Focus is presented as a Ladder of Progress.

However, as a reminder, the decision to analyse the domains separately in the next three Units is not intended to give the impression that the three key domains we have selected work in isolation. This is far from the case as all human activity is the outcome of highly complex inter-relationships between many human capabilities. In reality, following from the earlier description of human beings as being unavoidably holistic, the separation of progress into three domains is an impossible task as will be seen in the Units themselves. It is the case that all learning is taking place simultaneously in all three domains.

In Unit 5, analysis and discussion of the Physical Domain is the first domain to be featured as this is seen as of seminal concern in learning in physical education. This is followed by Unit 6, the Cognitive Domain and Unit 7, the Affective Domain. Unit 8 then draws the three domains together and explains how progress is best considered 'in the round' as the domains work together. This further highlights the complexity of learning in a holistic way. The argument that any progress will involve all three domains is reemphasised.

Unit 5   The Physical Domain

5.1 Introduction

As has been explained in Unit 4, in this book we concentrate on three generally recognised domains of learning which we also perceive to be particularly relevant in physical education; the Physical (sometimes called psychomotor), the Cognitive and the Affective Domains (see, for example, Bloom et al., 1956; Gagné, 1971). As physical education is a practical subject, the Physical Domain is at the heart of learning in the subject. It is therefore considered first.

If we consider that in physical education the main purpose is to progress in the Physical Domain, it is important to consider both knowing how and knowing what, i.e. what procedural knowledge a learner needs to progress in the subject, as well as what declarative knowledge the learner needs to underpin that (see Glossary, Unit 1 and Unit 6: the Cognitive Domain). After careful consideration of key components of learning in the Physical Domain that could most readily indicate important learning, two significant Aspects were identified. As a result, the two Aspects comprising the practical 'material' of physical education through which progress can be recognised are Movement Patterns and Movement Activities (see Glossary and below).

These two Aspects are divided into more detailed Foci (different components of learning within a particular Aspect), three each for the two Aspects. That is, for:

Aspect 1: Movement Patterns

> Focus 1: Acquiring an individual Movement Pattern
> Focus 2: Learning a repertoire of Movement Patterns and Movement Phrases, and
> Focus 3: Adapting Movement Patterns for different contexts.

And, for

Aspect 2: Movement Activities

> Focus 1: Applying conventions of a Movement Activity
> Focus 2: Enacting roles alongside other learners in the working space, and
> Focus 3: Participating effectively in a range of Movement Activities in different Movement Forms.

DOI: 10.4324/9781003172826-6

In this Unit these two Aspects of learning and the six Foci are considered separately as if they were discrete. However, this is purely for ease of description. It is not, in reality, the case as they are, in fact, very closely inter-related. Each Aspect and Focus is dependent on the others. A Movement Pattern is often learned in the context of a Movement Activity and effective participation in a Movement Activity depends on secure Movement Patterns. More specifically, for example, adapting Movement Patterns for different contexts is likely to occur in the context of a Movement Activity.

The first part of the Unit lays the ground for a detailed analysis of learning in these Aspects and Foci, each of which then culminates in a Ladder of Progress. The Ladders of Progress are instruments designed to identify and describe what progress might look like in each of the Aspects and Foci. They provide detail to recognise progress. The Ladders of Progress can be used in a number of ways to underpin decisions to facilitate and enhance progress in the various Aspects and Foci (see Unit 4).

Before continuing, it is important to describe what is meant by various terms used in this Unit and throughout this book, that is Movement Pattern, Movement Phrase, Movement Activity and Movement Form.

5.2 Descriptions of terms used in this Unit

In this Unit and book the meanings of the terms Movement Pattern, Movement Phrase, Movement Activity and Movement Form are as follows.

A **Movement Pattern** can be described as coordinated actions comprised of a number of components and body parts, designed to achieve a particular outcome. This could range from, for example, sending an object such as serving in tennis, performing a swimming stroke or a roll in gymnastics.

Movement Patterns are broken down into general, refined and specific Movement Patterns in this book, that is, in sequence:

General Movement Patterns are direct developments from a young learner's early movements. They include, for example, balancing, climbing, gesturing, inverting, jumping, receiving, rotating, running, sending, striking, travelling. The acquisition of general Movement Patterns is the prerequisite to developing refined Movement Patterns (see Murdoch and Whitehead, 2010, p. 179 and Annex 5.2).

Refined Movement Patterns are developments from general Movement Patterns such that a range of distinct Movement Patterns are identified, for example, the general Movement Pattern of sending is refined into bowling, shooting or throwing and striking is refined into batting, dribbling or driving.

Specific Movement Patterns are further developments of refined Movement Patterns in the context of the demands and conventions of specific Movement Activities. For example batting in cricket. In turn this is broken down into various types of batting stroke (e.g. cut shots, defensive shots, drives, glance shots, pulls and hooks and sweep shots), each of which can be further broken down (e.g. cover drive, off drive, on drive, square drive, straight drive, etc.)

In this book, the term Movement Pattern is preferred to either the term 'skill' or the term 'technique.' One reason for this is because there is considerable confusion concerning these two terms. The terms are often used interchangeably, without a clear definition and in different ways. For example, skill may be used to describe an applied technique. In a somewhat contrary way, skill is also sometimes viewed as comparatively simple while a technique is complex.

A Movement Phrase can be described as a number of Movement Patterns linked together to form a distinctive pattern or form. This could range from, for example, a jumping/bouncing routine on a trampoline or enacting a sequence of particular dance movements and steps.

A Movement Activity can be described as a purposeful, more or less structured, named event, which is carried out in larger or smaller groups, in pairs or by individuals, has specific conventions (i.e. rules, principles and protocols) to be followed and operates within a defined area. For example, Movement Activities in which:

* A number of learners work together include, e.g. a team game, group dance or gymnastics sequence, relay in athletics
* Learners work in pairs include, e.g. doubles in badminton or tennis, pair dance or gymnastics sequence, and
* A learner works individually include, e.g. most athletics events (except relays), singles play in badminton or tennis, some aspects of swimming, dance, gymnastics, outdoor and adventurous activities.

There are many and varied Movement Activities and in this book we group these into different Movement Forms.

A Movement Form can be described as a recognised and named group of the many and varied Movement Activities which share some common features or characteristics. In this book, five Movement Forms are identified, that is the Adventure Form, the Aesthetic and Expressive Form, the Athletic Form, the Competitive Form and the Fitness and Health Form (see below).

5.3 Parameters of learning in physical education in compulsory schooling

To lay the foundation for considering the nature of progress in the Physical Domain during compulsory schooling (generally approximately 5 to 16 years), it is useful to set out briefly the parameters of the learning. Below, these parameters, that is what might be expected with regards to learning prior to starting compulsory schooling and what might be expected on the completion of compulsory schooling, are considered briefly.

5.3.1 *Learning to be expected prior to starting compulsory schooling*

The pre-school years are both very significant and complex with regard to learning in the Physical Domain. It would be hoped, and expected that prior to starting compulsory schooling, learners have been involved in a range of opportunities in the physical field which have involved both free and semi-structured play as well as specific learning opportunities in which they are taught these explicitly (for example through attendance at pre-school). As a result of these opportunities, it would certainly be expected that when learners start physical education in Year 1 of compulsory schooling, there is clear evidence of both natural movement development and learning.

A great deal of study and debate has been undertaken by early years specialists to identify the movement abilities that learners should have developed by the time they enter compulsory schooling. These recommendations are presented in a number of ways. For example,

a)   In the form of a suggested Movement Vocabulary (i.e. a language to describe movement). This highlights the following: balance; construction; communication (non-verbal); flight; loco-motion; manipulation; projection (see Pickard and Maude, 2021; and Annex 5.1, in which the Movement Vocabulary particularly relevant to physical education has been highlighted), or

b)   In the form of Movement Patterns. The focus prior to compulsory schooling is on the development and learning of general Movement Patterns (see, definition above and in Glossary and examples in Annex 5.2 (adapted from Murdoch and Whitehead, 2010, p. 179)). These include locomotor and non-locomotor as well as object control Movement Patterns, for example, balancing, bouncing, catching, dodging, galloping, hopping, jumping, kicking, leaping, receiving, rolling, rotating, running, sending, skipping, sliding, striking, throwing (see Annex 5.2 for a summary of Movement Patterns)

In this book we use the term Movement Patterns.

It is important to stress that young learners at an early stage in their movement development may struggle to learn general Movement Patterns through free play alone. Hence, they need to be provided with learning opportunities in which they are taught these explicitly (see, for example, Brian and Taunton, 2018).

However, it is also important to stress that the development and learning of general Movement Patterns in the early years before learners have entered compulsory schooling and encountered the physical education curriculum, is only the start of learning in the Physical Domain. In order to maximise learning in physical education in compulsory schooling, general Movement Patterns developed and learned in the early years needs to be secure so that learners have the foundations, and are prepared, for the next stage of learning. If these general Movement Patterns are not secure, learners may be unable to learn the next, more complex, refined and specific Movement Patterns effectively. For example, a learner who has not learned to jump safely and effectively is not ready for refined and specific forms of jumping in different Movement Activities. To achieve this, in the early years, learners should be given opportunities to demonstrate general Movement Patterns in practice as well as describe the Movement Patterns, using specific vocabulary. For example, learners need to be able to physically demonstrate their competence in a Movement Pattern but also to be able to identify the key points in that Movement Pattern. Further, secure general Movement Patterns are important in building learners motivation and confidence in physical education and in participating in physical activity beyond physical education lessons (see, for example, Office for Standards in Education, Children's Services and Skills (Ofsted, 2023)).

Where learners have had the opportunity and encouragement to be active and thus have had a rich movement experience and developed the secure foundation of some general Movement Patterns, as described above, they will be ready to take full advantage of physical education throughout compulsory schooling, e.g. to learn refined and specific Movement Patterns, to develop a repertoire of Movement Patterns and Movement Phrases and adapt Movement Patterns for different contexts (including a range of different Movement Activities).

At the start of compulsory schooling learners natural growth and development and learning will open up opportunities for richer and wider play experiences and for learning in the movement field. In a reciprocal fashion, widening free play and semi-structured play and learning in physical education will make a positive impact on a learner's natural development in the Physical Domain.

It is not the role of this book to consider how young learners develop their Movement Patterns, nor the steps to be taken to ameliorate problems in developing and learning Movement Patterns, either when a learner commences schooling or during the first few years in school. However, to understand movement development and learning in the early years in relation to what learners should be able to do when they enter compulsory schooling and/or to enable any problems in movement development and learning to be addressed, it would be very valuable to follow up some of the very sound information which is available about young learners' development and learning in the Physical Domain.

5.3.2 *Learning to be expected at the end of compulsory schooling*

With respect to the progress it would be expected learners have made when they complete compulsory schooling, it is suggested that these include evidence of learning a wide range of Movement Patterns resulting in the ability to adapt these in a range of contexts, as well as the ability to participate effectively in a range of Movement Activities in different Movement Forms. More broadly, characteristics and constituents of movement at the end of compulsory schooling may include, for example:

- Accuracy, consistency, fluency, precision and proficiency of Movement Patterns
- Ability to select and apply, adapt, combine and transfer Movement Patterns across a range of Movement Activities, including those which are familiar and unfamiliar, in which learners work alone and with one or more others in both cooperative and competitive settings and with novel and/or unpredictable features
- Ability to participate effectively in a range of Movement Activities in different Movement Forms
- Aesthetic sensitivity, originality and proprioceptive acuity (body awareness)
- Ability to analyse, comment on, plan goals and monitor progress in respect of own and others movement
- Demonstrating commitment to physical activity beyond physical education by identifying and participating in school-based extra-curricular activity, other opportunities for physical activity outside school and physical activities in which the individual might participate beyond schooling.

5.4 Progress in the Physical Domain

As indicated above, after careful consideration of key components that could most readily indicate important learning in the Physical Domain, two significant Aspects were identified.

One is concerned with learning Movement Patterns and the other is concerned with participation in Movement Activities.

To reiterate, although Movement Patterns and Movement Activities are considered separately in this Unit, in reality they are very closely related. Movement Patterns are an integral part of involvement in Movement Activities and effective participation in Movement Activities depends on secure Movement Patterns which are adapted to meet the demands of each Movement Activity.

Within each of these two Aspects, three Foci have been identified.

With respect to learning Movement Patterns, the first focus is on acquiring an individual Movement Pattern. The second focus is on developing a repertoire of Movement Patterns and Movement Phrases. The third focus is on the ability to adapt the Movement Patterns for different contexts.

With respect to effective participation in Movement Activities, the first focus is on applying conventions of a Movement Activity. The second focus is on enacting roles alongside other learners in the working space. The third focus is on the ability to participate effectively in a range of Movement Activities in different Movement Forms.

These Aspects and Foci are now considered in turn.

5.4.1 Aspect 1: Movement Patterns

As has been explained above, Movement Patterns can be described as coordinated actions comprised of a number of components and body parts, designed to achieve a particular outcome. Movement Patterns are the currency of movement in all Movement Activities. Movement Phrases are a number of Movement Patterns linked together to form a distinctive pattern or form. Thus, recognising progress in respect of Movement Patterns is absolutely essential. This is a complex area.

Also, as described above, learners develop and learn general Movement Patterns in the early years through natural curiosity, normal growth, guided play and specific teaching. These general Movement Patterns need to be secure before learners are able to progress to learning a range of individual refined and specific Movement Patterns during compulsory schooling and are able to adapt a Movement Pattern for different contexts.

The three Foci in this Aspect are:

Focus 1 Acquiring an individual Movement Pattern
Focus 2 Developing a repertoire of Movement Patterns and Movement Phrases
Focus 3 Adapting Movement Patterns for different contexts

5.4.1.1 Aspect 1: Movement Patterns; Focus 1, acquiring an individual Movement Pattern

Progress in acquiring an individual Movement Pattern involves gradually developing the coordinated movement of different body parts (e.g. in a two-footed jump for distance, coordinating bending ankles, knees and hips, focusing eyes forward, swinging arms behind the body, then straightening legs with both feet leaving the ground together, swinging arms forward and up, then bending ankles, knees and hips to absorb the impact of landing on both feet at the same time).

Progress in acquiring an individual Movement Pattern also depends on the development of a number of Movement Capacities (described as the constituent abilities of an articulate, robust and secure Movement Pattern). Movement Capacities can be described as simple, combined and complex and include, for example, accurate placement of parts of the body, agility, balance, control, coordination, flexibility (see Murdoch and Whitehead (2010, p. 177); and Annex 5.3 for a summary of Movement Capacities). Without Movement Capacities, Movement Patterns could not be developed and fostered. In a reciprocal way, Movement Capacities benefit from use in various Movement Patterns, so that they can become stable and reliable. For example, in order to progress in a jump, a learner needs initially to develop their balance, core stability, placement of the body in space and explosive power and then, as a jump becomes more refined or specific (e.g. a long jump) needs to progressively develop other Movement Capacities, e.g. acceleration and deceleration, coordination of limbs).

Although there are a range of models that could be used to describe learning an individual Movement Pattern, Fitts and Posner's (1967) model of motor skill acquisition has stood the test of time and is perhaps the most frequently used. Their model is built around three stages of learning a Movement Pattern which they refer to as Cognitive, Associative and Automatic. For the sake of providing a relatively straight-forward basis for judgements of progress, we refer to the analysis of stages in learning as set out by Fitts and Posner (1967).

Briefly, in the early stages of learning an individual Movement Pattern, both physical and cognitive capabilities are important. At this Cognitive Stage, a Movement Pattern is consciously controlled; it requires conscious thought. A learner is engrossed in thinking about what they are doing and is paying considerable attention to attempting to achieve a particular outcome following a specific model. Characteristically, the Movement Pattern is enacted slowly and is somewhat erratic and inefficient.

As a learner continues to practice and progresses in learning a Movement Pattern, the amount of attention needed for the Movement Pattern decreases. Some parts of the Movement Pattern become automatic but other parts remain consciously controlled. At this Associative Stage, the learner is still relying somewhat on a specific model, but is establishing a clearer mental image of what they are attempting to do. The Movement Pattern begins to be more efficient and fluid, has some consistency, reliability and predictability. The intended learning outcome is more likely to be achieved.

When the basic requirements of a Movement Pattern have become virtually habitual and automatic, the learner is at the Autonomous stage. At this stage, enacting the Movement Pattern does not need conscious attention. Little or no cognitive activity is required. The learner has become more adept, the Movement Pattern is accurate, consistent and efficient and can be readily enacted when required.

Progress in acquiring an individual Movement Pattern, based on the stages of learning as set out by Fitts and Posner (1967) (Cognitive, Associative and Automatic), is shown in Table 5.1.

These stages of learning apply to learning any individual Movement Pattern – whether it is a simple, refined or specific Movement Pattern. Thus, whenever a new Movement Pattern is to be learned, this process is repeated. As new Movement Patterns are learned,

Table 5.1 Ladder of Progress in acquiring an individual Movement Pattern

Aspect 1 Movement Patterns
Focus 1 Acquiring an individual Movement Pattern

Baseline	Growing	Establishing	Consolidating
A learner is not assured in a Movement Pattern	A learner is generally assured in a Movement Pattern	A learner is becoming securet in a Movement Pattern	A learner is secure in a Movement Pattern
A learner is in the Cognitive stage of learning a Movement Pattern, therefore it requires conscious thought	A learner is in the Associative stage of learning a Movement Pattern, exhibiting a mixture of automatic and conscious control	A learner is moving into the Autonomous stage of learning a Movement Pattern, becoming able to enact a Movement Pattern largely without conscious attention	A learner is in the Autonomous stage of learning a Movement Pattern, requiring no cognitive activity
A Movement Pattern is somewhat erratic and inefficient	A Movement Pattern is becoming more efficient and fluid, has some consistency, reliability and predictability	A Movement Pattern is accurate, consistent and efficient	A Movement Pattern is accurate, consistent and efficient and can be readily enacted when required
A learner relies on a given model and verbal description	A learner relies on a model, but is establishing a clearer mental image of what they are attempting to do	A learner has a clear mental image of what they are attempting to do	A learner has a clear mental image of what they are attempting to do and can use this information to reflect on and refine their own Movement Pattern
A learner has limited movement memory	A learner is developing their movement memory	A learner has established their movement memory	A learner is able to draw on an established movement memory

throughout compulsory schooling this Aspect and Focus remains important. Further, as individual Movement Patterns are learned, a learner is developing a repertoire of Movement Patterns and Movement Phrases. This is considered next.

5.4.1.2 Aspect 1: Movement Patterns; Focus 2, developing a repertoire of Movement Patterns and Movement Phrases

As individual Movement Patterns progress from general to refined to specific and become more automatic and secure, learners are developing a repertoire of Movement Patterns. These Movement Patterns can be combined into different Movement Phrases. This allows

Table 5.2 Ladder of Progress in developing a repertoire of Movement Patterns and Movement Phrases

Aspect 1 Movement Patterns
Focus 2 Developing a Repertoire of Movement Patterns and Movement Phrases

Baseline	Growing	Establishing	Consolidating
A learner is developing a repertoire of general Movement Patterns	A learner is developing a repertoire of refined Movement Patterns	A learner is developing a repertoire of specific Movement Patterns for some Movement Activities	A learner is developing a wide repertoire of specific Movement Patterns for a range of Movement Activities
A learner is developing the ability to combine general Movement Patterns (e.g. run and kick) and to remember, repeat and link some of these to enact simple Movement Phrases	A learner is able to demonstrate smooth transitions between some general Movement Patterns and is developing the ability to combine some refined Movement Patterns to enact a range of more complex Movement Phrases to suit the context	A learner is able to combine and make smooth transitions between refined Movement Patterns and is developing the ability to use specific Movement Patterns in combination/ sequence in Movement Phrases, although transitions are not always smooth	A learner is able to make smooth transitions between a range of specific Movement Patterns which are used in combination/sequence in Movement Phrases

learners to gradually participate in various Movement Activities (see Aspect 2 below). Progress in learning a repertoire of Movement Patterns and Movement Phrases is shown in Table 5.2.

In order for learners to be able to take part in a physically active lifestyle outside and after they leave school, it is important that they have developed a repertoire of Movement Patterns and Movement Phrases which they can use in a range of Movement Activities in different Movement Forms (see Aspect 2, Focus 3 *Participating effectively in a range of Movement Activities in different Movement Forms*, below). In order to do this effectively, learners need to be able to adapt the Movement Patterns they have developed for different contexts. This is considered next.

5.4.1.3 *Aspect 1: Movement Patterns; Focus 3, adapting Movement Patterns for different contexts*

In this focus, different contexts includes, for example, different Movement Activities, novel or unpredictable circumstances or responding to other learners.

Aspect 1, Focus 1 concentrated on learners acquiring an individual Movement Pattern and Aspect 1, Focus 2 concentrated on learners developing a repertoire of Movement Patterns and Movement Phrases. In both, progress is principally based on learners developing a clear mental image of a model that is often viewed as most desirable. Although a model provides a sound foundation for the development of general, refined and specific Movement Patterns, Movement Patterns need to be considered in the context in which they are used.

It is the case that each time a Movement Pattern is used it needs to be enacted appropriately for the demands of the specific context. In many Movement Activities much more is asked from a learner than repetition or reproduction of Movement Patterns. A model response is unlikely to be appropriate; therefore a Movement Pattern needs to be adapted. In some movement contexts, adaptation is 'contained' (and is followed by replication). For example, in learning a gymnastics sequence, each Movement Pattern needs to be adapted to meet the particular requirements of the sequence, but then needs to be replicated exactly when performing the sequence. However, the ability to adapt a Movement Pattern to the ever-changing environment, context and specific circumstances is very significant in a number of Movement Activities. In such contexts Movement Patterns are 'tested' in situ, within particular limitations and changing circumstances (e.g. responding to other learners, unpredictability or a change of circumstance in a game). Thus, it is argued that far from viewing the Automatic stage (Fitts and Posner, 1967; see Aspect 1; Focus 1) as the end of the enterprise, it can be seen as the 'launch pad' to adapting a Movement Pattern for different contexts.

In this view, learning a Movement Pattern can be described using an hour-glass. The area above the restricted neck of the hour-glass represents the Cognitive and Associative stages of learning in which a Movement Pattern is honed into what is perceived as the ideal model. The narrow neck represents the Automatic stage of learning the Movement Pattern. However, at this stage not all necessary learning has been achieved as the specific model demonstrated at the Automatic stage is seldom, or practically never, used in exactly this way.

Rather, each time the Movement Pattern is used the learner is challenged to adapt the Movement Pattern according to the circumstances. The variations are endless (for example, a pass in a game will be different each time it is used). The area of the expansion of the hour-glass below the neck represents the adaptation of a Movement Pattern.

The representation of learning and adapting Movement Patterns as an hour-glass is shown in Figure 5.1.

Progress in adapting Movement Patterns for different contexts is shown in Table 5.3.

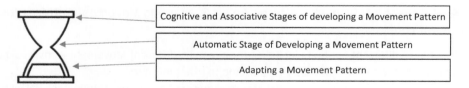

Figure 5.1 Learning and adapting Movement Patterns as illustrated by an hour-glass

Table 5.3 Ladder of Progress in adapting Movement Patterns for different contexts

Aspect 1 Movement Patterns
Focus 3 Adapting Movement Patterns for different contexts

Baseline	Growing	Establishing	Consolidating
A learner is able to enact a range of Movement Patterns in stable situations but, although aware that Movement Pattern models rehearsed in practice are seldom replicated exactly as they often have to be enacted in different contexts, finds it challenging to adapt Movement Patterns as appropriate for different contexts	A learner is aware of different contexts in which a range of Movement Patterns might need to be adapted and is developing the ability to adapt Movement Patterns in different contexts	A learner is becoming more adept at using key information related to a specific context to choose, adapt and modify a broad range of Movement Patterns for different contexts	A learner is able to use key information, perception, creativity and reflection related to the context to choose, adapt and modify a broad range of Movement Patterns for different contexts consistently

It is no use learners being consistently and securely able to do a range of decontextualised Movement Patterns; rather in making progress in the Physical Domain, being able to adapt a range of Movement Patterns for different contexts is important. Thus, it is important that learners not only learn a range of Movement Patterns, they also need to learn how to adapt them in order to apply them in different contexts, including in different Movement Activities (for example, different adaptations are needed for a jump for height in a dance, when used in a gymnastics sequence or high jump in athletics). Progress in Movement Activities is considered next.

5.4.2 Aspect 2: Movement Activities

As indicated at the start of this Unit, it was suggested that learning could be recognised from two perspectives; firstly in respect of Movement Patterns and secondly in respect of the Movement Activities that are the contexts in which Movement Patterns are applied. We have considered three foci in Aspect 1 (Movement Patterns). In this section we are concerned to look at progress with respect to Movement Activities, in which there are also three Foci.

As has been explained above, Movement Activities can be described as purposeful, more or less structured, named events which have specific conventions, are carried out in larger or smaller groups, in pairs or by individuals and operate within a defined space. Characteristically, they comprise a particular cluster of Movement Patterns. For example, Swimming has a cluster of strokes to propel the learner through water; a ball game comprises a particular set of Movement Patterns such as hitting, trapping, shooting and jumping.

Movement Patterns and Movement Activities have a similar relationship to that between Movement Patterns and Movement Capacities (see above). They are mutually beneficial to each other. Movement Patterns can be enhanced by use and adaptation in a Movement Activity setting and Movement Activities can develop markedly where a learner has well developed Movement Patterns which they are able to adapt appropriately.

There are three foci within this second Aspect: Movement Activities.

Focus 1 applying conventions of a Movement Activity
Focus 2 enacting roles alongside other learners in the working space
Focus 3 participating effectively in a range of Movement Activities in different
Movement Forms

These three foci are now addressed in turn.

5.4.2.1 Aspect 2: Movement Activities; Focus 1, applying conventions of a Movement Activity

All Movement Activities have a series of conventions that need to be learned and enacted so that progress can be made in relation to a specific Movement Activity. These conventions include the rules, principles and protocols for participating in a specific Movement Activity. These encompass, for example, choreographic principles (those compositional elements or factors to be considered to attain an aesthetically satisfying dance or gymnastics sequence) as well as principles of fair play and etiquette, established or official ways of doing something in a Movement Activity and explicit conventions governing a particular Movement Activity (for example rules in a game or for a change over in a relay in athletics or swimming). In turn these impact on how learners enact a Movement Activity (e.g. the strategies and tactics that can be adopted in a game within the rules). Progress in applying conventions of a Movement Activity is shown in Table 5.4.

Being able to apply conventions of a Movement Activity is key to a learner being able to participate fully in that Movement Activity. However, participating effectively in a Movement Activity may also require learners work alongside other learners. This is considered next.

5.4.2.2 Aspect 2: Movement Activities; Focus 2, enacting roles alongside other learners in the working space

All movement takes place in space. This space comprises personal space and common space. Thus, it is not appropriate for a learner to only consider movement from a 'personal' perspective. In all physical education contexts learners have to factor into the mix and adapt their own use of space to consider and accommodate other learners in the common space.

Common space comprises both the entire working space in which a class is working (e.g. a gymnasium) and the specific space in which an individual, pair or group are working (e.g. a mat, piece of equipment or court). In both spaces learners need to be aware of the other learners around them. For example a learner may be working on their own and therefore not interacting directly with other learners, or they may be working directly with other learner(s)

Table 5.4 Ladder of Progress in applying conventions of Movement Activities

Aspect 2 Movement Activities
Focus 1 Applying conventions of Movement Activities

Baseline	Growing	Establishing	Consolidating
A learner is able to follow instructions in relation to a few basic conventions for participating in a modified Movement Activity (e.g. what to do to restart a game when a ball goes outside the boundary of the playing space)	A learner is becoming aware of the conventions associated with a Movement Activity, accepts that these must be followed for the Movement Activity to be valid and, in appropriate activities, recognises that 'officials,' e.g. referees/ umpires, should be respected and their decision not disputed	A learner knows, is able to articulate and correctly interpret conventions relevant to participation in a Movement Activity and is developing the ability to apply them when participating in, or officiating, a Movement Activity	A learner understands and is able to apply the conventions consistently when participating in, or officiating, a range of Movement Activities to maintain the integrity of that activity
A learner is able to participate in some simplified/modified Movement Activities but is largely unaware of, or able to use approaches, strategies and tactics as appropriate for the conventions	A learner is aware of the need to use appropriate approaches, strategies and tactics in light of conventions of a Movement Activity, but has some difficulty in doing this	A learner is developing the ability to design appropriate approaches, strategies and tactics within the constraints of the conventions of a Movement Activity, but cannot do this consistently	A learner is consistently able to design appropriate approaches, strategies and tactics to solve problems in accordance with the conventions of a Movement Activity
A learner recognises and is able to follow instructions in relation to principles of fair play and etiquette in Movement Activities	A learner exhibits adherence to principles of fair play and etiquette in Movement Activities	A learner understands the need for, and is able to apply, principles of fair play and etiquette in Movement Activities without guidance	A learner positively embraces fair play and proper etiquette in all Movement Activities

where a level of co-operation is needed for the success of a Movement Activity (e.g. a pair or group sequence in dance or gymnastics, a relay baton change in athletics) and/or those where competition is an essential element (e.g. a game).

Other learners have different strengths and areas for development and can be unpredictable in, for example their movement or behaviour; hence, there are rules for working in a common space both in order for the space to be safe and for a Movement Activity to be valid (see above). The rest of this section focuses on use of space for a Movement Activity to be valid.

Progress in enacting roles alongside other learners in the working space is covered in Table 5.5.

How learners enact roles alongside other learners in the working space varies according to the Movement Activity. For example, in dance or gymnastics learners plan how to use the space cooperatively. In swimming the working space may be constrained within a lane. However, in a games context, the concept of 'open space' is important. As learners recognise this they can maximise their use of the space. This is an important part of being able to participate effectively in Movement Activities in different Movement Forms, which is considered next.

Table 5.5 Ladder of Progress in enacting roles alongside other learners in the working space

Aspect 2 Movement Activities
Focus 2 Enacting roles alongside other learners in the working space

Baseline	Growing	Establishing	Consolidating
A learner is developing an awareness of and confidence in the whole working space	A learner is aware of and pays attention to the whole working space	A learner is beginning to be able to determine how much working space is available and is starting to take this into account and use it productively	A learner understands the importance of using the working space effectively and is generally able to maximise the use of this space
A learner pays little attention to where others are in the entire working space, therefore is inconsistent in being able to move appropriately in the space in relation to other learners	A learner is beginning to realise that the entire working space is a shared space and to look to see where others are in the working space, in order to accommodate them and share space to work together safely and effectively	A learner is able to use and share the entire working space with others and is developing some consistency in being able to respond to the movement of others in order to use the working space effectively	A learner is well aware of others in the working space and demonstrates intelligent planning of using this space effectively
A learner pays little attention to the specific space for a Movement Activity, therefore whether working alone, in a pair or a group, is unable to use the working space effectively within the requirements of a Movement Activity	A learner is beginning to realise that in order to progress in a Movement Activity the use of the space available needs to be maximised. A learner is beginning to be able to move appropriately, but inconsistently, in the space available for the Movement Activity in relation to other learners	A learner is able to maximise the use of the working space available for the Movement Activity in order to progress, whether working alone, in pairs or groups	A learner evidences ability to adapt own movement in response to the movement of others within the working space allotted for a Movement Activity

5.4.2.3 Aspect 2: Movement Activities; Focus 3, participating effectively in a range of Movement Activities in different Movement Forms

Much of the focus in progress in physical education highlights depth of learning. Although this is very important, progress is also needed in breadth of learning, i.e. in the ability to both develop a repertoire of Movement Patterns (see Aspect 1, Focus 2) and to participate effectively in a range of Movement Activities. In this Focus we are particularly concerned with participating in a range of Movement Activities that display different characteristics of movement such as spelled out in respect of Movement Forms (by which we mean recognised and named groups of the many and varied Movement Activities which share some common features or characteristics).

Movement Activities cover a very wide field and there are a very wide range of Movement Activities which can be learned in physical education. These range from dance to swimming and from athletics to sailing. The list is endless. Limiting learning to only one or a few Movement Activities, for example, a variety of games, would not provide satisfactory evidence that progress has been made across the subject area and hence would be inadequate. As different Movement Activities have different characteristics, it is important that learners have a breadth of learning to enable them to make progress in Movement Activities with different characteristics. In order to aid this, Movement Activities with similar characteristics can be grouped together.

Over the years, a number of categorisations of Movement Activities have been suggested. For example, the National Curriculum in England in 1992 and 1999 explicitly cited Athletic activities, Dance activities, Games activities, Gymnastic activities, Outdoor and Adventurous activities and Swimming activities and water safety (Department of Education and Science and the Welsh Office (DES/WO), 1992; Department for Education and Employment and the Qualifications and Curriculum Authority (DfEE/QCA, 1999). Although these categories are not now included in the National Curriculum for Physical Education in England, they are generally recognised as categories of Movement Activities in the curriculum.

Other categorisations of Movement Activities have also been identified. For example, rather than simply naming specific Movement Activities, and to focus on particular characteristics shared by some Movement Activities, in the early 1980s the then Bedford College of Higher Education identified five 'Areas of Experience' which they called Adventure and Challenge, Aesthetic and Artistic, Body Management, Health and Wellbeing and Interaction. More recently, the six Movement Forms identified in the field of Physical Literacy have used the general approach of Areas of Experience (see Murdoch and Whitehead, 2010, pp. 181-183). Five of these Movement Forms which we perceive to be most relevant to schooling are entitled Adventure, Aesthetic and Expressive, Athletic, Competitive and Fitness and Health. Table 5.6 lists these five Movement Forms, describes features common to Movement Activities within that form and provides some examples of Movement Activities within the Movement Form.

Keeping in mind that, in this book, a physically active lifestyle has been identified as a key aim of physical education, breadth of learning in a range of Movement Activities from across all Movement Forms is important to enable learners to make informed decisions about which Movement Activities match their expertise, needs and interests; their personal preferences. Put another way, which Movement Activities they are most motivated to

Table 5.6 Movement Forms

ADVENTURE FORM: The common characteristics of Movement Activities in this Form are meeting risk and managing challenge, often in the outdoors in natural and often unpredictable environments, either carried out alone or as a group co-operative activity. *Examples of Activities include climbing, kayaking, orienteering*

AESTHETIC AND EXPRESSIVE FORM: The common characteristics of Movement Activities in this Form are using the human embodied dimension as an expressive medium within a creative, aesthetic or artistic context. *Examples of Activities include artistic gymnastics, dance, synchronised swimming*

ATHLETIC FORM: The common characteristics of Movement Activities in this Form are that a chief focus is on reaching a personal best in respect of speed, distance, power or accuracy, within the context of competition in a controlled environment. *Examples of Activities include events in athletics, gymnastics*

COMPETITIVE FORM: The common characteristics of Movement Activities in this Form are achieving predetermined goals through outwitting opponent(s) either individually or in teams, while (in some activities) managing a variety of implements and objects and coping with changing and challenging conditions and/or terrain. *Examples of Activities include basketball, hockey, tennis, volleyball*

FITNESS AND HEALTH FORM: The common characteristics of Movement Activities in this Form are gradually improving functioning within the Physical Domain both qualitatively and quantitively through regular repetitive participation. *Examples of Activities include aerobics, circuits, zumba*

See Murdoch and Whitehead (2010) and Murdoch and Whitehead (2013) for further detail

---

Note: Many Movement Activities can be experienced in a variety of different ways that mean they can be appropriate in a number of Movement Forms. For example, swimming in its various forms can be included in any of five Movement Forms.
Source: Adapted from Murdoch and Whitehead, 2010, pp. 181-183.

participate in outside physical education lessons and beyond compulsory schooling. Further, circumstances change throughout a lifespan (for example, at various times availability of time, money or facilities may be factors in decisions, as a result of, for example, getting a new job, moving to a different part of the country, having a family, motivation to take part in different activities, illness or aging). These may involve an assessment of choice of Movement Activity(ies) in which to take part. Hence, in order to accommodate changes in circumstances or life-style and cater for changing preferences throughout the life span, it is helpful for a learner to have developed a breadth of Movement Patterns and had meaningful learning experiences in a range of different types of Movement Activity across a range of Movement Forms during schooling (see Murdoch and Whitehead, 2010).

Progress in breath of learning; participating effectively in a range of Movement Activities that display different characteristics of movement such as spelled out in respect of different Movement Forms is covered in Table 5.7.

The issue of breadth is a challenging area. While breadth is an essential consideration in respect of learning, this must not be pursued at the expense of meaningful, deep learning. If learners are going to adopt a physically active lifestyle, they need time to engage in meaningful learning experiences to develop competence and confidence in participating in a range of Movement Activities. Depth of learning (as considered in progress in most of the other Foci in this Unit) is essential. In other words, learning experiences must be positive

Table 5.7 Ladder of Progress in participating effectively in a range of Movement Activities in different Movement Forms

Aspect 2 Movement Activities
Focus 3 Participating effectively in a range of Movement Activities in different Movement Forms

Baseline	Growing	Establishing	Consolidating
A learner is beginning to be able to participate in one or more individual, pair and small group simplified/modified Movement Activities (e.g. smaller group situations and conditioned games), representing at least three different Movement Forms	A learner is developing the ability to participate in one or more Movement Activities, some of which are simplified/modified, representing at least four different Movement Forms	A learner is able to participate in a number of Movement Activities representing all five Movement Forms with different levels of effectiveness	A learner is able to participate effectively and with confidence in a range of Movement Activities representing all five Movement Forms.

and in no way must learning be "a mile wide and an inch deep" (Guy, quoted by Kirk, 2010, p.7). This requires more than being introduced to a range of Movement Activities and then 'moving on to' a new/different one. Breadth and depth are considered further in Unit 11 in relation to the curriculum.

5.5 Summary and key points

This Unit has concentrated on progress in the Physical Domain which is at the heart of physical education. This (as well as progress in the Cognitive and Affective Domains) is complex. We have only touched the surface here.

To reiterate, despite separating out Movement Patterns and Movement Activities within this Unit for clarity of presentation, the two Aspects and the six Foci identified in this Unit are not mutually exclusive. There is overlap between these. Further, although learning may occur in different Aspects and Foci at the same time, learning in one Aspect and Foci might build on others. For example, while acquiring individual Movement Patterns, learners are at the same time learning a repertoire of Movement Patterns and Movement Phrases. Also, in order to adapt a Movement Pattern for a different context, learners need to have learned the Movement Pattern itself and in order to participate effectively in a range of Movement Activities in different Movement Forms learners need to have learned a range of individual Movement Patterns, be able to adapt them for the context, know and be able to apply the conventions of a Movement Activity and work alongside other learners.

The potential content for learning in the Physical Domain is vast. It is impossible to cover everything in one Unit. Whilst we have attempted to provide a range of examples, there may be other Aspects and Foci not identified in this Unit. Other Aspects and Foci, along with relevant Ladders of Progress, might therefore be identified in the Physical Domain.

As well as enabling progress in physical education, progress in the Aspects and Foci in the Physical Domain also stand learners in good stead to participate in, officiate, or watch a

Movement Activity they have learned. It also makes learners aware that there are a range of other Movement Activities in the different Movement Forms in which they can participate outside or after they leave school to which they can transfer their learning in physical education.

Finally, in physical education, it is difficult to separate out progress in the Physical Domain from progress in the Cognitive Domain. Learning in the Cognitive Domain in physical education is the focus of the next Unit.

ANNEX 5.1 Movement Vocabulary

Balance – vocabulary to enhance stable support and postural control

on front	on back	on side	on seat	on hands and feet	on hands and knees
on knees	on feet	on one hand and one foot	on one foot	sliding	upside down as in handstand
on elevated, wide and narrow surface	rocking	scooting	biking	floating	on unstable base

Locomotion – vocabulary to enhance travel from place to place

creeping	slithering	crawling	stepping	walking	gliding
trotting	jogging	running	dodging	pouncing	rolling
hopping along	skipping	galloping	bunny jumping along	cartwheeling	
pulling	pushing	swinging	climbing	wading	swimming

Flight – vocabulary to enhance projecting oneself off the ground and back down to land

landing on two feet	taking off	jumping up	jumping along	taking off from two feet	jumping around
jumping off	jumping over	jumping with turn	taking off on one foot	landing on one foot	hopping
hopscotch	leaping	assisted flight	abseiling		

Manipulation

holding	grasping	gripping	guiding	picking up	putting down
releasing	receiving a rolled object	receiving a thrown object			

Projection

placing	rolling	bouncing	throwing	striking	heading
aiming	kicking	punting	volleying	flicking	flinging
spinning	skimming	serving	driving	putting	goal shooting

Construction

adjusting	carrying	lifting	picking up

Communication (non-verbal)

leaning	turning away	turning towards

Source: Adapted from Maude and Pickard, 2021, p. 20 (focusing on vocabulary particularly relevant to physical education).

ANNEX 5.2 Movement Patterns

Examples of general Movement Patterns	Examples of refined Movement Patterns	Examples of specific Movement Patterns
jumping	hopping, leaping	Athletics – hop in triple jump
		Basketball – leaping for a rebound
receiving	catching, trapping	Netball – catching
		Football – chest trap
rotating	spinning, turning	Athletics – throwing a discus
		Gymnastics – barrel roll
		Dance – directional turns
running	dodging, sprinting	Netball – dodging to evade an opponent
		Athletics – running for speed, running for distance
sending	bowling, shooting, throwing	Rounders – underarm bowling
		Hockey – drive shot at goal
		Netball – chest pass
striking	batting, dribbling, driving	Cricket – forward drive
		Basketball – dribbling with both hands
		Football – outside foot pass

Source: Adapted from Murdoch and Whitehead, 2010, p. 179.

ANNEX 5.3 Examples of Movement Capacities

Simple capacities

These include, for example,

- Balance
- Coordination
- Control
- Core stability
- Flexibility
- Maintenance of stillness
- Moving at different rates/speeds
- Orienting in space and accurate placement of the body
- Proprioceptive awareness
- Stamina and endurance
- Use of power

Combined capacities

These comprise an amalgamation of simple capacities and include, for example,

- Agility which incorporates balance, coordination and flexibility
- Dexterity which incorporates coordination, flexibility and accurate placement of body parts
- Equilibrium which incorporates balance, core stability, orientation in space and maintenance of stillness
- Fluency which incorporates balance, coordination, proprioceptive awareness
- Poise which incorporates balance and core stability
- Precision which incorporates accurate placement of body parts and core stability

Complex capacities

These comprise an amalgamation of both simple and combined capacities and include, for example,

- Bi-lateral coordination
- Control of acceleration/deceleration
- Hand-eye coordination
- Inter-limb coordination
- Rhythmic movement
- Turning and twisting on a variety of rotational axes

Source: Adapted from Murdoch and Whitehead, 2010, p. 177.

Unit 6   The Cognitive Domain

6.1 Introduction

Physical education is a practical subject. However, in order for learners to progress, it is not enough for them to copy and reproduce a Movement Pattern or aspect of a Movement Activity, even though they may copy and reproduce them accurately. Rather, progress in physical education involves a combination of doing and thinking (and doing involves both declarative (facts and information about a topic – or knowing what) and procedural (how to do something – knowing how) knowledge; it is a physical and cognitive exercise. For example, progress in the Physical Domain is enhanced by learners developing their thinking to enable them to make decisions prior to, during and after movement (e.g. what Movement Pattern shall I use, how effectively am I doing the Movement Pattern, how can I improve or adapt it for the context?). In order to think about what they are doing, learners need relevant declarative knowledge which they can apply as procedural knowledge to a Movement Pattern or Movement Activity. For example, knowledge about constituents and principles of movement which they apply to learning a Movement Pattern (e.g., how the principle of levers helps with a swimming stroke). Further, progress in the Physical Domain also requires a positive attitude. Hence, although the outward manifestation of learning in physical education is the physical, this is underpinned by the Cognitive and the Affective Domains.

In this book we view the subject matter taught in physical education as part of the compulsory curriculum is Movement Patterns and Movement Activities which can be grouped into Movement Forms (See Unit 5). The subject matter is not biomechanics, exercise physiology or psychology. As a result, the view taken in this book is that progress in the Cognitive Domain underpins, facilitates and enhances progress in the Physical Domain, rather than knowledge being learned for its own sake, i.e. declarative knowledge underpins procedural knowledge.

Thus, it is not enough for learners to accumulate factual and conceptual knowledge (see Anderson and Krathwohl, 2001 and Table 6.1); what is generally referred to as declarative knowledge (or knowing what) (see above; Glossary; Office for Standards in Education, Children's Services and Skills (Ofsted), 2022; Unit 2). It is the purposeful use of this knowledge that is important in physical education; learners should be able to use knowledge to engage thoughtfully in their actual movement experience, *in a practical way*. This is generally referred to as procedural knowledge (or knowing how) (see Ofsted, 2022). For example,

DOI: 10.4324/9781003172826-7

knowledge about constituents and principles of movement should be demonstrated in the context of a learner's own actual movement experience, not as a theoretical exercise (we explore types of knowledge in more detail later in the Unit).

It is sometimes difficult to separate out progress in the Physical Domain from progress in the Cognitive Domain. For example, applying conventions of Movement Activities has been identified as an Aspect/Focus in the Physical Domain. However, in order to apply conventions in practice, and to participate effectively and fully in a Movement Activity, learners need to know and understand what these conventions are. Thus, application of knowledge in the Physical Domain is underpinned by knowledge developed through the Cognitive Domain (see, for example, Unit 5 Aspect 1: Foci 1 and 3, and Aspect 2: Focus 1).

In this Unit we start by looking at the nature of the Cognitive Domain, highlighting what is perhaps the most commonly used framework for considering progress in the Cognitive Domain in education generally as well as in physical education specifically; the taxonomy of educational objectives by Anderson and Krathwohl (2001) (adapted from the original by Bloom et al, 1956). We then consider Aspects and Foci of the Cognitive Domain we perceive to be relevant for the aim of learners adopting a physically active lifestyle. Progress in these Aspects and Foci is identified in Ladders of Progress which are based on the cognitive processes identified in the Anderson and Krathwohl (2001) framework.

6.2 The nature of the Cognitive Domain

The Cognitive Domain focuses on learners thinking and the acquisition of knowledge. But, what is meant by thinking and knowledge?

Simply, thinking is using the mind to do something; it is the activity of using the brain by considering a problem or possibility or creating an idea (Collins Dictionary, n.d.) or the process of forming an opinion or idea about something (Cambridge dictionary, n.d.). Knowledge is information and understanding about a subject gained by experience or study, either known by one person or by people generally (Cambridge Dictionary, n.d.). Following Anderson and Kratwohl (2001), thinking involves not only remembering and recalling appropriate knowledge from previously learned content but also applying, deliberating or reflecting on it in various ways, e.g. analysing, evaluating the facts and information and creating new knowledge. These meanings are used in this Unit. As stated above, it is the application of knowledge in a practical way which is key in physical education.

We next consider briefly the taxonomy of educational objectives by Anderson and Krathwohl (2001). This theoretical framework was identified for use in this Unit because it is commonly used for considering progress in the Cognitive Domain in education generally and physical education specifically. In this Unit, this framework is described and then used to underpin progress in Aspects and Foci we perceive to be important for learners to progress in the aim of adopting a physically active lifestyle.

The taxonomy identifies:

- The level of cognitive process required of a task (i.e. the cognitive process to be used in acquiring knowledge) (remembering, understanding, applying, analysing, evaluating and creating)

- Types of knowledge (i.e. the kind of knowledge to be learned) (factual, conceptual, procedural and meta-cognitive).

6.2.1 Levels of cognitive process

A brief description of each level of cognitive process is given in Table 6.1.

The levels of cognitive process are hierarchical. This is based on the belief that learners must first learn basic, foundational knowledge about any given topic before they can progress to more complex processes in relation to that knowledge, such as analysing and evaluating it. If higher levels of cognitive processing can only be attempted once lower levels have been mastered for any topic, learners must therefore work through these levels of cognitive process in order and master one level before they can progress to the next. In relation to physical education, learners must have mastered basic knowledge about a topic before they can start applying their knowledge in practice. Thus, for example, learners need to have a basic knowledge of the rules of a game in order to apply them in practice. In turn, as they apply the rules in practice, they gain greater understanding about them, and are able to respond appropriately and creatively within the rules.

Although they are hierarchical, the levels of cognitive process are not age-related. By this we mean that different learners may be at different levels of cognitive process at the same time. This may be for a number of reasons, including for example, a learner taking longer to progress through the levels or, on the other hand a learner progressing faster through the levels. Furthermore, a learner may have missed out on some learning already undertaken by the rest of the class as underpinning new learning, e.g. through illness or joining a school from another school where they did not cover pre-requisite content. Such learners will need to start at a lower level of cognitive process than other learners in the class.

Table 6.1 Level of cognitive process (Anderson and Krathwohl, 2001) (lowest level at the top to highest level at the bottom)

Cognitive process	Brief description of the cognitive process
Remembering	Recognise, retrieve or recite previously learned knowledge (basic concepts, facts, information, principles and procedures) from memory
Understanding	Construct meaning from this knowledge, explain ideas and concepts or interpret material
Applying	Use knowledge in a practical way; apply it to a new context
Analysing	Break knowledge down into its component parts in order to better understand it, determine how the parts relate to one another or to an overall structure or purpose
Evaluating	Make a judgement about the effective use of the knowledge by checking against criteria
Creating	Put elements of knowledge together or reorganise elements into a new pattern or structure to produce something new

Table 6.2 Anderson and Krathwohl (2001) Four types of knowledge

Types of knowledge	Brief description of each type of knowledge
Factual (knowing what)	• Knowledge of specific facts or items of information which a learner must know in a subject • Forms the underpinning for other knowledge and allows the learner to solve problems in a subject
Conceptual (knowing what)	• Separate or disconnected facts are brought together so that the interrelationships among them give a broader perspective and enable generalisations to be made
Procedural (knowing how)	• The application of factual and conceptual knowledge to practice • Discipline specific knowledge and competences and criteria, or rules, to be followed to determine how to do a specific task
Metacognitive (Knowing how)	• Learning how to learn • Knowledge of general strategies for learning and thinking; when and how to use cognitive strategies appropriately, both in general as well as by self (self-knowledge) • Knowledge of own thinking processes and of own strengths and weaknesses in relation to cognition and learning.

6.2.2 Types of knowledge

The four types of knowledge: factual; conceptual, procedural and metacognitive are shown in Table 6.2, along with a description of each type of knowledge.

In this Unit and book, we collapse factual and conceptual knowledge (Bloom et al., 1956) into declarative knowledge (knowing what) and procedural and metacognitve knowledge into procedural knowledge (knowing how).

The four different types of knowledge are not hierarchical, nor are they discrete steps. Rather, these types of knowledge can be developed at the same time. For example, learners can learn about the effects of physical activity on breathing at the same time as they apply this, for example, when running for a distance a learner will feel an increase in their breathing rate and be able to recognise that this is a result of the activity they are undertaking, and that to maintain this activity they will need to consider how they control their breathing. Likewise, knowledge of a specific rule can be learned at the same time as it is applied in a game situation in practice.

Cognitive processes and types of knowledge do not operate in a vacuum. Rather, they have to be applied in a specific context; in our case physical education. The next section considers progress in the Cognitive Domain in physical education. Throughout the rest of the Unit progress in the Cognitive Domain is linked to Anderson and Krathwohl's (2001) framework but using the words declarative and procedural knowledge.

6.3 The Cognitive Domain in physical education

6.3.1 Aspects and Foci of knowledge

Because cognitive processes and types of knowledge are applied in a specific context, this raises the question of 'What knowledge is important for learners to learn to facilitate and enhance their progress in the Physical Domain in physical education?' More specifically, in relation to this Unit and book, 'What knowledge is important for learners to learn to work towards an aim of adopting a physically active lifestyle in physical education?'

In our view, two different Aspects of learning are essential in the Cognitive Domain, that is knowledge about:

Aspect 1: Constituents and principles of movement
Aspect 2: Adopting a physically active lifestyle

These two Aspects were identified because, in our view, this knowledge underpins progress in the Physical Domain in working towards an aim of adopting a physically active lifestyle. For example, underpinning knowledge about constituents and principles of movement (including what makes a Movement Pattern efficient and effective and why, as well as how the body responds to physical activity) can be applied to facilitate and enhance progress in physical education. Thus, Aspect 1 facilitates and enhances learning of Movement Patterns and Movement Activities. However, learners also need knowledge about the nature and purpose of Movement Activities, the importance and benefits of physical activity and to be able to plan for participation in physical activity in order to adopt a physically active lifestyle (Aspect 2). The two Aspects (and Foci) are considered below.

In considering progress in each of these Aspects, it is important to take into account not only the content, but also the cognitive processes and the types of knowledge being developed (as identified by Anderson and Krathwohl, 2001; see Tables 6.1 and 6.2). However, to reiterate, because in physical education progress in the Cognitive Domain underpins progress in the Physical Domain, knowledge is not learned theoretically, for its own sake; rather it is the application of knowledge in practice, in learning and adapting Movement Patterns in accordance with the demands of the context and participating in Movement Activities that is important.

6.3.1.1 Aspect 1: Constituents and principles of movement

This Aspect refers to components or foundations which underpin movement and the effect of physical activity. These include, for example, the constituent parts of a Movement Pattern, how different parts of the body work together, what makes them efficient and effective, principles such as balance, force or motion, exercise intensity, aerobic and anaerobic respiration, adaptations of the body to exercise both immediately and over time (acute and chronic responses), and why the body responds in this way. Having knowledge, thinking about and applying in practice constituents and principles of movement is important in physical education to enable learners to progress in their own Movement Patterns and in participating effectively in Movement Activities.

This Aspect is divided into two Foci which, in our view, are central to progress in learning Movement Patterns and Movement Activities. These Foci are:

• Knowing how to move efficiently and effectively
• Recognising the effects of physical activity

6.3.1.2 *Aspect 2: Adopting a physically active lifestyle*

Aspect 1 considered supporting learners to effectively develop Movement Patterns and to participate effectively in a range of Movement Activities. Although these are important underpinnings to enable learners to work towards an aim of adopting a physically active lifestyle, alone they are not enough. To enable learners to adopt a physically active lifestyle, it is also important for them to have a broader understanding of Movement Activities and their importance in supporting the adoption of a physically active lifestyle. In doing so they become better informed and can apply this understanding to a specific Movement Activity. It is also important for them to know and think about the value and benefits of participating in physical activity and be able to plan their own participation in physical activity. There are three Foci central to progress in this Aspect:

- Knowing the nature and purpose of Movement Activities
- Knowing the importance and benefits of participating in physical activity
- Planning for participation in physical activity

6.4 Progress in the Cognitive Domain

As explained in Unit 4 – for each of the Aspects and Foci in each of the three domains in this book, we identify four levels of progress in the Ladders of Progress, i.e. baseline, growing, establishing and consolidating. However, the widely used work of Anderson and Krathwohl (2001) which underpins progress in the Cognitive Domain in this Unit identifies six levels of cognitive process. In order to reconcile these differences, we have attempted to categorise the six levels of Anderson and Krathwohl into the four levels used in this book. This is shown in Table 6.3. However, the boundaries are not hard and fast between different cognitive processes, as shown by the wavy lines. Table 6.3 also gives examples of words which may be used to describe the level as well as some examples from physical education.

6.4.1 *Aspect 1: Constituents and principles of movement*

Knowledge about constituents and principles of movement and the ability to apply these in practice enables learners to take responsibility for developing, improving and extending their own Movement Patterns.

   There are two Foci central to progress in this Aspect:

- Knowing how to move efficiently and effectively
- Recognising the effects of physical activity.

These two Foci are considered in turn below.

6.4.1.1 *Aspect 1: Focus 1, knowing how to move efficiently and effectively*

This focus is on the what, how and why of movement. It includes knowing the constituent parts of a Movement Pattern, how the different parts work together, what makes them efficient and effective and why.

Table 6.3 Links between the four levels of progress in the Ladders of Progress and Anderson and Krathwohl's (2001) six levels of cognitive process

Cognitive process	Levels used in this Unit	Examples of words which can be used to recognise process/level	Examples from physical education Learners are able to:
Remembering	Baseline	Define, describe, identify, illustrate, label, list, locate, match, memorise, quote, recall, recite, recognise, record, select, state, tell	• identify technical vocabulary related to Movement Patterns and Movement Activities • name the positions in netball and which parts of the court each position is allowed to move in • list the key points for performing a sitting dive
Understanding	Developing	Arrange, associate, classify, compare, comprehend, contrast, convert, discuss, distinguish, examine, explain, explore, extract, extend, illustrate, indicate, infer, inquire, interpret, predict, relate, see, summarise, translate	• explain why it is important to follow the safety rules in athletics • summarise the role of force in stopping or landing in a still position from a jump • discuss how they feel after involvement in physical activity
Applying		Act, articulate, change, complete, demonstrate, discover, employ, interpret, involve, manipulate, predict, prepare, produce, relate, report, respond, show, sketch, solve, teach, transfer, use	• demonstrate knowledge of momentum in learning how to do a headstand • transfer knowledge of defensive strategies in hockey to playing a game • show how body, effort, shape and space (see, for example, Laban's (1974) principles; also Annex 6.1) have underpinned a dance sequence
Analysing	Establishing	Adapt, analyse, break down, calculate, categorise, conclude, connect, contrast, correlate, deduce, devise, illustrate, infer, order, problem-solve, reason, relate, subdivide, support, take apart	• subdivide a warm up into activities that focus on different parts of the body • analyse how effectively a number of Movement Patterns were combined in a sequence • break down a tactic in a game to better understand what is needed to improve
Evaluating		Appraise, argue, combine, compose, criticise, decide, defend, design, evolve, judge, plan, prioritise, re-design, refine, reframe, reorganise, revise, support, value	• redesign a gymnastics sequence, based on own critique of current performance • refine or revise long jump technique based on a video analysis of performance • plan a simple and safe exercise programme and monitor personal activity levels

(Continued)

Table 6.3 (Continued)

Cognitive process	Levels used in this Unit	Examples of words which can be used to recognise process/level	Examples from physical education Learners are able to:
Creating	Consolidating	Appraise, assess, collaborate, construct, defend, design, develop, devise, evaluate, formulate, generate, imagine, initiate, invent, judge, modify, organise, pivot, rewrite, role-play, write	• formulate an appropriate strategy for maximising the use of space in a game situation • design appropriate practices to develop and improve existing Movement Patterns as well as learn new Movement Patterns • develop a synchronised swimming sequence to improve its flow

Knowing how to move efficiently and effectively can be considered in different ways. For example, an anatomical and biomechanical approach looks at knowledge of the components of movement, such as bones, joints and muscles and the structure of the skeleton as well as how these components work together in different Movement Patterns including, for example, alignment, balance/stability, direction, dynamics, effort/force, levers, momentum, motion, muscular tension and velocity (e.g. bending the knees lowers the centre of gravity and increases stability). It is this framework that we adopt in this Unit.

An alternative way of looking at how to move efficiently and effectively is through Laban's (1974) principles – an approach which is frequently used in the context of dance. This focuses on four categories of movement; body, space, effort and relationships (see Table 6.3). Whilst we do not consider Laban's (1974) framework further in this Unit, we have provided a brief summary in Annex 6.1 for those who have not encountered this and are interested in pursuing this further.

Knowledge about how to move efficiently and effectively is important because it not only supports learners in developing individual Movement Patterns, but also enables learners to transfer learning across Movement Patterns. For example, being able to apply the principles of balance in learning a shoulder stand can then be transferred to learning how to do a head-stand. Likewise, being able to apply knowledge of levers to hitting a ball with a racket can be transferred to kicking a ball in football.

Progress in knowing how to move efficiently and effectively is shown in Table 6.4.

Knowing how to move efficiently and effectively is important in facilitating and enhancing progress in physical education. However, it is also important to recognise the effects of physical activity. This is considered next.

6.4.1.2 Aspect 1: Focus 2, recognising the effects of physical activity

In this Focus the what, how and why of the effects of physical activity are considered. Specifically, it considers what the effects of physical activity are on the body, how the body responds when participating in physical activity and why the body responds in this way, both immediately and over time (acute and chronic responses). Some knowledge of the effects of

Table 6.4 Ladder of Progress in knowing how to move efficiently and effectively

Aspect 1 Constituents and principles of movement
Focus 1 Knowing how to move efficiently and effectively

Baseline	Developing	Establishing	Consolidating
A learner is able to recognise and remember the names of different parts of the body used in a Movement Pattern.	A learner is able to distinguish and explain the use of the main parts of the body relevant in a Movement Pattern.	With the help of others, a learner is able to recognise and break down how different parts of the body are used individually and together in a Movement Pattern and use this information to improve own Movement Pattern.	A learner is able to analyse independently how effectively different body parts are used individually and together in a Movement Pattern and use this information to improve own Movement Pattern.
A learner is able to describe a basic Movement Pattern using correct vocabulary.	A learner shows some knowledge of movement concepts and principles and is beginning to apply them to, for example, underpin progress in learning a Movement Pattern.	A learner is able to apply information about some movement concepts and principles to learning and improving a Movement Pattern.	A learner is able to transfer concepts and principles learned in one Movement Pattern to other Movement Patterns.

physical activity is important because it facilitates and enhances learners' ability to participate effectively in Movement Activities.

Progress in recognising the effects of physical activity is shown in Table 6.5.

As a reminder, and as should be clear in the Ladders of Progress, in both Foci in Aspect 1 (knowing how to move efficiently and effectively and recognising the effects of physical activity), we are not advocating learners learn anatomy, biomechanics and physiology theoretically. Rather, we are advocating that knowledge of core principles in both Foci is developed which learners apply in practice to facilitate and enhance their progress in the Physical Domain.

Knowing how to move efficiently and effectively, alongside recognising the effects of physical activity, are important in enabling a learner to progressively develop their Movement Patterns and to participate effectively in a range of Movement Activities. However, if learners are to adopt a physically active lifestyle, this knowledge needs to be supplemented by an understanding of the benefits of participating in physical activity and the ability to plan for this. This is considered next.

6.4.2 Aspect 2: Adopting a physically active lifestyle

The knowledge and application developed through Aspect 1, considered above facilitates and enhances learners to progressively develop their Movement Patterns and to effectively participate in a range of Movement Activities. This is important underpinning to support an

Table 6.5 Ladder of Progress in recognising the effects of physical activity

Aspect 1 Constituents and principles of movement
Focus 2 Recognising the effects of physical activity

Baseline	Developing	Establishing	Consolidating
A learner can recognise differences in their body and describe how their body feels when they are still and when they are participating vigorously in physical activity. For example, they are short of breath/ puffing, feel hot and have a red face after vigorous physical activity which they do not have when they have been walking slowly or sitting down.	A learner understands and can explain the reasons for differences in their body before, during and after physical activity as well as when participating in different types of Movement Patterns and Movement Activities, e.g. running fast, holding a balance, dancing.	A learner is beginning to use knowledge of the effects of physical activity on the body to monitor their own response and think about what they might do to improve their response to physical activity. A learner is beginning to understand that there are long-term or accumulative effects of physical activity on the body. A learner is able to make connections as to why changes are happening.	A learner uses knowledge about the short and long term effects of physical activity on the body to monitor the effects on their body, to plan and take action to improve their response to physical activity to enable them to participate effectively in specific Movement Activities in the short and longer term.

aim of adopting a physically active lifestyle. However, it is not enough. In order to increase the likelihood that a learner will adopt a physically active lifestyle within and outside school and after they leave school, it is also important for them to progressively develop knowledge of the importance and benefits of participating in physical activity and to be able to plan for participation in physical activity.

Adopting a physically active lifestyle is divided into three Foci central to progress in this Aspect:

- Knowing the nature and purpose of Movement Activities
- Knowing the importance and benefits of participating in physical activity
- Planning for participation in physical activity.

6.4.2.1 Aspect 2: Focus 1, knowing the nature and purpose of Movement Activities

By nature of Movement Activities we mean the basic or inherent features, characteristics or qualities of a Movement Activity, and by purpose we mean the reason for participating in a Movement Activity. Knowing the nature and purpose of Movement Activities provides a broader perspective on Movement Activities which can help learners when learning and participating in a specific Movement Activity as well as help them to identify which types of

Table 6.6 Ladder of Progress in knowing the nature and purpose of Movement Activities

Aspect 2 Adopting a physically active lifestyle
Focus 1 Knowing the nature and purpose of Movement Activities

Baseline	Developing	Establishing	Consolidating
A learner can recognise that different Movement Activities have different characteristics, features, qualities and purposes (e.g. a tag game involves running and dodging, whereas hopscotch involves throwing and hopping and the purpose of dance is different to the purpose of these games).	A learner can describe the key characteristics, features, qualities and purposes of a number of different Movement Activities. They are able to explain what they like or not about the different Movement Activities.	A learner is able to use their knowledge of the characteristics, features, qualities and purposes of a Movement Activity to identify their own preferred Movement Activities.	A learner understands similarities and differences in characteristics, features, qualities and purposes between Movement Activities in the same and different Movement Forms and uses this information to decide which Movement Forms and Movement Activities to participate in outside physical education lessons and after they leave school.

Movement Activity they prefer to participate in. In turn, this provides a rationale, and fosters an informed motivation, for choices they make in adopting a physically active lifestyle. Progress in knowing the nature and purpose of Movement Activities is shown in Table 6.6.

6.4.2.2 Aspect 2: Focus 2, knowing the importance and benefits of participating in physical activity

Knowing the importance and benefits of physical activity can support the learner to understand the value of learning Movement Patterns and Movement Activities. Further, it is important that learners are aware of why it is important to adopt a physically active lifestyle outside physical education lessons, with a view that this knowledge will encourage them to participate throughout their life. Table 6.7 shows progress in knowing the importance and benefits of participating in physical activity.

Understanding the importance and benefits of participating in physical activity is important if learners are going to adopt a physically active lifestyle. However, in order for this knowledge to make a difference, learners need to plan for participation in physical activity. This is addressed in the third Focus in this Aspect.

6.4.2.3 Aspect 2: Focus 3, planning for participation in physical activity

Focus 3 extends Focus 2 by progressively enabling learners to plan their own participation in physical activity. This involves learners knowing about opportunities to take part in physical activity safely as well as considering their own participation in physical activity outside physical education lessons, both at school and in the community. For example, what they

Table 6.7 Ladder of Progress in knowing about the importance and benefits of participating in physical activity

Aspect 2 Adopting a physically active lifestyle
Focus 2 Knowing about the importance and benefits of participating in physical activity

Baseline	Developing	Establishing	Consolidating
A learner is able to describe why regular physical activity is important and beneficial in the short term, e.g. feel good/ alert, gives them energy.	A learner can articulate the importance and benefits of participating in physical activity in the short term and is beginning to recognise the longer-term benefits, e.g. strengthening bones, muscles, heart and lungs.	A learner recognises the importance and benefits of participating in physical activity in the short and long-term and is beginning to be able to apply these to their own participation in physical activity outside lessons and outside school.	A learner uses their knowledge of the importance and benefits of participating in physical activity in the short and long-term to underpin decisions about their participation in physical activity outside lessons and outside school.

enjoy and why, their current levels of physical activity and how they can increase this, when, where and how they can be active in school as well as in the community and being able to plan a physical activity programme, monitor their progress and adapt as appropriate. As a result learners take personal responsibility for, and make a commitment to, adopting a phys-ically active lifestyle outside physical education, outside school and beyond. Table 6.8 shows progress in being able to plan for participation in physical activity.

Developing the ability to plan for participation in physical activity enables learners to bring together the knowledge learned in the Aspects and Foci we identify as important for learners to progress in physical education. However, it is not something that develops 'by chance.' It needs to be explicitly incorporated into facilitating and enhancing progress.

6.5 Summary and key points

This Unit has considered progress in the two different Aspects of the Cognitive Domain we have identified as important in physical education, specifically with the aim of learners adopting a physically active lifestyle. These two Aspects are knowledge about; constituents and principles of movement, and adopting a physically active lifestyle. Although two different Aspects of the Cognitive Domain have been considered in this Unit, there may be other Aspects which can be identified. When considering these Aspects and their various Foci (as well as any other Aspects identified as important for progress), it is important to remember that:

- The subject matter taught in physical education as part of the compulsory curriculum is Movement Patterns and Movement Activities. Hence, the purpose of developing thinking and knowledge in the Cognitive Domain in physical education is not for this to learned theoretically in a classroom for its own sake. Rather, its purpose is to underpin, facili-tate and enhance progress in the Physical Domain, to enable learners to work towards an aim of adopting a physically active lifestyle. The focus at all times should therefore

Table 6.8 Ladder of Progress in planning for participation in physical activity

Aspect 2 Adopting a physically active lifestyle
Focus 3 Planning for participation in physical activity

Baseline	Developing	Establishing	Consolidating
A learner takes opportunities to participate in physical activity within and outside the school day (e.g. they are active with their friends before school, at playtimes and at lunch time).	A learner actively identifies and explores formal and informal opportunities to participate in physical activity within and outside the school day.	A learner is able to identify their own physical activity preferences and strengths and use this information to decide which physical activity contexts to participate in. The learner knows how and where they can participate in these physical activities.	A learner is able to take responsibility for a personal commitment to participating in physical activity, based on their preferences and strengths and taking account of, and addressing, any constraints or factors affecting their participation.
A learner knows how to participate in physical activity safely.	A learner is able to explain how to participate in physical activity safely and use this information in participating in physical activity safely.	A learner can apply basic safety principles to plan a simple and safe physical activity programme which reflects their strengths, preferences and opportunities and can then monitor their participation and personal activity levels.	A learner is able to plan an appropriate and safe physical activity programme into their lifestyle, based on their preferences and strengths, opportunities available and their knowledge of relevant scientific information.

be the application of knowledge to practice, i.e. declarative to procedural knowledge or knowing what to knowing how. As a result, in our view, progress in the Cognitive Domain in physical education should be developed through the physical, as far as possible, not in a classroom.

- Progress in the Cognitive Domain will not occur automatically or by absorption, therefore deliberate decisions need to be made about what content, cognitive processes and types of knowledge learners should develop to facilitate and enhance progress in the Physical Domain and when and how this is taught.
- Progress in the Cognitive Domain could seem overwhelming, both on its own and in conjunction with progress in the Physical and Affective Domains. Therefore, in order for progress in the Cognitive Domain to be manageable, attention cannot and should not be given to the different Aspects and Foci at the same time. Rather, different Aspects within the Cognitive Domain are better developed within some of the Aspects of the Physical Domain than others and hence one or another Aspect will be prioritised at different times. For example, knowing how to move efficiently and effectively is better developed in relation to facilitating and enhancing the development of a specific Movement Pattern, whilst knowing the nature and purpose of Movement Activities is best developed in relation to specific Movement Activities.

To reiterate, this Unit only provides a start in this complex area. There is a large amount of material readily available which can be referred to for content to facilitate and enhance progress in each of the Aspects in the Cognitive Domain (as well as any others identified).

The next Unit (Unit 7) focuses on progress in the Affective Domain in facilitating and enhancing progress in the Physical and Cognitive Domains.

Annex 6.1 gives a basic outline of Laban's analysis of movement. In order to use the Laban Principles to support teaching, further information can be obtained from several sources but Laban Guild International is a good place to work. Their work, as the name suggests, focuses on the work of Rudolph Laban. Their website (https://labanguildinternational.org.uk) includes a range of resources and a bibliography which can be used to understand this framework better to underpin its use.

Annex 6.1 A basic outline of the content of Laban's analysis of movement

Category of movement	Examples of analyses
What is the body doing?	*The body and its parts* can bend/stretch/twist (fundamental to all movement) *Actions* of the whole body: Travel, e.g. step, run, dash, gallop, sprint Turn, e.g. pivot, spin, spiral, rotate Jump, e.g. skip, leap, vault, bound (five varieties of footwork) Gesture, e.g. contract, extend, spiral, arch Transfer the weight of the body, e.g. roll, cartwheel, fall, slide, vault Hold still, e.g. stop, freeze, balance, halt *Body parts* can lead a movement, can support other body parts, relate to other body parts, be used in isolation from the rest of the body, be used simultaneously or successively *Body shape* may need to be narrow, wide, twisted, symmetrical or asymmetrical, round
Where is the body moving?	General space/personal space Size of movements Levels: low, medium, high Shape in space: curved/straight, angular, twisted Directions: up/down, forward/backward, left/right
How is the body moving?	Time: slow/sustained/lingering; fast/sudden/rapid/quick; medium speed, accelerating/decelerating Weight/tension: strong/firm/maximum tension; light/soft/fine/minimal tension; moderate tension, relaxed/no tension In space: direct/piercing/focused; multidirectional/flexible/unfocused Flow: bound/restrained/stoppable; free/unrestrained/ongoing
In what relationship is the body to others and to the environment?	Relating to the space: floor; walls; pitch; arena; court; stage Relating to objects: small apparatus (balls, hoops, mats etc.); large apparatus (benches, climbing frame, horse etc.); goals; weights Relating to people: alone/partner/small group/large group/whole class, positioning in relation to a partner/team members/opposing team members

Source: Adapted from Killingbeck and Whitehead, 2021, p. 253.

Unit 7 The Affective Domain

7.1 Introduction

As stressed throughout this book, learners are holistic. Therefore, the Physical, Cognitive and Affective Domains all need to be considered for learners to progress. Units 5 and 6 considered progress in the Physical and Cognitive Domains of learning, respectively. This Unit considers progress in the Affective Domain.

The Unit starts by describing the Affective Domain as used in this Unit, then considers the importance of attitudes in physical education. It explains how this Domain is similar to, and differs from, the Physical and Cognitive Domains in respect of considerations concerning progress. It then considers theories relevant to the Affective Domain and highlights the Self-determination theory (Deci and Ryan, 2000) which underpins analysis in this Unit. Finally, it looks at progress in the Affective Domain. While the Affective Domain covers a wide range of human characteristics, it has been decided that in this Unit it is best to focus on three key Aspects of this Domain in the context of physical education; that is Motivation, Confidence and Autonomy (see below for the rationale for selecting these three Aspects).

7.2 The Affective Domain

Generally, the Affective Domain refers to a person's feelings, emotions and attitudes. According to the Oxford Learners Dictionary (n.d.), feelings are defined as 'a person's emotions rather than their thoughts or ideas.' Emotions are defined as 'a strong feeling such as love, fear or anger; the part of a person's character that consists of feelings.' Attitudes are defined as 'the way that you think and feel about somebody/something; the way that you behave towards somebody/something that shows how you think and feel.' Further, in Enclyclopaedia.com (n.d.) attitudes are defined as 'a settled way of thinking or feeling about someone or something, typically one that is reflected in a person's behaviour.'

Although feelings, emotions and attitudes are separate constructs, they are closely related. For example, feelings are close to emotions and attitudes are shaped by feelings and emotions. A person's emotional state is related to their mental state, and this is related to attitude. In turn, these impact on a person's behaviour.

Krathwohl, Bloom and Masia (1964) describe the Affective Domain as the manner in which people deal with things emotionally, such as appreciation, attitudes, enthusiasms, feelings, motivations and values. It is this description which underpins this Unit. Further, in light of attitudes being 'a settled way of doing something' we argue that attitudes are reflected in the

DOI: 10.4324/9781003172826-8

three Aspects of the Affective Domain which are the focus of this Unit; Motivation, Confidence and Autonomy. Specifically, we focus on: a person's motivation (interest in, drive to effect or willingness to persist in something – whether due to an emotion, feeling or attitude); confidence (how a person sees themselves; trust or a belief in oneself and one's own abilities to do things and be successful); and autonomy (feeling one has a choice; an ability to think for one's self; being creative; willingly endorsing own behaviour and having assurance to express and justify a personal point of view). Although we consider Motivation, Confidence and Autonomy separately in this Unit, they are, in fact, very closely inter-related. Each of these three Aspects and Foci is dependent on the others. For example, if a learner is confident and/or has a good degree of autonomy, they are likely to be more willing to persist in an activity.

We next consider attitudes as an important factor in learners making progress in physical education.

7.3 The importance of attitudes in progress in physical education

The view of the Affective Domain used in this Unit encompasses a particular aspect of human nature that includes dispositions (the natural and inborn tendency of a person to behave in a certain way in a specific situation) and attitudes (a partly natural but predominantly learned way of a person thinking or feeling about something or behaving in a certain way which has become established).

Human beings usually have a general disposition to life. For example, they may be optimistic or pessimistic. They may be outward-going and extrovert or more withdrawn and introvert. They may be happy-go-lucky or cautious and questioning. These examples describe the broad nature of a person as they engage in all the activities of life. In this respect, individuals 'carry with them' a general outlook on life in whatever context they may find themselves. However, it is certainly the case that each person also has particular attitudes in respect of a specific context. For example, one person may be frightened of flying in an aeroplane while another may revel in the ambience of mountain scenery. Another may love the creativity that is part of cooking, while another may be irritated with the procedures for preparing all the ingredients needed.

A person's attitudes are the outcome of previous experiences which colour all human perceptions. In the context of physical education, a learner will likely present differently, based on their general outlook on life but more importantly their prior interactions with physical education and with physical activity outside lessons. For example, a learner who has had a positive experience of one or a range of Movement Activities in physical education lessons and/or physical activity outside lessons is likely to demonstrate more positive attitudes towards the subject than a learner who has had a negative experience of one or a range of Movement Activities in physical education lessons and/or physical activity outside lessons. Further, a learner may also have a particular attitude to a specific Movement Activity such as swimming or dance.

Because the Affective Domain works in concert with the Physical and Cognitive Domains, attitudes are very powerful in that they can block effective progress in other domains. For example, lack of confidence may inhibit an individual learner's progress in, for example, an athletic event or self-consciousness may limit progress in, for example, dance choreography. The aim of adopting a physically active lifestyle rests as much on nurturing positive attitudes as it does on mastery of Movement Patterns, participating in a range of Movement Activities, a sound understanding of constituents and principles of movement or knowing the value of adopting a physically active lifestyle. The success on which progress in the Affective Domain is founded arises from progress in the Physical and Cognitive Domains. Likewise, progress in these two Domains relies on the Affective Domain. This creates a challenging situation in which progress in respect of the Affective Domain can be seen as both complex and critically important.

As stated above, within this Unit we consider three key Aspects of the Affective Domain; Motivation, Confidence and Autonomy. Individually and together, Motivation, Confidence and Autonomy impact on learner behaviours both in physical education lessons and in relation to participating in extra-curricular activities and physical activity outside (and after leaving) school.

7.4 Theory related to the Affective Domain

Whilst there are various theories related to Motivation, Confidence and Autonomy (see for example, achievement motivation (Atkinson, 1964; McClelland, 1961), achievement goal theory (Ames, 1992a, 1992b; Dweck, 1986; Dweck and Leggett, 1988; Duda, 2004; Nicholls, 1984, 1989), attribution theory (Weiner, 1972), expectancy theory (Rosenthal and Jacobson, 1968); hierarchy of needs theory (Maslow, 1970); self-attribution theory (Weiner, 1972); self-efficacy theory (Bandura, 1977) (for summary refer to McLellan, 2022), most of these theories focus on one Aspect – Motivation, Confidence or Autonomy. Therefore, in this Unit we have selected to concentrate on Deci and Ryan's (2000) Self-determination theory because it is relevant to Motivation, Confidence and Autonomy.

Self-determination refers to a firmness of purpose and a willingness to persevere in the face of obstacles. A learner who is self-determined:

1. Is self-motivated and not driven by the standards of others or external factors
2. Shows confidence in their own ability
3. Determines their own actions based on own internal values and goals, as appropriate
4. Believes they are in control of their own life
5. Takes responsibility for their own behaviour (taking credit or blame, as warranted).

Thus, a learner who takes responsibility for their actions and does things because they align with their own personal values and goals is self-determined. A learner who blames others, sees themself as a constant victim and does things solely for external approval or recognition, is not.

Self-determination theory posits that there are two main types of motivation – intrinsic and extrinsic. This is covered in Motivation, below. It also identifies three core psychological needs that must be met for a person to flourish and succeed: competence, autonomy and relatedness. Refer to Deci and Ryan (2000) for further detail on each of these, as well as on the theory as a whole.

7.5 Comparing progress in the Affective Domain to progress in the Physical and Cognitive Domains

Unit 2 stresses that for progress to be achieved learning has to take place; indeed, learning is a pre-requisite to progress. This is certainly the case in respect of the Physical Domain and the Cognitive Domain. In the Physical Domain, learning has to take place to progress from, for example, performing a Movement Pattern in a practice situation to its effective use in a game situation or a gymnastics sequence. Similarly, learning has to take place between the development of Movement Patterns on an indoor climbing wall to the adept use of these patterns when climbing a rock face in a mountain range. In the Cognitive Domain, learning is needed to progress from a basic knowledge of constituents and principles of movement to being able to apply these in order to make progress in learning a Movement Pattern or from a basic understanding of muscle function to appreciating the theory underpinning the management of lactic acid build up to being able to apply these in practice (from declarative to procedural knowledge).

This also applies in relation to some Aspects of the Affective Domain; in the Aspects considered in this Unit, it applies to Autonomy – in which progress requires a learner to, for example, increasingly act independently, take ownership of their own decisions, take responsibility for their own actions, be creative, innovative and open to new possibilities, demonstrate self-management, self-control and honest self-assessment, show self-reliant and self-sufficient behaviour and be eager to explore and experience new challenges.

However, in relation to other Aspects of the Affective Domain; in the Aspects considered in this Unit, to Motivation and Confidence, progress does not take this form. It neither depends directly on ever more challenging practice as in the Physical Domain nor the grasp of declarative knowledge as in the Cognitive Domain nor increasingly being able to act independently. Rather it depends on personal experience.

Positive, meaningful experiences (Whitehead, 2019) have the power to facilitate and enhance progress while negative experiences can stunt progress. Although this progress in motivation and confidence can be seen as a type of learning, it is more about change in respect of the self rather than learning per se (although it does impact progress in the Physical and Cognitive Domains). Changes in motivation and confidence are likely to be more the result of how learning is presented and experienced; for example how new information is presented, modelled, rehearsed and reinforced (Simonson and Maushak, 2001; Smith and Ragan, 1999) or the nature of the interaction between the teacher and the learner (the emotional investment), and less on account of what content is being presented.

As a result, progress in some Aspects of the Affective Domain (Motivation and Confidence) does not necessarily follow the more straightforward pattern set out in relation to the Physical and Cognitive Domains and in some Aspects of the Affective Domain (in this Unit; Autonomy). In those two Domains and in Autonomy, evidence of learning builds from baseline, through developing and establishing to consolidating. Thus, the Ladders of Progress can be read from left to right and be interpreted as indicating desirable progressive steps in learning. In some situations, such as a serious accident, there might be evidence of regression to the left. Nonetheless, this would be seen as an exception. However, this progress is not the case in respect of some Aspects of the Affective Domain (Motivation and Confidence).

As this relies on life experiences in general, as well as experiences in physical education and physical activity outside physical education lessons, it is not surprising to find that matching behaviours with descriptors does not always follow the left to right pattern. In some cases attitudes may change, fluctuate and wax and wane. Thus, there can be regression as well as progression (for example, motivation or confidence may be reduced) and hence there may be movement from right to left as well as left to right in the Ladders of Progress.

For example, an individual learner's attitude to schooling, including physical education, may be affected by a significant change in life-circumstances (sometimes referred to as a trauma; see, for example, Department for Education (DfE, 2022), such as a death in the family or a sudden redundancy of the principal earner in the family. The learner may become demotivated and try to opt out of learning in physical education. As another example, an individual learner may react to change by losing confidence. This could be the case if, for example, groups are radically reorganised, such as moving from single sex to mixed sex groups, there is a new teacher, or learners are learning a challenging new activity such as sailing. In addition confidence could be lessened by, for example, the experience of a sudden growth spurt, leaving the individual learner less coordinated and/or embarrassed by physical changes. Progress in Aspects of the Affective Domain will therefore not be unidirectional and recognising any variation in progress is essential if learners are to be supported to return to a more positive attitude. This highlights the need for learners to be known and understood as unique individuals so that they can be supported appropriately.

7.6 Progress in the Affective Domain

As stated above, while the Affective Domain covers a wide range of human characteristics, it has been decided that in this Unit it is best to focus on three key Aspects of this Domain in the context of physical education: Motivation, Confidence and Autonomy.

With an aim of physical education being for learners to adopt a physically active lifestyle, motivation was considered as essential. Motivation broadly covers interest in and drive to effect learning and participation. Confidence is viewed as a belief in oneself and one's own abilities to do things and be successful; being the security an individual learner feels concerning learning in physical education. Positive learning experiences and progress in learning are generally viewed as self-affirming and fostering self-belief. Growth in confidence can make a significant contribution to the development of a positive attitude towards, and motivation in, learning in physical education, participation in physical activity outside lessons and adopting a physically active lifestyle. Autonomy was selected on the grounds that for an individual learner to make a personal decision regarding participation in physical activity outside lessons as part of adopting a physically active lifestyle, independent initiative is essential. At root, autonomy describes an ability to think for oneself, be creative and have the assurance to express and justify a personal point of view. Autonomy builds on both motivation and confidence; it requires the motivation and confidence to follow personal goals. In respect of adopting a physically active lifestyle the development of autonomy is essential. Without a clear and rationally developed commitment it is unlikely that an individual will be able hold to a resolve to be physically active through life. Unit 9 looks in more detail at how learners can be supported to take greater responsibility for their own learning.

While Motivation, Confidence and Autonomy are distinctive Aspects of the Affective Domain they are closely related; they influence and feed off each other. For example, more confident learners are usually motivated to plan their own work and take some responsibility for achieving their own goals. Equally, learners who are less confident are likely to be less motivated to plan their own work and less likely to take responsibility for achieving goals. This may be due, at least in part, to them being apprehensive about how far they can fulfil the task.

However, each of these three Aspects may manifest itself in different ways. For example, a lack of motivation may manifest itself in a lack of engagement or application to learning in a lesson or to participating in physical activity outside a lesson. Confidence may manifest itself through self-efficacy and/or self-belief that participation in a wide range of Movement Activities or adopting a physically active lifestyle can be rewarding. Autonomy may manifest itself in a learner's self-awareness in how they set their own goals, solve problems or create new ideas or in them participating in physical activity outside lessons. The complex nature of the Affective Domain meant that we felt it inappropriate to generate a number of different Foci in each Aspect to cover different ways each Aspect may manifest itself. However, in each Aspect two or three different examples are given of how progress in that Aspect manifests itself.

7.6.1 *Aspect 1: Motivation*

As indicated above, motivation can be described as the interest, drive and desire to participate in a particular activity. Motivation can energise, enthuse and inspire. The word 'motivation' has roots in the notion of having a motive and is closely related to the commitment to achieve goals. It is suggested that this positive commitment is essential to learning in physical education, participation in physical activity and to adopting and maintaining a physically active lifestyle.

We have previously indicated that attitudes reflect a learned way of a person thinking or feeling about something, demonstrated through behavioural responses (see above). This is shown in, for example, motivation of a learner in relation to their willingness to persist in their learning. The stage of motivation shown by a learner is reflective of three key aspects, these being a learner's acceptance of the need to learn; which is related to their attitude towards the learning; and their belief in being able to make progress. This is also linked to their confidence and expectation; and the value or priority they assign to the learning.

There has been a significant amount of work on motivation in general and in school and learning in particular (including learning in physical education) to which reference can be made. Among the theories that unpack and explain human motivation, in our view Deci and Ryan's Self-Determination Theory (2000) is particularly useful to physical education as it marries well with practices in this subject area. In this context it is therefore useful to look briefly at Deci and Ryan's exposition in relation to motivation. However, references should be made to other sources for a more detailed explanation.

Deci and Ryan (2000) start from the presumption that a basic human need is to fulfil human potential and achieve competency. They assert that the fundamental motive for human behaviour is the desire to meet one's own innate needs. Sun et al (2017) identify physical potential as a human resource and therefore among human needs. Thus it follows that progress in physical education and participation in physical activity outside lessons can be the focus of motivated behaviour.

Deci and Ryan (2000) look broadly at motivation ranging from a state they name amotivation, that is the lack of any motivation to intrinsic motivation. Amotivation is described as a lack of drive, interest or application in respect of putting energy into a task. This, Deci and Ryan explain, is often caused by an individual seeing no value in the activity and/or feeling incompetent to do the activity, thus having little chance of making progress or experiencing any satisfaction. At the opposite end of the spectrum of stages of motivation they identify intrinsic motivation, where an individual is motivated by the expectation that genuine satisfaction will be the outcome of participation in physical activity.

Deci and Ryan (2000) describe stages between *amotivation* and *intrinsic motivation* as forms of extrinsic motivation. Broadly, extrinsic motivation refers to motivation that is external to the individual. Incentives such as rewards and punishments are the motivators and thus an activity is not engaged in for its own sake but for the purpose of some sort of 'external' recognition. The stages of extrinsic motivation gradually move external regulation towards more intrinsic regulation.

Ryan and Deci's (2000) stages of motivation are shown in Table 7.1.

These stages of Motivation are described broadly below, using exemplars to show key observable characteristics.

Progress made in respect of motivation starts with general disinterest and works steadily towards a clear commitment to adopting a physically active lifestyle. At the least motivated stage an individual learner tends to distance themself from the lesson activity, is not engaged in the learning activities and seldom shows any sign of applying themself to the challenges set. They show little interest in taking part in new activities or in working in different environments. They tend to take steps not to need to be involved, never taking an active role and finding a place on the periphery of any group. These individuals often absent themself or bring an excuse note. They have no involvement in physical activity outside lessons.

Progress can be seen when an individual learner begins to show some spasmodic and cautious interest in the learning activities. There is an occasional dialogue with other learners to clarify the task. Teacher feedback is reluctantly acknowledged and there is evidence of short periods of sustained application, however there is little progress. The teacher is the key motivator. The learner is less often absent or less often brings an excuse note. They have some tentative discussion with others about participating in physical activity outside lessons and may occasionally go with others to physical activities outside lessons, but tend not to become involved and keep a distance.

Clear progress can be seen when an individual learner begins to apply themself thoughtfully to learning activities, engages with others and refers to the teacher for guidance. They persist in applying themself through periods in which they make some progress. This effort usually results in some success. In turn this initiates an increase in motivation. The experience of success, acknowledged by the teacher, enhances further determination, further effort, further interest, further mastery and further motivation. There is ample evidence that there is an established pattern of participation in physical activity outside lessons.

Table 7.1 Stages of motivation

Motivation	Non self-determined	Self-determination continuum				Self-determined
	Amotivation	Extrinsic motivation				Intrinsic motivation
Regulatory style	Non-regulation (no drive to speak of; struggling to have any of their needs met).	External regulation (Acts out of the desire for external rewards or fear of punishment. Motivation is exclusively external and regulated by compliance, conformity, external rewards and punishments).	Introjected regulation (motivation from partially internalised activities and values, e.g. avoiding shame, seeking approval, and protecting the ego. Motivation is driven by self-control, efforts to protect the ego and internal rewards and punishments).	Identified regulation (motivation is somewhat internal and based on conscious values and what is personally important to the individual).	Integrated regulation (motivated by intrinsic sources and the desire to be self-aware).	Intrinsic regulation (self-motivated and self-determined, driven by interest, enjoyment and the satisfaction inherent in the behaviour or activity in which engaging).
Source of motivation	Impersonal	External	Somewhat external	Somewhat internal	Internal	Internal
Regulation of motivation	Non-intentional, Non-valuing, incompetence, lack of control	Compliance, external rewards and punishments	Self-control, ego-involvement, internal rewards and punishments	Personal, importance, conscious valuing	Congruence, awareness, synthesis with self	Interest, enjoyment, inherent satisfaction

Source: Adapted from Ryan and Deci, 2000.

An intrinsically motivated individual takes more initiative in relation to learning in physical education and participation in physical activity. Not only do they participate in school lessons with commitment, effort and enthusiasm, but they are also eager to participate in a wide range of physical activities outside lessons and outside school. Such an individual takes the initiative to research where different physical activities are going on in the locality and exhibits a strong indication that participation in physical activity will be a life-long commitment.

Keeping track of the stage of motivation – from amotivation to intrinsic motivation is of key importance in learning in physical education. The aspiration is for individual learners to be intrinsically motivated to progress in the subject and should there be any signs of apathy and/or disinterest it is essential that this negative attitude is eliminated. This is critical both because motivation is the trigger for learning and because it lies at the heart of adopting a physically active lifestyle.

The information in the Ladder of Progress in respect of Motivation (Table 7.2) gives examples of motivation in relation to engagement and application in lessons and to participating in physical activity outside lessons. However, motivation can also be demonstrated in other ways, and we would encourage consideration of how other ways of demonstrating motivation can be incorporated into the Ladder of Progress.

In Table 7.2, the descriptor for baseline aligns with amotivation, the descriptors for growing and establishing broadly with progress through extrinsic motivation and the descriptor for consolidating aligns with intrinsic motivation.

Alongside and in very close association with motivation in the Affective Domain, it is important that learner confidence is also monitored. Confidence is considered next.

7.6.2 Aspect 2: Confidence

As alluded to above, in this book, confidence can be described as the self-assurance that an individual has in respect of successfully making progress in a particular activity or on a particular task. Thus, it is viewed as a belief in oneself and one's own abilities to do things and be successful, being the security an individual learner feels concerning learning in physical education.

Confidence is identified as a key Aspect of the Affective Domain both because, in partnership with motivation, it provides an essential prerequisite for learning and also in the way that it forms an indispensable foundation for developing autonomy. Confidence lies at the heart of progress in learning and plays a significant part in continued participation in physical activity and adopting a physically active lifestyle.

As has previously been alluded to, the relationship between confidence and motivation is very close in that motivation is forward looking and is the drive or resolve to take action. In addition confidence builds from the past and is fed by the memory of successful learning and progress and participation in various challenges. Confidence usually plays a part in generating motivation, while motivation leads to active involvement that can add to the development of confidence.

Confidence is important in learning in physical education. Learner confidence will ensure that there is no block to exploring movement possibilities. There is no fear of a lack of ability

Table 7.2 Ladder of Progress in developing Motivation

ASPECT 1 *Developing Motivation*

Baseline	*Growing*	*Establishing*	*Consolidating*
Amotivated	Exhibits extrinsic motivation	Developing intrinsic motivation	Intrinsically motivated
A learner opts out of a lesson whenever possible e.g. absents themself, brings an excuse note.	A learner opts out of a lesson only occasionally.	A learner seldom opts out of a lesson.	A learner never opts out of a lesson and only misses a lesson when unavoidable.
When participating in a lesson, a learner engineers to do the minimum, seldom engages fully or applies self in a lesson, therefore shows very little evidence of any progress.	A learner tends to rely on the teacher for guidance and encouragement to apply self and persist for a short time. A learner tends to have a very short concentration span which limits progress.	A learner shows evidence of self-motivation and concentrates, persists and applies self. This interest results in the learner trying hard with encouragement and productive work with others as well as initiating questions to the teacher. Experience of progress leads to further effort.	A learner is clearly self-motivated and readily concentrates, applies self thoughtfully, is happy to persist and persevere when problems arise, or success is hard to come by and reflects on learning in the interests of future progress.
A learner has no interest in trying or participating in physical activity outside lessons.	A learner may show some interest in giving extra time to participating in physical activity outside lessons, with appropriate teacher encouragement, and friends with whom to work.	Following positive experiences in the school extra-curricular programme, a learner begins to seek out a range of opportunities for physical activity in local facilities in which they can participate.	A learner participates as much as possible in both school extra-curricular activities and physical activity outside school.

or even failure. An aspiration in physical education is for each individual learner to perceive participation in physical activity as a source of the development and enhancement of confidence. On a broader front, confidence is a key characteristic of a learner, necessary to lay the ground for, and develop a positive attitude to, participation in physical activity outside lessons and the adoption of a physically active lifestyle.

Where confidence is not in evidence there is a possibility that a learner may begin to perceive themself as having no prospect of progress in this area of the curriculum or in participating in physical activity outside lessons. Lack of confidence can stunt motivation and threaten progress in physical education and participation in physical activity outside lessons, and beyond school. Indeed, the outcome could well be a withdrawal from involvement in physical activity. It goes without saying that where an individual has no confidence it is unlikely that a physically active lifestyle well be realised both outside lessons and after schooling is complete.

A positive attitude towards participation in any area of life depends on confidence generated by meaningful, successful and rewarding experiences.

In relation to Self-determination theory (Deci and Ryan, 2000), confidence is built on a solid foundation of ability or competence. Learners are likely to be more confident if they have autonomy and they and the teacher has faith in their abilities. People like to feel in control of, and manage, their own lives, to have the ability to make their own

Table 7.3 Ladder of Progress in developing Confidence

Aspect 2 Developing Confidence			
Baseline	Growing	Establishing	Consolidating
A learner lacks confidence and is cautious to take part in all but the simplest/ most familiar of learning activities. A learner is quick to (try to find an excuse to) withdraw from a learning activity when not confident or little progress is being made.	A learner shows some signs of the development of confidence in own ability to make progress.	A learner is generally confident in own ability to make progress.	A learner is confident in making progress in Movement Patterns and Movement Activities which enhances global confidence and develops self-assurance, self-efficacy and self-esteem.
A learner fears failure and shies away from challenging tasks. Focuses on what they cannot do rather than what they can do. Easily loses faith in own abilities.	A learner is receptive to failure, and is developing the ability to persist with an activity. There is some realisation that where effort is expended, progress can be made, and this can enhance self-image and self-esteem.	A learner does not fear failure, rather uses this to resolve to apply self whole-heartedly.	A learner views challenges as something to be mastered rather than threats to be avoided. Recovers quickly from failure and is more likely to attribute failure to a lack of effort.
A learner is self-conscious concerning own movement and is nervous to expose any inability.	A learner shows some confidence in learning new Movement Patterns and participating in new Movement Activities.	A learner is prepared to explore new contexts in the confidence that new challenges can be met, and that new Movement Patterns and Movement Activities have the potential to build confidence.	A learner is intrigued and excited to explore new Movement Patterns and Movement Activities in the secure belief that these will be rewarding.

choices and, indeed, to make confident choices (Deci, 1971). Further, a sense of belonging and social connections (relatedness) are important for confidence because they provide a strong support network, regular feedback from peers – both good and in terms of keeping a learner grounded if needed and opportunities for social learning (see also theories of learning, Unit 2).

Progress in relation to Confidence is shown in Table 7.3. Developing confidence can be demonstrated in multiple ways. The information in the Ladder of Progress in Table 7.3 gives examples of confidence that participation in a wide variety of Movement Patterns and Movement Activities in lessons and physical activity outside lessons will be rewarding. However, confidence can also be demonstrated in other ways. Other ways of demonstrating confidence can be incorporated into the Ladder of Progress, as appropriate.

The final Aspect of the Affective Domain on which progress is considered in this Unit is identified as Autonomy. This is considered next.

7.6.3 Aspect 3: Autonomy

At root Autonomy describes an ability to think for oneself, be creative and have the assurance to express and justify a personal point of view. Autonomy is identified as a key Aspect in the Affective Domain as it is seen to be an essential personal attribute in the context of achieving an aim of adopting a physically active lifestyle. It builds on, and requires, both confidence and the motivation and desire to follow personal goals.

To sustain involvement in physical activity throughout life depends on long term commitment, with individuals having to make a number of personal choices as age and circumstances change. This commitment may well need to be weighed against other possibilities of spending, for example, time and money. In most cases the decision rests with the individual, although of course much may depend on the views of others. There will always be repercussions from selecting physical activity over other activities and this could call on the individual justifying the choice made. Autonomy, alongside motivation and confidence in respect of a wide range of physical education and physical activity experiences augers well for adopting a physically active lifestyle over the long term.

The aspiration of this Aspect is that participation in physical activity will be maintained once the learner has completed schooling. However, there is always a danger of learners getting into the habit of deferring to the teacher, relying on them to set goals, to help to solve problems and to make a judgement of future goals, providing the strategies to reach these. To realise a physically active lifestyle the responsibility rests with each individual to act in accordance to needs and potentials throughout different periods of life.

Autonomy includes a range of personal skills. Characteristically a person might be described as being autonomous if they exhibit the ability to, inter alia:

- Act independently
- Make, justify, defend and take ownership of own decisions
- Take responsibility for own actions
- Be creative, innovative and open to new possibilities
- Demonstrate self-management, self-control and honest self-assessment

- Show self-reliant and self-sufficient behaviour
- Be eager to explore and experience new challenges.

Acting independently in the context of physical education involves an individual learner making personal decisions without significant reliance on the teacher or other learners. These decisions will be thoughtfully chosen and thus the individual will be able to explain and justify their selection. In this way the individual will take ownership, as appropriate, of a chosen pathway and particular goals.

This independence may be concerned with learner creativity that springs from an assured 'open mindedness' and may well involve 'thinking outside the box' or using divergent thinking. The individual will be adept at exploring new ground and keen to be involved in novel and challenging physical activity environments.

In all participation in physical activity outside lessons an individual learner will evidence behaviour that is symptomatic of someone who is able to be self-reliant. They will be well able to plan, enact and monitor endeavours in physical activity.

Progress in the Autonomy Aspect of the Affective Domain is illustrated by three examples of how autonomy is manifested. These are:

- Awareness by an individual learner that they exhibit particular strengths and areas to be developed. Thus particular goals will be apposite to a particular learner. Each learner needs to develop self-sufficiency in monitoring progress.
- The ability of a learner to be imaginative and solve problems. Ideally here, there needs to be evidence that a learner can act independently. Participation in physical activity throughout life will depend on an individual taking the initiative to find what opportunities are available within reach of their home.
- The ability of an individual learner to plan and enact schemes to be involved in preferred Movement Activities. This will involve considerable effort to make the personal arrangements to effect participation.

Progress in relation to Autonomy is shown in the Ladder of Progress in Table 7.4. Developing autonomy can be demonstrated in many ways. The information in Table 7.4 gives examples of autonomy in relation self-awareness and setting goals, developing creative ideas and problem solving with others/on own and participating in physical activity outside lessons, outside school and after schooling is completed. However, Autonomy can also be demonstrated in other ways. Other ways of demonstrating autonomy can be incorporated into the Ladder of Progress.

Autonomy is key in learners being able to take responsibility for their own learning, which is considered in Unit 9.

7.7 Summary and key points

The aim of this Unit has been to demonstrate the fundamental importance of the Affective Domain in relation to progress in physical education, participating in physical activity outside lessons and in adopting a physically active lifestyle. It has sought to highlight how people deal with things emotionally which might manifest itself in the attitudes and behaviours

Table 7.4 Ladder of Progress in developing Autonomy

Aspect 3 Developing Autonomy

Baseline	Growing	Establishing	Consolidating
A learner pays minimal attention to the learning outcomes.	A learner pays some attention to the learning outcomes provided for them.	A learner identifies own learning outcomes, with support from the teacher.	A learner takes the lead in identifying own learning outcomes.
A learner relies on the teacher to plan how progress can be made towards achieving the success criteria of the learning outcomes.	A learner shows an interest in planning how progress can be made to achieve the success criteria of the learning outcomes, although is largely still reliant on the teacher.	A learner begins to plan how progress can be made to achieve the success criteria of the learning outcomes. A learner is more prepared to reflect on what has been learnt and ways in which learning can be fostered.	A learner takes significant responsibility for own progress to achieve the success criteria of the learning outcomes and to solve problems and create new movement solutions.
A learner has no confidence to use imagination or create new ideas to solve problems/ identify solutions that enable them to work towards achieving the learning outcomes; rather is reliant on others to solve problems/identify solutions for them.	A learner generally relies on others to solve problems/identify solutions that enable them to work towards achieving the learning outcomes but shows some interest in what has been achieved.	A learner works with others in contributing to finding new ideas to solve problems/ identify solutions that enable them to work towards achieving the learning outcomes.	A learner suggests ideas to solve problems/identify solutions that enable them to work towards achieving the learning outcomes without being called on or relying on others. A learner is prepared to discuss/ justify, explain own initiatives.
A learner has no aspirations to participate in physical activity outside lessons or once schooling is completed.	A learner shows some interest in participating in physical activity outside lessons in school, although attendance at extra-curricular activities is sporadic and only when friends attend. Has no interest in participating in physical activity outside school or once schooling is completed.	A learner regularly attends some extra-curricular activities, both on own and with friends. A learner participates in physical activity outside school on their own or with friends and engages in some debate with friends about continuing to participate in physical activity once schooling is completed.	A learner is committed to adopting a physically active lifestyle outside lessons and after schooling is completed. A learner is interested to discuss the benefits of being physically active now and in the future.

exhibited by learners. This, in turn impacts both positively and negatively on learner progress in the Physical and Cognitive Domains. Deci and Ryan's (2000) Self-determination theory has been used to underpin progress in the three Aspects of the Affective Domain we have highlighted in the Unit: Motivation, Confidence and Autonomy.

As outlined in Unit 4, the Physical, Cognitive and Affective Domains work hand-in-hand, and all three domains are critical both for progress in physical education and for learners to adopt a physically active lifestyle both whilst in school and in the future. However, it is suggested that the Affective Domain 'holds the key' to both progress in physical education and to participation in physical activity outside physical education lessons. Widespread anecdotal evidence would suggest that neither mastery of Movement Patterns and participating in a range of Movement Activities, nor a sound understanding constituents and principles of movement and knowledge of the value of adopting a physically active lifestyle, 'automatically' result in committed participation. Lifelong habits rest on perceived value and on a consistently positive experience of rewarding and meaningful learning experiences. As a general rule, if progress and participation in the past has resulted in experiences that bring pleasure, acceptance by others and a boost for the learner's self-respect and self-esteem, there is a strong likelihood of continued learning and involvement. On the other hand, if progress and participation has seldom been rewarding, little recognition of effort has been exhibited by others or on occasion an individual learner has experienced embarrassment or humiliation and has suffered a loss of confidence, there is little likelihood of continued progress and participation. In this context the Affective Domain needs serious attention and should be part of any consideration of progress. While not being an easy area in which to consider progress it is critical that attitudes are monitored, and action taken to ensure that they are positive.

Unit 8 refocuses attention on the importance of integrating the three Domains for learners to progress.

Unit 8 Viewing the Physical, Cognitive and Affective Domains Holistically

8.1 Introduction

Unit 3 highlighted the importance of recognising learners as holistic and unique. Unit 4 identified the three domains of learning we deem particularly important in physical education and explained that these would be considered separately in Units 5 (the Physical Domain), 6 (the Cognitive Domain) and 7 (the Affective Domain), respectively. This separation of the three domains of learning was deliberate in order to explain each domain clearly and, we hope, provide clarity in progress in each of the three domains.

However, we recognise that addressing the three domains separately is an artificial way of considering progress in physical education. It is accepted that there is something of a conflict between this approach and the perspective that at all times a learner should be perceived as a whole; as a doing, thinking and feeling human being. At any one time an individual is experiencing all three modes of being simultaneously.

Thus, in reality, the three domains of learning cannot be considered separately. Throughout the book there are frequent reminders that learners are holistic; the Physical, Cognitive and Affective Domains are never in evidence individually; they never function alone. Rather, they are interrelated and interdependent. Indeed, links or overlaps between progress in the three domains can be identified in the previous three Units. In order to reinforce this point, the purpose of this short Unit is to highlight how the three domains need to be considered together in order for individual learners to progress.

The Unit starts with a brief comment on the holistic nature of individual learners. The rest of the Unit provides some scenarios which highlight the complex web of inter-relationships of human potential in their totality in facilitating, enhancing and recognising the progress of individual, holistic learners and, hence, which illustrate the complexity of both learning and teaching in physical education.

8.2 The holistic nature of progress for individual learners

Learning in the Physical Domain involves doing, thinking and feeling. The Office for Standards in Education, Children's Services and Skills (Ofsted, 2022) argues that learners

DOI: 10.4324/9781003172826-9

who lack knowledge and/or structure to their knowledge (including both declarative and procedural knowledge, see Unit 2), are denied the opportunity to develop competency and to flourish in and beyond physical education lessons. However, learners also need a positive attitude to learning; to be motivated, be confident and take responsibility for their own learning.

Progress in the different domains is generally mutually reinforcing. Indeed, a considerable amount of research has shown that higher competence is generally positively correlated with more knowledge and understanding, higher motivation, higher confidence and higher enjoyment. If a learner develops secure Movement Patterns which they can apply in a range of Movement Activities, it is more likely that the aim of physical education that is the focus of this book will be achieved (that is, to adopt a physically active lifestyle, participating in physical activity beyond timetabled lessons (both in and out of school) and after leaving school). Therefore, learners with higher competence are likely to have higher rates of participation in physical activity outside physical education lessons and improved health and fitness. On the other hand, low competence in physical education is generally correlated with limited knowledge and understanding, lower motivation, lower confidence, lower enjoyment and lower rates of participation in physical activity outside physical education lessons. This can be self perpetuating. For example, if the learning challenge for a learner with a lower level of competence and/or knowledge and understanding is too high, it can negatively impact on their competence, motivation, confidence, enjoyment, participation in physical activity outside timetabled physical education lessons and reduced health and fitness. (See, for example, Barić, et al., 2014; Bernstein, Phillips and Silverman, 2011; Bureau, et al, 2022; Coppens, et al., 2021; Garn, Cothran and Jenkins, 2011; Hastie and Mesquita, 2017; Ntoumanis, 2001; Simón-Chico et al., 2023; Utesch et al. 2019; Washburn and Kolen, 2018; Williams et al, 2008.)

Despite this generally positive correlation, learners are individuals. Thus, not all learners who have high physical competence have high motivation or confidence, enjoy the subject or participate in physical activity outside physical education lessons. Likewise, not all learners who have lower physical competence have lower motivation or confidence, do not enjoy the subject and do not participate in physical activity outside physical education lessons. As a result, learning in physical education is complex. Likewise, teaching in physical education is also complex.

Thus, whilst the initial focus of physical education teachers might be on progress in the Physical Domain, to reiterate, it is not enough just to focus on progress in the Physical Domain and hope that progress also occurs in the other domains. In order for progress to be made by individual learners, the Cognitive and Affective Domains must also be taken into account in relation to each individual learner.

The scenarios below are designed to demonstrate the holistic nature of learning which needs to be considered for any one learner in a lesson.

8.3 Scenarios of individual learners illustrating the holistic nature of learning

---

Scenario 8.1 Developing a Movement Pattern for a specific Movement Activity; throwing a javelin

The story about Jaikishan is used to illustrate the importance of declarative knowledge (the Cognitive Domain) to facilitate and enhance progress in the Physical Domain.

Jaikishan (aged 14; year 9) has developed general and refined Movement Patterns of throwing and is learning the specific Movement Pattern of throwing a javelin. To support learning how to throw the javelin, modelling has been used. Jaikishan has tried to copy the Movement Pattern modelled, but when he is unable to effectively coordinate the various body parts needed to be able to throw the javelin effectively, he is unable to analyse why this is the case. As a result he is unable to analyse his own movement to be able to understand what he needs to do to be able to progress in throwing the javelin. Therefore, he is unable to take advantage of the time he is given to practice the Movement Pattern. Although he generally demonstrates a positive attitude towards the activity and is motivated to be able to progress his javelin throw, Jaikishan gets frustrated about his inability to construct an appropriate response and hence his lack of progress. This affects his confidence.

The teacher identifies a lack of declarative knowledge of how different body parts work together, both individually and together, in being able to throw the javelin as a major issue in preventing Jaikishan from making progress and leading to his frustration. The teacher puts learners in pairs to help progress their javelin throw. The teacher provides worksheets which highlight the main body parts and how they work together which one learner, acting as the teacher, uses to support the other learner in learning the javelin throw. He pairs a learner who has a clear understanding of how different body parts work together with Jaikishan. In addition, the teacher provides some further resources to help Jaikishan understand the different body parts and how they work together and also asks him to revisit the content covered in class about different body parts in throwing the javelin. With support and a focus on developing his declarative knowledge of the role of different body parts in throwing a javelin, Jaikishan develops his ability to plan how he can apply this new learning to help him progress in this activity. In turn, this increases his levels of success, which is reflected in improvements to his motivation and his confidence.

Scenario 8.2 Encouraging participation in physical activity outside lessons

The story about Judith is used to illustrate the importance of declarative knowledge as well as a positive attitude to progress in the Physical Domain.

Judith (aged 11; year 7) enjoys school and although she participates in her physical education lessons, she does not always apply herself fully. This is because she does not really enjoy the subject and does not have a positive attitude towards learning in the subject. A major reason for this is that, to date, the physical education curriculum has focused largely on competitive games, which were included in the curriculum Judith followed in her primary school and which she does not enjoy. There has been little time spent on learning other activities which Judith enjoys or on developing knowledge of the effect of physical activity for physical and mental health and the importance of adopting a physically active lifestyle.

The teacher talks to Judith to establish any reasons for her general lack of application in physical education. Emerging from this conversation is the identification of the narrow curriculum offering as being a major influence and Judith's lack of enjoyment of competitive activities. The teacher discusses the upcoming curriculum as a means of reassuring Judith that other activities are going to be included in the curriculum later in the school year and throughout her time in secondary school. She also highlights extra-curricular opportunities which may interest Judith, including yoga, zumba and circuit training. She tells Judith that a classmate attends these and encourages the classmate to bring Judith along to these activities. Judith agrees to attend to try them out. She finds that she enjoys them and starts to attend on a regular basis. This motivates her to apply herself more in physical education, resulting in progress in both the physical and cognitive domain. This progress continues as Judith experiences an increasing range of Movement Activities within the curriculum.

Scenario 8.3 Developing a Movement Capacity to underpin learning a Movement Pattern and increase motivation and confidence

The story about Blake is used to illustrate the importance of motivation to overcome a challenge in physical education. It provides an example of how two seemingly similar situations (i.e. Judith's and Blake's engagement in physical education) are likely to be the result of two very different issues and hence a different response is needed for each learner to progress in physical education.

Blake (aged 12; year 8) enjoys school but does not always apply himself fully in physical education. Indeed, he enjoys and makes an effort in learning Movement Patterns and Movement Activities in physical education which do not require hand-eye coordination (for example the Athletic Form, Aesthetic and Expressive Form). However, he does not make much effort in games-based activities in which hand-eye coordination is needed for some Movement Patterns. Both the teacher and Blake recognise his hand-eye co-ordination is not very good and hence he is making limited progress in activities which require this. (Blake puts this down partly to being hit in the face with a ball he did not catch when he was younger).

The teacher and Blake agree a plan to help him improve his hand-eye coordination so that he can progress in Movement Patterns which require this. These include, for example, juggling, bouncing a ball against a wall, rolling/throwing a ball back and forth with another person. The teacher provides teaching points to help Blake succeed in these, particularly always watching the ball rather than looking away as the ball comes towards him. Blake asks a friend to help him with these Movement Patterns outside school. They practice together and Blake gradually improves Movement Patterns which involve hand-eye coordination, such as catching. This increases his confidence and motivation to learn in relevant Movement Activities during physical education lessons. As a result, he increases the range of Movement Activities and Movement Forms which he is willing and able to participate in outside physical education.

Scenario 8.4 Developing Motivation

The story about Jack is used as an example of progress from baseline to developing in Motivation. It illustrates how peer friendship can help to kick start some interest in physical activity.

Jack (aged 13; year 8) is habitually absent or excused from physical education. When he does attend it is hard for him to take part satisfactorily as he has missed a good deal of work. As a result, he does not have the underpinning knowledge needed for the learning which the class are now doing. The teacher realises that there is little chance of progress as long as this situation continues.

Following discussions with other teachers Jack's physical education teacher establishes that Jack is not an overly enthusiastic participant in his schooling. However, they have found out that Jack does show an interest in history and seems to enjoy talking about history lessons as he walks home with Peter, who lives nearby.

Peter is a quiet boy but is a keen athlete. The teacher decides to talk to Peter and ask him if he would try to help Jack to catch up with some of the work in physical education. Following agreement from Peter, the teacher talks to both boys together and suggests that they identify opportunities outside lessons to be physically active in school. In the first week Peter suggests to Jack that they might just run round the football pitch together. This they do as they chat about an issue in history.

The following week Peter suggests that they start running together after school to try and improve their fitness. Healthy Active Lifestyle was the focus of the physical education lesson that week – which Jack did not attend. Jack and Peter are then involved in some physical activity outside lessons for a number of weeks and Jack begins to attend physical education more regularly. Where possible the teacher rewards Jack for his participation and offers encouraging feedback on the progress Jack is making. As a result Jack's interest in physical education grows and he becomes a regular attendee at physical education lessons.

Scenario 8.5 Developing Confidence

The story about Mary is used as an example of progress from baseline to developing in Confidence. It illustrates how a teacher can set up safe situations which encourage a learner to move beyond the known and develop self-confidence in their ability.

Mary (aged 14; year 9) is a capable mover and enjoys physical education. However, the teacher has noticed that she seldom participates beyond her comfort zone and always opts for an easier or more familiar learning activity. While the grouping in class broadly reflects ability, Mary always manages to be in a group of friends who are happy to work within their comfort-zone and take the easy option. It seems that Mary is lacking in confidence to attempt a new challenge. The class is involved in work on a climbing wall and the learners are in groups that match the level of difficulty presented in different areas of the wall. Mary can readily climb at the level of the group to which she has assigned herself. The teacher feels that there is little chance of realising any progress unless Mary can be persuaded to 'move out of her comfort zone' (which the teacher is confident she can manage). At the end of a lesson the teacher shares with the learners that she wants to create a new configuration of holds for next week and asks four learners, one from each activity-level group, to help her before school one day. Mary is one of these. In the course of the re-arrangement members of the group try out moves to decide which level of the new configuration might be appropriate, and Mary finds herself working beyond her previous 'level' of difficulty. This is what the teacher is hoping for and as a result of this Mary is moved up a group, indicating that she has already reached that level of challenge. Mary's confidence is strengthened and is further supported by the teacher's positive feedback. One result of this is Mary's enquiry about on what day of the week she might attend the Climbing Club after school.

Scenario 8.6 Developing Autonomy

The story about Haydn illustrates the need to focus on the Cognitive and Affective Domains in order to progress in developing Movement Patterns.

Haydn (aged 14; year 9) is progressing in developing her Movement Patterns. However, she is not able to adapt or apply these effectively in Movement Activities. One reason for this is that she follows instructions and copies and repeats a model of what she is being asked to do. Further, whilst Haydn shows some evidence of being intrinsically motivated, she has a tendency to rely on teacher instruction and encouragement to apply herself to her learning rather than taking any responsibility herself. To support her progress, Haydn is given more scaffolded activities that allow her to gain success. As a result, she is able to take greater responsibility for her own learning, resulting in her being less reliant on input from the teacher, and becoming more confident within lessons. This is further reflected in an increase in her levels of engagement. In turn, this helps her to adapt and apply Movement Patterns in Movement Activities.

Scenario 8.7 Developing Autonomy

The story about Saul is used as an example of progress from baseline to consolidating in Autonomy. It illustrates how a teacher can enhance commitment through carefully planned groupings.

Saul (aged 15; year 10) is an able learner in all subjects in the curriculum. He has a wide range of interests from music to archaeology and regularly attends clubs relating to these activities in and out of school. Physical education is a subject on the curriculum and so he has to take part. Although he takes part willingly, he is not interested in reflecting on the value of the subject or to participating in physical activity outside lessons. The teacher feels that this almost dismissive attitude is unlikely to change for the better without some carefully planned challenges to engage Saul.

The class are working on a module in physical education that is concerned with holistic health and fitness. The class comprises individuals who have a wide range of interests outside school. The teacher puts the class into groups of four and as homework asks each group to meet outside the lesson to create a training programme to support the development of their holistic health and fitness perhaps based on an area of interest they share.

Saul was immediately interested in this task and began to think about the fitness needed to play a musical instrument. He then turned to consider archaeology and fitness. He was challenged to find links by another group member who rather light heartedly said that of course there is nothing to be said about physical activity, holistic health and fitness in relation to archaeology. After doing some research, Saul was pleased to present a list of 15 objects that had been found on recent 'digs' that clearly indicated that throughout history people have been involved in physical activity. The group were impressed by this list, as was the teacher. The group built their training programme around the training which this group of people might have undertaken to support the physical activity in which they were engaged.

8.4 Summary and key points

The purpose of this Unit was to focus attention on, and serve as a reminder of, the holistic nature of learning and hence the importance of considering the three domains of Physical, Cognitive and Affective together in order for individual learners to progress in physical education, even though one domain might be a priority at any one time.

The Unit started with a brief comment on the holistic nature of individual learners. The rest of the Unit offered a number of scenarios which highlighted the different needs and hence the need for different approaches which need to be taken for individual learners to progress in the subject. Together these highlight the complexity of learning and teaching in order for all learners to progress in the subject with an aim of them adopting a physically active lifestyle.

We recognise that progress in the three domains could seem overwhelming, both individually and together. Therefore, in order to make progress manageable, attention cannot and should not be given to all the domains, and indeed to the different Aspects and Foci within the domains, at the same time. Rather, consideration should be given to how and when to prioritise different domains and different Aspects and Foci within each domain. Consideration should also be given to where progress in different domains or different Aspects and Foci within a domain can be developed at the same time. For example, some Aspects of progress in the Cognitive Domain are best developed within some of the Aspects of the Physical Domain. For example, knowing how to move efficiently and effectively can be developed in relation to facilitating and enhancing the development of a specific Movement Pattern, whilst the nature and purpose of Movement Activities can be developed in relation to specific Movement Activities.

Thus, to reiterate, in order for learners to progress, the teacher's role is to plan for, teach and recognise each learner's progress in the relevant Aspect of each domain in relation to the learning outcomes towards which learners are working and to make a decision as to how best to support them in the next steps in their learning to achieve the success criteria. This is the focus of the next Unit (Unit 9) which looks at teaching to facilitate and enhance progress.

Unit 9   Teaching to Facilitate and Enhance Progress

9.1 Introduction

This book is concerned both with establishing the importance of progression in providing enabling conditions for learners to progress towards the long-term aims of the physical education curriculum and providing some guidance on how progress by individual learners might be facilitated and enhanced. In the Units to date we have concentrated largely on the progress of individual learners. In this and the following Units, the focus is on progression; i.e. the conditions which need to be in place to make progress possible. In this Unit we focus on teaching.

As stressed throughout this book, the main function of teaching in schools is to enable learners to make progress in relation to intended learning. Indeed, Gage (1997) describes teaching as any activity undertaken by one person which is intended to promote learning by another person. The role of the teacher is therefore to facilitate and enhance the progress of individual learners.

So far the Units in this book have focused on:

- progression, progress and learning (Units 1 and 2)
- the learner as holistic and unique (Unit 3)
- progress within and across the Physical, Cognitive and Affective Domains in physical education (Units 4-8).

These Units have alluded to teaching; however, this has not been their main focus. This Unit turns attention squarely to teaching in facilitating and enhancing progress. In this Unit, we start by considering the importance of rational, reflective and responsive teaching, before considering learner-centred teaching. Teaching is then considered in relation to learners as holistic and unique. The Unit then refocuses attention on the principles for facilitating and enhancing progress which were first introduced in Unit 2 and followed up in Unit 3. In this Unit the focus is on constituents of teaching which underpin each of the principles so that individual learners are more likely to progress. Finally, it looks at one of these principles in more depth, learners taking responsibility for their own learning. Throughout the Unit some of the content included in previous Units is considered from the perspective of teaching.

DOI: 10.4324/9781003172826-10

9.2 Rational, reflective and responsive teaching

Teaching is an art as well as a science. There is no magic formula for effective teaching to facilitate and enhance progress to enable all learners to progress in all instances. A teacher cannot apply the various constituents of teaching routinely or mechanistically or in exactly the same way to facilitate and enhance progress for all learners – or even the same learner at different times. The art of teaching is in adapting, applying and combining constituents of teaching appropriately in each specific context.

As it is not possible to say exactly what a teacher should do to facilitate and enhance progress, a book such as this can only highlight some constituents of teaching that we consider to be particularly relevant and share both our experience and some of what has worked elsewhere. It is only individual teachers who can decide what they need to do to facilitate and enhance progress for individual learners in the specific context in which they are working. This requires each teacher to reflect on, and respond to, the progress of individual learners in lessons. This must be a deliberate and rational process which is ongoing throughout a teaching career.

We call this the three Rs of teaching to facilitate and enhance progress:

- Teaching has to be **rational**, requiring
- A teacher to **reflect**, then
- Make a deliberate, appropriate **response**.

We stress that in asking teachers to use the three Rs of teaching, we are not asking them to do more; rather we are asking them to consider if they need to do things differently, to ensure that each and every learner is progressing in their lessons.

Rational (and deliberate) decisions are needed at all stages in the cycle of planning-teaching-evaluating in order for all learners to progress. Thus, for example, teachers need to:

- deliberately plan inclusive and differentiated/adapted learning that is progressive for specific classes, groups of learners and individual learners, with appropriate scaffolds, to facilitate and enhance progress towards achieving the learning outcomes and to ensure that the lesson learning outcomes feed into medium term objectives for the unit of work and long term aims for the scheme of work and curriculum. This plan needs to be based on deliberate decisions made in light of the outcomes of evaluation of progress in the previous lesson
- teach the lesson, reading cues given by a class, group of learners and individual learners through, for example, observing and questioning in order to monitor each learner's progress towards the learning outcomes throughout the lesson (through achievement of the success criteria), thinking carefully about options in making adjustments to the learning activities and/or constituents of teaching during the lesson to further facilitate and enhance progress during the lesson
- use the evidence to evaluate the lesson after it has finished in relation to what and how much each learner progressed, whether each learner has or has not achieved the success criteria for the learning outcomes and reasons why this is the case

- make a rational response based on deliberate decisions about what is going to be most effective in moving learning forward; what each learner and the teacher need to do in the next lesson to build on the progress made, based on all the information available.

This cycle engages a teacher in a process of reflection. Whilst reflection is generally considered to be central to effective teaching in order to facilitate and enhance the progress of individual learners, it is a skill which a teacher may need to spend time working on.

In developing this skill, it is important to recognise that decisions about how best to facilitate and enhance progress are influenced by many factors. These include, for example, a teacher's beliefs about how learners learn, about learning and teaching in the subject as well as about the subject itself. Beliefs develop due to socialisation, as a result of the teacher's background and experiences. Whilst we do not explore either beliefs or socialisation in this book, it is well worth exploring the literature which considers this area further (as a start you may want to refer to, for example, Richards and Gaudreault, 2017; Richards, et al., 2020; Tse Sheng, 2022).

In order to be able to reflect and make rational decisions teachers need, for example:

- To understand their own beliefs, why they hold these beliefs, and how they impact both learner progress and their own practice, including the assumptions and decisions they make about what and how they teach, learner progress and how teaching can facilitate and enhance progress. If a teacher's beliefs are not questioned, it is likely that, for example, they teach as they were taught because it 'worked for them,' teach something as they have always taught it and/or assume learners are learning and do not reflect on the impact of their teaching on learners and their learning
- Good knowledge of each learner they are teaching
- Clarity about what learners are working towards, that is the learning outcomes and the associated success criteria of a particular lesson, the objectives of the unit of work and the aims of the scheme of work and curriculum. To maximise progress, the learning outcomes and the associated success criteria towards which learners are working need to be clear, transparent and understood by the learners as well as the teacher
- Good knowledge of a range of approaches to assessment
- Good subject content knowledge - both declarative and procedural (see Unit 2), including progressions in learning
- Good pedagogical content knowledge, including a repertoire of teaching approaches which can be used.

We do not look at how to reflect in detail in this Unit. However, there is a considerable amount of literature on reflection in both libraries and on-line to which reference can be made in order to develop skills of reflection (see for example, Bin Mizzy, 2022; Lawrence, 2017; Leask et al., 2022).

We now turn our attention to learner-centred teaching.

9.3 Learner-centred teaching

As stressed previously, for learning to occur, all teaching, and all decisions made by a teacher, must have learner progress at its heart. Learner-centred teaching requires the teacher to, for example:

- teach learners, not a lesson. Thus, for example, a teacher should not teach a class specific content identified in a unit of work if the learners are not ready for it or teach content in a specific way because, for example, 'it worked for me,' 'it has worked with other classes before' or 'this is how we teach this.' Likewise, it is important not to assume that learners are learning what is being taught
- focus on, and check, what learners are learning and continually try to facilitate and enhance their progress
- continually examine how effectively they plan for, teach and engage learners in the progressive process of learning
- not assume a problem with learners not learning effectively lies with the learner; rather consider what the teacher needs to do differently to facilitate and enhance progress
- be a learner themselves, to continually try to improve their teaching to facilitate and enhance progress. It is important to remember that if the teacher is not also a learner, they don't make learners out of those they teach.

However, learner-centred teaching is more than just putting learners at the centre of everything the teacher does; it also involves giving learners greater responsibility for their own learning. To achieve this learners need to be engaged in active learning. As explained in Unit 2, just because learners are physically active does not mean they are engaged in active learning. Rather, active learning means that learners are actively engaged in constructing their own learning by working things out for themselves, rather than being told. This may involve learners in, for example, solving problems, asking and answering questions, discussing, explaining, debating, brainstorming, planning during a lesson. In physical education this may include discovery learning (for example, the guided discovery, convergent discovery or divergent discovery styles of Mosston and Ashworth, 2002; see below), self and peer evaluation or paired teaching. Learners taking responsibility for their own learning is considered further below.

In addition, all decisions teachers make, including those in relation to learner-centred teaching, need to take into account that learners are holistic and unique. This is considered next.

9.4 Taking account of learners as holistic and unique

As stressed throughout this book, the premise on which this book is written is that learners are holistic; the Physical, Cognitive and Affective Domains are interdependent and inextricably linked. As well as being holistic, each learner is also unique.

Despite physical education being a practical subject, if each learner is to progress in their learning, a teacher cannot just focus on progress in the Physical Domain. Instead, connections need to be made in planning and teaching between the Physical, Cognitive and Affective Domains in each and every lesson for each learner. Learners seemingly making similar progress may have different learning needs in the Physical, Cognitive and/or Affective Domain in order to make further progress. For example, three learners are all capable movers. However, learner A lacks motivation to participate in physical education. Whilst learner B and C are motivated in and enjoy physical education, learner B is less able to apply declarative knowledge of how to move efficiently and effectively to their learning in the physical context, whilst learner C lacks confidence to attempt a new challenge. In order for the three learners to progress, the teacher needs to iden-tify different components of learning for each learner to work on and try to find the appropriate balance to facilitate and enhance progress for each learner. Some specific examples of progress in different domains being prioritised for different learners are given in Unit 8.

Further, because each learner is unique, they are at different places in their learning, making progress at different rates and encountering different hurdles. As stated in Unit 3, learning is age-related, not age-dependent. All learners are on a similar learning journey in physical education, but each learner is unique in relation to, for example, abilities, back-ground, endowment, learning needs, level of readiness to learn something, knowledge, potential, progress, interests, experiences. Further, each learner has beliefs about phys-ical education which may be similar to, or different from, those of other learners and from the teacher. Together, these frame, for example, a learner's perceptions of and attitudes towards the subject, how they respond in lessons, their aspirations, and their progress in the Physical, Cognitive and Affective Domains.

A teacher therefore needs to take into account how different learners can benefit from, and learn in, physical education. Thus, to achieve the fundamental professional responsi-bility of all teachers to enable all learners to progress, teaching cannot be 'one size fits all'; it needs to be inclusive and differentiated/adapted, with scaffolds in place to support learners. Thus, to stress, an individual is more likely to progress if their unique potential, abilities and characteristics are recognised, considered and planned for and their individual needs met. In agreement with Office for Standards in Education, Children's Services and Skills (Ofsted, 2022), there is no single way of achieving what they call high-quality physical education. Rather, a teacher needs to try to find the best solution for each learner in each lesson.

A teacher should therefore:

- Plan a specific lesson for a specific class, specific group of learners and specific learners in that class at a specific time rather than teach what is written in a unit of work just because it is written as the next lesson, use a generic lesson plan or recycle a lesson exactly as taught previously
- Plan a lesson so that all learners are included in the learning, barriers to learning are removed and learning is differentiated/adapted and scaffolded so that each learner has suitable learning challenges
- Identify a realistic range of expectations of what counts as a satisfactory response to a learning activity and lesson when differentiating/adapting by outcome
- Provide appropriate opportunities and use a range of teaching approaches to enable learners to achieve the learning outcomes

- Allow a learner more time to engage in a learning activity as needed to ensure learning has occurred before moving the learner on
- Take account of the learning of all learners in reflecting on the effectiveness of the lesson and planning next lesson.

(Note: consideration also needs to be given to recognising progress, including feedback and assessment. This is the focus of Unit 10 next.)

Thus, as no two learners or contexts are exactly the same, the same teacher may make different decisions at different times, depending on the needs of a class, group of learners and individual learners. Further, as with learners, teachers are unique, therefore different teachers may make different decisions in similar contexts. This is the art of teaching.

In considering the progress of each holistic and unique individual learner, a teacher may ask questions such as,

- 'Where is this learner currently in their learning in relation to the Physical, Cognitive and Affective Domains,' and
- 'What does this learner need to do next in the Physical, Cognitive and Affective Domains in order to continue to make progress towards the learning outcomes?' and, in relation to the aim of physical education in this book,
- 'What does this learner need to do next in the Physical, Cognitive and Affective Domains in order to continue to make progress towards the aim of adopting a physically active lifestyle?'

Recognition of each learner as holistic and unique should underpin the focus on the progress of each learner in physical education.

9.5 Using the Ladders of Progress to support the holistic progress of each individual learner

Units 5, 6, and 7 looked at the Physical, Cognitive and Affective Domains separately. However, as we have stressed throughout the book, in reality, as learners are holistic, the three domains are inter-related and cannot be considered separately. Thus, the Aspects, Foci and Ladders of Progress in the Physical, Cognitive and Affective Domains should not be considered separately when used to inform teaching to facilitate and enhance the progress of each individual learner. In addition, as learners are unique, the different domains (and their respective Aspects, Foci and Ladders of Progress) need to be prioritised differently for different learners at different times. This is a complex enterprise. To help deal with this complexity, the Ladders of Progress can be used to help reflect on the progress of learners (as a class, group of learners and as individual learners) and to use this information to plan next content, learning activities and teaching approaches as appropriate to facilitate and enhance their progress.

For example, when performing an overarm throw from a stationary position, a learner is able to demonstrate aspects of the consolidating level. However when asked to combine this Movement Pattern with others, for example when moving towards the ball, collecting it and then throwing, they show characteristics of the establishing level in

Table 9.1 An example of the use of the Ladders of Progress across the Physical, Cognitive and Affective Domains for an individual learner

Aspect	Foci	Baseline	Growing	Establishing	Consolidating
Physical					
Aspect 1 Movement Patterns	Acquiring an individual Movement Pattern				▓
	Developing a repertoire of Movement Patterns and Movement Phrases			▓	
	Adapting Movement Patterns for different contexts		▓		
Aspect 2 Movement Activities	Applying conventions of a Movement Activity		▓		
	Enacting roles alongside other learners in the working space		▓		
	Participating effectively in a range of Movement Activities in different Movement Forms		▓		
Cognitive					
Aspect 1 Constituents and principles of movement	Knowing how to move efficiently and effectively			▓	
	Recognising the effects of physical activity			▓	
Aspect 2 Adopting a physically active lifestyle	Knowing the nature and purpose of Movement Activities			▓	
	Knowing the importance and benefits of participating in physical activity			▓	
	Planning for participation in physical activity			▓	
Affective					
Aspect 1 Motivation			▓		
Aspect 2 Confidence			▓		
Aspect 3 Autonomy			▓		

Note: The shading represents the current level of progress.

developing Movement Patterns and Movement Phrases. Further they are only showing evidence of the growing level of being able to adapt Movement Patterns in different contexts. In addition, the learner is demonstrating characteristics in the establishing level across the Cognitive Domain and the growing level across all Aspects in the Affective Domain. This is represented in Table 9.1.

In addition, in making rational, deliberate decisions in relation to planning (and teaching) what is going to be taught and how it is going to be taught to facilitate and enhance progress, as well as recognise progress for each and every learner, relevant Aspects, Foci and Ladders of Progress can be selected in relation to, for example:

- planning a unit of work and lesson taking account of the holistic nature of learning. For example, if learners are learning a new Movement Pattern, their learning needs to be planned so that they have enough time to practice as they work through the stages of motor skill acquisition (see Fitts and Posner's (1967) model of motor skill acquisition in Unit 5) and the relevant constituents and principles of movement need to be applied at the appropriate level to underpin this learning. In addition, learners attitudes to the learning need to be taken into account.
- planning and teaching to take account of the needs of each individual learner. To achieve this it is important to understand each learner's level of progress in the relevant Aspects and Foci in each domain in relation to the learning outcomes towards which learners are working.

9.6 Principles for facilitating and enhancing progress

So far we have looked at the need for teaching to take account of each learner as holistic and unique and using the Ladders of Progress identified for each Aspect and Focus in each of the three domains. However, it is also important that consideration is given to constituents of teaching which underpin each of the nine principles or facilitating and enhancing progress (see Table 9.2). The nine principles for facilitating and enhancing progress in the first column of Table 9.2 were first introduced in Unit 2 (progression, progress and learning). In Unit 3 (the individual learner), these were included, but with a second column which identified how the principles might be interpreted so that individual learners are more likely to progress. In Table 9.2, a third column has been added which identifies constituents of teaching which underpin each of the nine principles so that individual learners are more likely to progress. The constituents identified are not comprehensive and other constituents of teaching can be added to extend the list.

It is not claimed that there is anything new in Table 9.2. Rather, it is assumed that teachers are familiar with the nine principles for facilitating and enhancing progress and constituents of teaching in relation to the nine principles. However, by highlighting these principles and constituents we may encourage teachers to identify and reflect on their strengths and areas for development in relation to their teaching. This may include, for example, gaps or weaknesses in knowledge and understanding or constituents of teaching which are given lower priority or ignored. This may then encourage a teacher to take appropriate action to develop their teaching skills in light of knowledge about what individual learners need in order for progress to be made in each of the three domains.

Table 9.2 Constituents of teaching which underpin each of the principles for facilitating and enhancing progress so that individual learners are more likely to progress

Principles for facilitating and enhancing progress	Individual learners are more likely to progress if, for example, ...:	Constituents of teaching: A learner is more likely to progress if, for example, ...:
1. Each learner is holistic, with Physical, Cognitive and Affective Domains all inter-related	• they are recognised as a whole with physical, cognitive and affective capabilities operating in concert • Learning in the Physical Domain is underpinned by relevant declarative knowledge, thinking is promoted and affective responses are monitored, as appropriate for the individual learner	• knows the progress of each learner in each of the three domains • can apply knowledge and understanding about each of the three domains to facilitate and enhance progress, as appropriate for each learner
2. Each learner is unique, therefore needs to be treated as such	• Their uniqueness (endowment, potential and biography) is recognised and catered for • Learning activities and challenges are appropriate for their personal strengths and needs (in both the Physical and Cognitive Domains) and take account of the Affective Domain • Learning activities and challenges support the development of confidence and motivation to make it more likely that they will adopt a physically active lifestyle	• knows each learner by name and has some knowledge of their particular characteristics, including what interests and motivates them, their strengths and areas for development and reasons why they are working at their current level • is responsive to, and prepared to adjust plans as appropriate, to meet the needs of the learners • differentiates/adapts work to enable each learner to access the learning • scaffolds learning as appropriate for each learner • allows time for interaction with individual learners • observes and gives feedback relevant to the individual learner's specific needs • is sensitive and flexible to modify their teaching as needed
3. Learning is purposive – towards achieving an aim	• They are clear about the learning outcomes and related success criteria, objectives and aims towards which they are working as well as the steps they are going to take to get there • They engage in purposeful learning activities that enable them to work towards achieving the success criteria of learning outcomes which are used to guide learning towards medium term objectives and the long term aims	• formulates clear learning outcomes and success criteria, consistent with the medium-term objectives and longer-term aims • plans learning activities which: • are appropriate to enable learners to work towards achieving a specific learning outcome • provide building blocks to scaffold learning to enable learners to achieve the learning outcomes • promote active learning • communicates learning outcomes and associated success criteria clearly to learners at the start of a lesson

Table 9.2 (Continued)

Principles for facilitating and enhancing progress	Individual learners are more likely to progress if, for example, ...:	Constituents of teaching: A learner is more likely to progress if, for example, ...:
		• supports learners to set their own learning outcomes and success criteria as they take responsibility for their own learning
		• enables learners to demonstrate a match between what they are intended to know, the opportunities they receive to practice and learn, and how their learning is demonstrated. In turn, this promotes more worthwhile and meaningful learning for learners
4. Learning is an ongoing process that takes time, practice, application and effort	• The speed at which each learner is able to progress through the steps in learning is considered and planned. If a learner has learned the prerequisite for next learning they are able to progress, whereas if prerequisite learning has not been achieved they will need to spend time learning the prerequisite(s) and progress more slowly • they are given an appropriate amount of time to practice in order to learn, consolidate and embed learning • Learning activities are challenging and stretching within each learner's capability so that learning is not out of reach or is not too easy • they are actively engaged in learning, apply themself fully and put effort into learning rather than just going through the motions of learning	• plans appropriate learning activities so that learners can progress and have rewarding and motivating experiences that can influence them in adopting a physically active lifestyle • plans adequate time for learning activities for optimal learning to occur • allows different amounts of time for individual learners to practice and learn • returns to learning at a later date to enable learners to consolidate, embed and apply it (but practices build on rather than repeat exactly what learners were required to do previously in exactly the same way) • focuses on the nature and quality of practice as well as the amount of practice for learners to progress • ensures learners are actively engaged in their learning
5. Learning attempts to move the learner on; new learning builds from where the learner is in respect of current learning	• Evidence of prior learning is used as the basis for judgements about whether or not they are ready to move on to future challenges • New learning builds on their current learning – what they already know and can do • clear connections are made for each learner to previous learning	• Uses evidence of current learning as the basis of judgements about whether or not an individual learner has the pre-requisites and is ready to move on to new learning • Not only builds new learning from old but also plans that current learning leads into future learning. It is important to know what learners are going to move onto and to make connections between past, current and future learning

(Continued)

Table 9.2 (Continued)

Principles for facilitating and enhancing progress	Individual learners are more likely to progress if, for example, …..:	Constituents of teaching: A learner is more likely to progress if, for example, ……:
	• Current learning leads into future learning; hence it is important that each learner knows what they are going to move onto and can make connections between past, current and future learning	• Plans for an appropriate level of challenge for each learner. If there is too much difference between what has already been learned and what is to be learned next, then the dissonance is too great for the process to move on smoothly • Learning activities are differentiated/adapted so that they are challenging and stretching within each learners capability. Learning should not be out of reach, or too easy, for an individual learner • Provides sufficient support, prompts and scaffolding for learners. Scaffolding may initially involve modelling and support from the teacher. Teacher input will gradually involve monitoring, with intervention only being made when necessary • Gaps in knowledge and misconceptions in learning are identified and addressed
6. Learning is coherent, with a logical order, going step by step	• they have learned the steps that form the underpinning foundations or pre-requisites before they progress to the next step in the learning. If a learner has not learned one step, they will not be ready to progress to the next. Where an individual learner has not learned the previous steps in the sequence they may need more time on the same or different practices or may need to take a backward step along the continuum • careful consideration is given to the speed at which each learner progresses through the sequence of clear, coherent, continuous steps, each of which builds from the previous one • the scaffolding needed for each learner is carefully considered and planned	• Is clear about the logical sequence of learning and then plans and teaches a sequence of clear, progressive, coherent, continuous steps in a logical order, each of which builds from the previous one. Illogical links in what is being asked of the learner results in the breakdown of the learning process • Plans learning activities that empower the learner to achieve more complex or better things over time • Breaks learning down into manageable chunks; not giving learners too much information/too many instructions at the same time

Table 9.2 (Continued)

Principles for facilitating and enhancing progress	Individual learners are more likely to progress if, for example, ...:	Constituents of teaching: A learner is more likely to progress if, for example, ...:
7. Learning is presented in such a way that motivates learners to apply themselves	• The learning environment is considered and planned such that each learner has a positive, satisfying learning experience in a secure learning environment • learning is perceived by an individual learner as of value, interesting, relevant and meaningful • Personal factors which impact an individual learner's motivation are considered and action taken to increase motivation • A learners basic needs are met in order for them to be motivated to learn	• takes a proactive approach to the Affective Domain so that motivation and interest are maintained, self esteem is nurtured and learners apply themselves fully during a learning activity • plans learning activities that are positive, interesting, relevant, meaningful, satisfying and valuable for learners of a specific age and for different individual learners which engender a positive attitude to learning • presents learning to ensure that learners are actively engaged in learning activities, apply themselves fully, put effort into learning and are not just going through the motions of learning • develops an alignment between learning outcomes and success criteria, the learning activities and teaching approaches employed to facilitate and enhance progress and which make learning meaningful and assessment for learning that provides evidence of learners' progress toward those outcomes • establishes a positive, secure and purposive learning environment for the lesson to provide a clear rationale for the nature of the tasks in order to motivate learners • recognises that personal factors and factors outside the lesson may impact on learning and motivation to learn (e.g. a learners basic needs are not met) and does what can to address these

(Continued)

Table 9.2 (Continued)

Principles for facilitating and enhancing progress	Individual learners are more likely to progress if, for example, ….:	Constituents of teaching: A learner is more likely to progress if, for example, ……:

8. Learning accommodates opportunities for feedback to the learner	• Each learner receives specific information, given constructively, about their current learning so that they know what they are doing well (in whole or in part) and what they need to work on further in order to progress their learning
	• they take action on the feedback in order to learn from it and progress
	• it is recognised that a learner may not like public feedback and hence, unless it is general feedback to the whole class, feedback is given privately to an individual learner
	• In addition to feedback from others (a teacher or peer), each learner develops their ability to receive feedback from themselves, e.g. through video recording or kinaesthetic feedback.
		• observes learners carefully to be able to be able to give constructive feedback
		• provides constructive feedback to enable learners to know how they are progressing in their learning
		• focuses on feedback *for* learning (Education Endowment Foundation (2021) and Unit 10), i.e.
		  • where am I going?
		  • how am I doing?
		  • where to next?
		• ensures feedback comments on areas for development and provides suggestions on how to improve, and at least one positive comment
		• provides feedback related to achievement against the learning outcomes (and success criteria). The more specific the learning outcome, the more specific feedback can be to bridge the gap between current learning and the desired learning. Feedback is constructive and meaningful when learners are clear about what they are learning and what they need to do
		• recognises that individualised feedback cannot be given to each learner in each lesson, therefore provides opportunities for learners to develop skills to receive feedback from peers and themselves, e.g. through video recording or kinaesthetic feedback
		(Feedback is considered further in Unit 10.)

Table 9.2 (Continued)

Principles for facilitating and enhancing progress	Individual learners are more likely to progress if, for example, ...:	Constituents of teaching: A learner is more likely to progress if, for example, ...:
9. Learning provides opportunities for learners to take responsibility for their learning, thus enhancing their learning	• Each learner gradually develops a set of skills that enables them to take responsibility for their own learning (e.g. they learn how to learn and how to plan and evaluate their own learning) so that they develop into a lifelong learner who is able to make choices to enable them to adopt a physically active lifestyle	• supports learners to develop skills involved in taking responsibility for their own learning; rather than expect learners to absorb such skills • engages learners in a process of planning, performing and evaluating (Department of Education and Science and the Welsh Office (DES/WO, 1991)) their own learning, because these are integral to all movement and can enable learners to take increasing responsibility for their own learning • allows time for learners to plan, perform, evaluate and reflect on own learning and • uses learning activities and teaching approaches which gradually enable learners to make their own decisions, be proactive and take responsibility for their own learning, e.g. teaching approaches which do not tell learners what to do all the time, rather, those that require learners to take an active role in constructing their own learning through open-ended tasks (Learners taking responsibility for own learning is considered further below.)

Table 9.2 highlights the multi-dimensional or multi-faceted nature of teaching which makes it a complex operation. To this end, the different constituents of teaching in Table 9.2 should be viewed as interdependent. The interdependency between constituents of teaching such that a learner is more likely to progress means that each affects, and in turn is affected by, the others. When one is enhanced, others are enhanced and when one is diminished, others are diminished. Likewise, one constituent of teaching (or indeed, one of the principles for facilitating and enhancing progress) cannot be weak or ignored without impacting on the others or having an impact on the effectiveness of teaching and/or the lesson as a whole and on the progress of individual learners.

As an example, the learning environment (both the physical and affective) affects everything that happens, and each learner's progress, in a lesson. A learning environment which, inter alia,

- Is physically clean, well cared for
- Is affectively inviting, affirming, positive, supportive, trusting
- Is responsive to the needs of each learner
- Is purposeful and has a culture of learning in which each learner feels they are part of a community that values all learning
- Focuses on mastery of the learning, self-improvement and effort
- Enables each learner to see themself as a learner who can learn and progress and that their learning is not fixed (Evidence Based Education, 2020) has a positive impact on learning.

On the other hand, if, for example,

- Does not recognise learners as holistic
- A teacher is not responsive to the needs of each learner
- A lesson does not have clear learning outcomes and success criteria, is not purposeful and learning is not prioritised
- A lesson is not inclusive and/or not differentiated/adapted
- The content is not meaningful to each learner, does not challenge or is too challenging
- Does not provide appropriate support and scaffolds for each learner
- Teaching approaches are not appropriate for the learners, or
- Learners are not given constructive feedback about how to improve there is a negative impact on the learning environment and hence learning.

The principles for facilitating and enhancing progress and the constituents of teaching in Table 9.2 are self-explanatory. Further, there is a lot written elsewhere in relation to teaching in general and in relation to many of these nine principles for facilitating and enhancing progress and the various constituents of teaching to which reference can be made. The exception is point 9, 'learners taking responsibility for their own learning,' for which, in our view, less is written specifically in relation to physical education. Hence, although we do not provide further explanation on most of Table 9.2, we consider learners taking responsibility for their own learning in a bit more detail next.

9.7 Supporting learners to take responsibility for their own learning

We consider learners taking responsibility for their own learning here because we believe that, although learners developing their capacity to take responsibility for their own learning has developed across subjects more generally, the extent to which this is reflected in physical education is, in our view, less well developed. For example, there is a continuing reliance on and dominance of command and practice styles in physical education, teaching styles in which all decisions are made by the teacher (see Mosston and Ashworth, 2002 and below) (see, for example, Ofsted, 2022). Simply telling learners to do something is less likely to support learners to take responsibility for their own learning. If learners are passive recipients of knowledge in the learning situation, copying and repeating what the teacher does or asks them to do, they may see learning as something which a teacher provides for them and therefore which they receive. A constructivist approach to learning guides much current thinking about learning and teaching. In this approach, rather than transmitting facts to learners which are not connected or understood, the teacher provides the conditions which increase the likelihood that learners construct understandings themselves.

There are a number of reasons why it is important that learners develop their ability to take responsibility for their own learning. These include, for example:

- a learner is the only person who knows exactly what progress they are making
- a teacher can only spend a certain (limited) amount of time with each learner and, in the remaining time, a learner needs to be able to work out for themself how to address a problem to move their own learning forward to make progress
- learning is a personal process and the teacher can only do a certain amount. Indeed, as Haydn (2016, p. 462) states "You [the teacher] can't do the learning for the pupils; they have to do it themselves, and your job is to show them how to do this" (bracket added)
- learners have to make their own decisions about adopting a physically active lifestyle, so it is important that they take responsibility for this.

Indeed, Kapfer (1970, p.148) stated that "learning is a natural human enterprise … students want to learn, and they will learn voluntary and efficiently when given opportunities to become responsibly involved in determining the character of their learning experiences."

According to the Education Endowment Foundation (EEF, 2018a, 2018b), developing learners ability to take responsibility for their own learning is most effective when applied to challenging tasks rooted in the usual curriculum content. This is endorsed by Ofsted (2022) who state that "pupils need to practise and be taught domain-specific knowledge (rather than more generic cognitive strategies about, for example, how to problem-solve)" (p. 27). Thus, in the context of our subject, strategies need to be applied that relate specifically to supporting learners learning how to take responsibility for their own learning in physical education.

9.7.1 Planning, performing and evaluating

Just as teachers are engaged in a cycle of planning, teaching and evaluating, learning involves learners in a cycle of planning, performing and evaluating (DES/WO, 1991). These inter-related components of planning, performing and evaluating form the process of learning (see Figure 9.1). The cycle also forms the basis of learners reflecting on their learning.

The process of learning forms the bridge between a learner and the achievement of a learning outcome, i.e. the product of learning (a product of learning could be, for example, an isolated Movement Pattern such as a handstand in gymnastics or being able to engage effectively in a Movement Activity such as a group dance at a particular point in time), as illustrated in Figure 9.2.

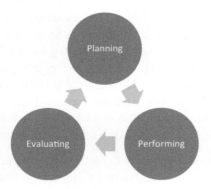

Figure 9.1 The process of learning

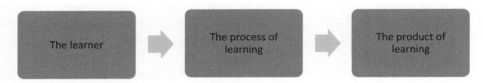

Figure 9.2 The relationship between the learner, the process and the product of learning

9.7.1.1 The importance of planning, performing and evaluating in physical education

There are strong arguments to more clearly focus on the process of learning rather than the product of learning in physical education. For example, planning, performing and evaluating:

- provide a framework for learners to take responsibility for developing their Movement Patterns and ability to participate in Movement Activities
- provide an underpinning for ongoing participation in a range of Movement Activities in different Movement Forms which make it more likely that a goal of learners taking responsibility for adopting a physically active lifestyle will be achieved
- provide a structure for learners to organise and take increasing responsibility for their own learning, rather than rely on the teacher

Although the process of learning is worthy of serious attention, it is often overlooked as compared to the product of learning. There are several reasons for this, including:

- it is harder to know that learning is taking place than it is to see the end product of learning
- each of the concepts of planning, performing and evaluating are complex and it is a challenge to understand and be able to develop them, individually or together

In our view, planning, performing and evaluating is a valid structure for learners to organise and take increasing responsibility for their own learning. Being actively involved in these processes encourages the development of learners' metacognition ("the ways learners monitor and purposefully direct their learning" (EEF, 2018a, p. 9)), allowing them to reflect on and identify the next steps they need to take to support their own learning.

We next consider how teachers can provide conditions to support learners to take responsibility for their own learning through their teaching.

9.7.2 *Teaching to support learners to take responsibility for their own learning*

Many learners are used to physical education lessons being teacher led, e.g. the teacher chooses the learning outcomes and success criteria, how they might be realised through specific content and learning activities; directs the way in which a learner engages with the learning activity; manages the timing and duration of the work; determines the outcome of the learning; assesses and evaluates the learning and provides feedback to the learner. This results in a learner being told what they are learning, given a demonstration, engaging in learning activities set by the teacher to develop a particular component of their learning, being observed and assessed and being given feedback by the teacher. Thus, the learner is dependent on the teacher. Although we recognise that being dependent on the teacher is appropriate at some times in some contexts, learners need to become independent if they are to progress.

Gradually devolving responsibility to learners over time to enable them to take increasing responsibility for their learning themselves enables learners to move from depending on the teacher to working with increasing autonomy with the eventual aim of them learning largely independently of the teacher. This requires learner-centred teaching, with a learner taking an active role in all components of learning, for example, choosing the purpose of the learning and identifying the learning outcomes and success criteria, selecting the content and appropriate learning activities and how they might engage with these, determining the timing and method of learning, determining the outcome of the learning, assessing and evaluating the learning and providing own feedback) (see, for example, Demos, 2005, pp. 18-19).

Taking responsibility for their own learning requires learners to develop their ability to plan, monitor their performance and evaluate in progressively more sophisticated ways, in different movement contexts and situations. As a result, learners develop both their understanding that learning is a *process* which develops over time, as well as what is required to progress. Further, the greater involvement in, ownership of, responsibility for, and ability to self-regulate their own learning is motivating for learners (EEF, 2018a, 2018b).

Rather than expecting learners to absorb skills involved in taking responsibilities for their own learning, learners need to learn and practise relevant skills. There are a number of ways learners can be supported to develop these skills and gradually take responsibility for their own learning, some of which are highlighted below. For example, a teacher can:

- Ensure learners are clear about the learning outcomes towards which they are working and the success criteria for achieving these and, over time, support learners to learn how to set their own learning outcomes and success criteria. This enables learners to better self-regulate their learning to enable them to achieve the learning outcomes (Brookhart and McMillan, 2020)

- Establish a supportive learning environment that allows learners to plan their own learning, explore and make mistakes, ask questions, make decisions, have opportunities to work collaboratively with peers, evaluate and reflect on their progress
- go beyond simple procedural instructions and give a commentary which demonstrates a structure for what learners need to do in a learning episode. Following the teacher commentary, learners could be encouraged, and guided, to identify and verbalise their own thoughts and ideas (focusing on important details) during a learning activity
- ensure that learners are involved in active learning (See above and Unit 2); that they are actively engaged in contributing to their own learning by thinking about what and how they are learning
- engage learners in a process of planning, performing and evaluating (DES/WO, 1991; also see above) their own learning and
- allow time for learners to engage fully in the process of planning, performing the learning activity, evaluating the outcome, reflecting on what they have learned and to subsequently respond through next planning and performing in order to develop their Movement Patterns and ability to participate in Movement Activities. For example, where learners are working co-operatively to create a sequence that includes balances, jumps and rolls, they need time to discuss how they are going to develop the sequence (for example, how they are going to meet the criteria for including different Movement Patterns, how they are going to use the space etc.), practice the sequence, then have time to consider together how effective they were in performing the sequence – what worked well and what they need to change to improve their sequence. They then need time to put the learning into action to change and/or develop the sequence.
- use learning activities and teaching approaches which require learners to make decisions for themselves, be proactive and take responsibility for their own learning rather than being told what to do. This requires learners to take an active role in constructing their own learning through having opportunities to work on open-ended tasks and in problem solving situations in which they make their own decisions, reflect on and monitor their strengths and areas for development, and plan how to overcome current difficulties. The extent of decisions should increase over time. For example, deciding how to differentiate/adapt and scaffold a learning activity to try and achieve a learning outcome that they would otherwise struggle with or moving from a decision about which of two Movement Patterns to use, to making decisions about adopting a physically active lifestyle. Learners take time to adjust to new teaching approaches; hence, teachers need to use the same teaching approaches over time, allowing them to become embedded rather than just introducing a new teaching approach in one lesson and then reverting to a command and practice/copy and repeat type practice moving forward.

Although there are other frameworks, one framework to support teachers in being able to devolve responsibility to learners is Mosston's spectrum of teaching styles (Mosston and Ashworth, 2002). The rationale for this framework was gradually devolving responsibility to learners through the decisions they make. The styles in the framework are shown in Table 9.3.

Table 9.3 Summary of teaching styles (Mosston and Ashworth, 2002)

Style	Decision making	Role of the teacher	Role of the learner
A: Command	Teacher makes all the decisions. Learners follow instructions and copy the teacher	Teaching	Copying, Replicating
B: Practice	Teacher sets up opportunities for learners to work at own pace on set learning activities, then gives feedback on learning	Establishing	Repeating, refining and improving
C: Reciprocal	Learners work in pairs, one acting as the teacher. The learner receives feedback from their partner acting as the teacher, using a checklist of reference points provided by the teacher. Teacher communication is with the learner acting as the teacher.	Supporting	Performing and peer assessing
D: Self-check	Teacher sets criteria for success. Learners check their own performance against the criteria	Directing, managing	Self-assessing
E: Inclusion	Teacher sets out a variety of learning opportunities, ranging from easy to complex. Learners select the task to work on most appropriate to their ability and/or motivation	Facilitating, encouraging	Selecting, choosing
F: Guided discovery	Teacher uses questions and learning activities to gradually direct learners towards a pre-determined learning outcome	Questioning	Uncovering, Discovering
G: Convergent discovery	Teacher sets or formulates a problem. Learners attempt to find out and explore the most appropriate solutions	Guiding, Coaching, Showing	Finding out, Figuring out
H: Divergent discovery	Teacher sets or formulates a problem. Learners attempt to explore and create possible solutions	Prompting	Creating
I: Learner designed	Teacher decides on area of focus. Learners select what to do within this area, drawing on teachers' experience and expertise	Advising	Initiating, starting
J: Learner initiated	Learners decide what they are aiming for and how they are going to get there. Teacher provides support as needed	Mentoring	Deciding
K: Self-teach	Learners engage in development on their own (note, this style is rarely used in a school context).	N/A	Self-determined, Autonomous

Styles A to E are what are called reproductive styles; whereas styles F to K are what are called productive styles. In order for learners to take responsibility for their own learning, the emphasis should be on productive styles. Thus, for example, instead of using command (style A) and practice (style B), teachers should gradually introduce Styles C to K.

Below are some examples of how teaching can support learners to develop their capacity to take responsibility for their own learning.

• Include scaffolds which support learners to gradually take more responsibility for their decisions. By leaving gaps in the scaffolds in which learners have to think for themselves and monitor their learning, learners are encouraged through guided practice to independent practice. As learners develop their skills to plan, perform and evaluate, scaffolds can be reduced, then removed. Thus, teacher input gradually changes to monitoring, with intervention only being made when necessary (Note, it is important that learners have the pre-requisites to engage in the learning activity)

- Model own practices in learning effectively. To be most effective, a teacher needs also to communicate what they are modelling or demonstrating, e.g. verbalising their thinking as they undertake a task or solve a problem, e.g. 'What do I know about problems like this?' 'What ways of solving them have I used before?' Learners then do this, with prompts as to where their thinking may have broken down or did not work. Further, Newton (2023) said that it may help learners to know that if they are frustrated with their ability to complete a learning activity, this may be a sign that the approach they are taking is not working, therefore they need to take a different approach or need some support, e.g. from a more knowledgeable other (teacher, other adult in the learning situation or more competent peer) (see Vygotsky, 1978)

- Use physical education specific vocabulary and expressions with frequent reminders of their meaning in the specific contexts where they are used to enable learners to articulate what they are learning

- Use peer and self-assessment. This requires learners to be clear about the learning outcomes towards which they are working, have an accurate mental model of the success criteria for achieving these, be able to observe and analyse their movement against the model and be able to give themselves accurate and meaningful feedback (Topping, 2005) (see Unit 10)

- gather information from observation and questions to enable the teacher to identify how learners are progressing and provide appropriate feedback. By modelling observation and feedback the teacher can gradually enable learners to learn these skills. In giving feedback about the process of learning, the teacher provides information about how well learners correct their mistakes and uses prompts to enable them to better understand the details of the task (see Unit 10)

- Ask questions of learners (and later for learners to ask themselves) which require them to move beyond answering closed questions in a sequence which involves 'teacher question–learner response–teacher feedback.' Rather, questions should require learners to think hard and make decisions, based on their current level of learning in the Physical and Cognitive Domains (see, for example, Evidence Based Education, 2022 (first published in Evidence Based Education, 2020)).

- A few examples of questions to support learners to develop their ability to take responsibility for their own learning are given below. A teacher can select those appropriate, or can use these as a basis to develop their own questions for a class, group of learners or an individual learner in the context in which they are working. Over time, learners can ask such questions of themselves. These questions are divided into questions for planning, monitoring learning and evaluating.

Examples of **Planning** questions to ask learners before they start planning their own learning:

- What are you trying to learn?
- What do you already know about this area of learning?

- What approaches will you use to make progress towards the learning outcomes?
- Where do you start?
- Are there any approaches you have used before that might be useful?

Examples of **Monitoring** questions to ask while learners are working on their learning:

- How are you doing in this learning?
- Are you getting closer to meeting the success criteria for the learning outcomes? How do you know?
- What parts of your approach for learning are effective and what parts are not effective? Do you know why?
- What can you do differently? Or what other approach might you take?
- What should you do next?

Examples of **Evaluating** questions to ask learners after the learning has been completed:

- Did you get the results you expected, meet the success criteria and/or achieve the learning outcomes? Why? Why not?
- How effective was the approach you used in helping you progress in your learning and/or achieve the success criteria and learning outcome?
- What factors affected how you progressed (e.g. the amount of effort you put in during the lesson)?
- What other choices could you have made?
- If you are going to work on this area of learning again to progress further, what will you do differently?
- How can you apply your learning to another similar area of learning?

- To enable the responses to the questions to be used effectively, learners need to be engaged in learning conversations to help them understand how to improve their learning
- Support learners to keep an ongoing record of their learning, for example, success criteria and learning outcomes met, progress made, milestones achieved and barriers overcome. This record may be in the form of, for example, a personal diary/journal, developing a physical education dictionary or chart listing and defining key words (subject specific language) which they keep up to date as they learn new subject specific vocabulary to help them articulate their learning

9.7.2.1 What does progress in learners taking responsibility for their own learning look like?

Lastly, a quick word on what progress in learners taking responsibility for their own learning might look like. There might be, for example, an increase in the:

- extent to which learners are able to consider all components of the requirements of a learning activity in planning in relation to specific learning outcomes and associated success criteria

- extent to which learners are able to adopt an appropriate method of approaching a learning activity
- difficulty of concepts or procedures learners incorporate in a learning activity appropriate for own current progress
- extent to which learners are able to recognise factors involved in meeting the success criteria for the learning activity
- thoroughness and depth of learners analysis of and ability to select appropriate ways to describe their progress
- selection and use of appropriate and accurate knowledge and understanding to discuss what they have learned
- accuracy and understanding of evaluation of achievement on the learning activity (for example, are statements made appropriate to the learning outcome and success criteria)?
- Use of evidence to support statements
- ability of learners to express themselves in increasingly sophisticated and subject specific language
- ability of learners to recognise the limitations of the approach to a problem and awareness of ways to improve it
- ability of learners to recognise their progress (in relation to the learning outcomes and success criteria)
- ability of learners to identify factors which mean they are more likely to adopt a physically active lifestyle.

9.8 Summary and key points

Teaching is any activity undertaken by one person which is intended to promote learning by another person. This Unit initially focused on rational, reflective and responsive teaching, then on learner-centred teaching. We then considered teaching individual learners who are holistic and unique, before looking at how the Ladders of Progress in the Physical, Cognitive and Affective Domains might be used by teachers to facilitate and enhance progress. Constituents of teaching were then identified in relation to the principles for facilitating and enhancing progress so that individual learners are more likely to progress. Lastly, one of the principles for facilitating and enhancing progress was considered in more depth, learners taking responsibility for their own learning. This was selected as, in our view, it is less well covered than the other principles for facilitating and enhancing progress in physical education.

What has been covered in this Unit is, however, only part of the story. In considering teaching to facilitate and enhance progress, it would be remiss not to consider how progress is recognised and charted. The next Unit (Unit 10) focuses on recognising progress. It includes sections on assessment, observation, feedback and charting progress.

Unit 10 Recognising and Charting Progress

10.1 Introduction

Teaching does not necessarily result in learning. Therefore, it is no good teaching without recognising and charting what progress is being made. Indeed, if progress is not recognised and charted, a teacher may plan and teach regardless of or, even worse, despite the progress made by each learner. Thus, recognising and charting progress must be integral to teaching, not an add-on.

We have deliberately chosen to use recognising progress as a broad term to cover observation, assessment and feedback – all of which are considered in this Unit. We have chosen to use charting progress in order to highlight an approach to noting progress which is designed to facilitate and enhance future progress. Although we might have used recording progress, in our view, this is frequently linked to assessment *of* learning, with a grade which is not appropriate in terms of focusing on the progress that a learner is making.

Recognising and charting progress against the intended learning outcomes enables a teacher and learner to:

- Understand where a learner is now in their current learning, i.e. the learner's current progress in relation to the success criteria for the learning outcomes
- work out where a learner needs to go next and how they are going to get there, i.e. what still needs to be done to enable the learner to make progress against the learning outcomes.

In this Unit we cover four areas which we identify as important in relation to recognising and charting progress:

- observation *for* learning
- assessment *for* learning
- feedback *for* learning, and
- charting progress *for* learning.

We deliberately use the words '*for* learning' here as a reminder that it is progress towards the learning outcomes that is being recognised. Further, we use the words '*for* learning' rather than the words '*for* progress' as used in the rest of the book because the words '*for* learning' are generally recognised in relation to assessment *for* learning and feedback

DOI: 10.4324/9781003172826-11

for learning. Hence, it makes sense to also use '*for* learning' in relation to observation and charting progress. Further, *for* learning emphasises the formative use of observation, assessment, feedback and charting progress (see below), which aligns with moving towards a learner-centred approach (see Unit 9). However, throughout the Unit the focus is on the progress made by individual learners in relation to learning outcomes in each of the three domains of learning on which we focus in this book – the Physical Domain, the Cognitive Domain and the Affective Domain.

As a result, observation, assessment, feedback and charting progress *for* learning should be considered in relation to the learning outcomes for the lesson and the objectives for the unit of work. In turn, these enable learners to progress towards the intended aims of the curriculum. Despite this, Green (2008) identified an abiding issue in physical education in ensuring that assessment is fit for purpose in facilitating and enhancing future progress (and this could also apply to observation, feedback and charting progress); that is, a lack of clarity in what learners are aiming to achieve in terms of aims of a scheme of work and curriculum, objectives of a unit of work and learning outcomes of a lesson. Without clear aims, objectives and learning outcomes, it is not clear what progress should be observed, assessed, on which feedback should be given and charted (see also Unit 1 on aims of the subject). Further, research has found discrepancies between what teachers identify as the aims of physical education (and hence, objectives and learning outcomes) and their assessment practices (e.g. Borghouts, Slingerland and Haerens, 2017) and between the methods of assessment and what learners are expected to have learned (e.g. Moura, Graça, MacPhail and Batista, 2021). Such discrepancies can, at times, make it unlikely that learners will make progress towards achieving the aims, objectives and learning outcomes. As a consequence, the information generated may not appropriately inform the next steps in learner progress (The Office for Standards in Education, Children's Services and Skills (Ofsted) 2022).

Despite their importance, observation, assessment, feedback and charting progress are constituents of teaching physical education that, in our view, are not always done well. There may be a number of reasons for this. For example, they need to be planned, they take time which might be regarded as taking time away from teaching or from learners being active in a lesson, the learning outcomes might not be clear (see above), the teacher may not be clear what they are looking for or the learners may not be clear of the success criteria to demonstrate progress on achieving the learning outcomes.

Despite recognising that observation, assessment, feedback and charting progress may not always be done well in physical education, in this Unit we deliberately do not look at 'How to;' i.e., how to observe *for* learning; how to assess *for* learning; how to give feedback *for* learning; and how to chart progress *for* learning. There are other sources on 'How to do' these to which reference can be made. As a start, reference can be made to Capel, Cliffe and Lawrence (2021a; 2021b) and Lawrence (2017).

Before considering observation, assessment, feedback and charting progress separately, we look briefly at recognising progress in relation to holistic, individual learners. It is difficult to separate out holistic and individual, therefore although we start by considering the holistic, followed by individual learners, there is inevitably some overlap between these two characteristics of learners.

10.2 Recognising and charting the progress of holistic, individual learners

The importance of viewing learners as holistic applies equally to recognising and charting the progress of individual learners, as it does to, for example, planning, teaching and to the curriculum.

It is a challenging task to recognise and chart progress in the complexity of learning in the Physical, Cognitive and Affective Domains. Hence, at some times and in some contexts, one or other of the domains might be prioritised. We acknowledge that, most frequently, it is progress in the Physical Domain that is prioritised. There may be a number of reasons for this including, for example, the Physical Domain has been prioritised in teaching and it is easier to observe, assess, give feedback on and chart progress in the Physical Domain. It may also be that a teacher feels more confident in recognising and charting progress in the Physical Domain than in the Cognitive and Affective Domains. However, prioritising the Physical Domain alone is unlikely to facilitate and enhance progress; therefore, the Physical Domain must not be the sole focus of attention, nor the only domain in which progress is recognised and charted. For example, principles of choreography in a group sequence in gymnastics or selecting the most appropriate stroke in a specific situation in tennis show evidence of the application of relevant declarative knowledge in practice. In addition, progress in the Physical Domain may be due to, for example, motivation or confidence. As a result, progress in the Cognitive and Affective Domains should also be recognised.

Recognising and charting progress in the Physical, Cognitive and Affective Domains must be in relation to the progress of individual learners. This is important because progress can only be recognised and charted in relation to, for example, who is doing the movement, their experience of that movement and the context in which the movement is occurring (Ford et al., 2011; Lloyd et al., 2015a, 2015b). Although learners are on broadly the same learning journey and tend to follow a similar pattern in the Physical, Cognitive and Affective Domains, as progress is a personal journey that is unique to each individual learner, it is unlikely that they all follow it at the same rate. Some learners make steady progress, whilst the progress of others is uneven. For example, Murdoch (2004) highlights that a learner may make expected improvement followed by an apparent drop in level before they consolidate at an appropriate level or there may be a period of acceleration perhaps followed by a delay (or vice-versa) in one or more of the domains. Thus, learners are at different stages in their learning. It is therefore important to know each learner as an individual in order to recognise and chart how each learner is progressing in the three domains and take into account the particular needs of individual learners. This enables next steps in learning to be planned, with appropriate differentiation/adaptation and scaffolding, based on a realistic expectation of progress for each learner. It also enables teaching to be adjusted in the moment. Thus, it is no good a teacher planning and teaching individual learners if their individual progress is not recognised and charted.

As learners are unique, it is not appropriate, and indeed, it is irrelevant to recognise and chart their progress in comparison with other learners. Further, it is not appropriate to recognise and chart progress by reference to a 'norm'; learners do not conform to a norm (see

Unit 3; see also Glossary). Rather, an individual learner's progress should be recognised and charted in relation to their own starting point against the success criteria for a learning outcome. Success criteria identify the criteria against which progress is to be assessed. In turn, this should inform the next steps the learner needs to make to show progress towards meeting the success criteria for achieving the learning outcome. Such progress is called ipsative and criterion-referenced (see Glossary).

Recognising and charting progress in relation to the Physical, Cognitive and Affective Domains over time for each learner is important to build up a picture of each learner's progress. This, for example, provides essential information which:

- identifies strengths and areas for development in each of the three domains and how the strengths can be built on and areas for development can be addressed
- informs next steps in learning
- promotes continuity in learning,

all of which facilitate and enhance the progress of each individual learner.

In this section, we have highlighted the importance of recognising and charting the progress of individual learners in the three domains. Before considering some salient points in relation to each of the four component parts of recognising and charting progress: observation; assessment; feedback; and charting progress, we briefly consider recognising progress.

10.3 Recognising progress

It is important to bear in mind at all times that it is progress in learning which is to be observed, assessed, on which feedback is given and which is charted – NOT performance. But, what makes recognition *for* progress in learning different from recognition *of* performance?

First, observation, assessment, feedback and charting progress *for* learning focus on what a learner can do at a particular point in time in relation to the success criteria for achieving a learning outcome compared with what they could do previously. It should focus on what an individual learner is doing (i.e. be ipsative and criterion-referenced), rather than making comparisons between learners (i.e. norm referenced (see above)). Thus, in order to make inferences about progress, it is important to know what an individual learner could or could not do previously. This requires observation and assessment of the same learner over time. This enables a teacher (and a learner themself) to know at what level a learner is working and how they are progressing in order to facilitate and enhance further progress. On the other hand, observation, assessment, feedback *of* performance and charting progress of that performance focuses on what a learner can do at a particular time without reference to how they did this previously. It therefore does not take into account the progress made by a learner over time. One consequence of this might be that the learner has stayed at the same level over time (or even regressed), i.e. has not progressed.

Second, in order to facilitate and enhance progress in the Physical Domain, consideration has to be given to the whole person, that is to the contribution of the Cognitive and Affective

Domains to progress. For example, observation, assessment, feedback and charting progress of whether a learner: understands what they are trying to do and why; is able to apply knowledge to the movement or is just copying and repeating effectively; is motivated in the learning (e.g. is applying themselves to the learning); is confident in the learning or is taking responsibility for their learning are important considerations in facilitating and enhancing progress in the Physical Domain. This is more likely to occur if the focus is on observation, assessment, feedback and charting progress *for* learning. On the other hand, observation, assessment, feedback and charting progress *of* performance may only focus on the Physical Domain. For example, how well did the learner throw the javelin or execute a dive off the springboard? How well did the group perform a dance motif or execute a tactic to overcome a zone defence? Where the focus is on the performance, this may not help the reasons for the performance to be understood in order to facilitate and enhance progress.

Focusing on *for* learning therefore enables questions such as the following to be addressed:

- What is the learner able to do now that they were not able to do previously?
- Where is the learner in relation to the success criteria for achieving the learning outcomes?
- Is the learner able to identify what they can now do that they could not do previously?
- How is the learner applying themselves to the learning to enable them to progress towards achieving the success criteria for the learning outcomes?
- Is the learner making an effort and trying to achieve the success criteria for the learning outcome, that is, are they motivated?

We now move to consider briefly some points in relation to observation *for* learning, assessment *for* learning, feedback *for* learning and charting progress *for* learning separately.

We start by considering some aspects of observation *for* learning.

10.4 Observation *for* learning

In our view, observation is one of the (or perhaps even the) most important skills a physical education teacher possesses. It is central to learners learning effectively in physical education and hence to their progress. It is also an important skill for learners to develop as they take increasing responsibility for their own learning (see Unit 9).

As progress is the priority in physical education, an ability to observe whether learners are progressing or not is obviously critical. For example, information from observation is key to identifying:

- what progress is (or is not) being made by the class, group of learners and individual learners, and
- whether the success criteria for the learning outcomes have been met (or not)

In turn, this enables:

- feedback to be provided to facilitate and enhance progress and
- progress to be charted so that

- next steps in learning can be planned to facilitate and enhance progress for each learner (e.g., select suitable learning activities and teaching approaches, differentiate/adapt and scaffold learning in order to help learners close the learning gap).

Thus, "In order to promote learning, you must strive to become a perceptive observer of human movement" (Marsden, 2010, p.46).

In describing observation, Marsden (2010, p. 46) cited Graham (2008) who state "Observe the children. Analyse their movement. Make a decision whether to change the task, provide a cue, offer a challenge or provide feedback. Seems easy." However, physical education teachers who observe *for* learning know that this statement is far from accurate. As with all constituents of teaching, observation is certainly *not* easy. There are a number of reasons for observation *for* learning being a challenging and daunting skill to develop, including:

- observation is more than just looking; rather it involves astute awareness of the whole class, groups of learners and individual learners
- learners are distributed over a large area and are seldom still
- It is difficult to balance teaching, organising and managing with observation in the limited time available in a lesson
- It requires good knowledge and understanding of:

  - individual learners, where they are in their progress across the Physical, Cognitive and Affective Domains, what they can/cannot do and their individual needs
  - the content of a lesson (and hence the focus of the observation) as well as of the specific focus of the learning, i.e. the specific learning outcomes and success criteria, including, for example stages of learning a Movement Pattern, key features of different Movement Activities, relevant declarative knowledge, common mistakes, misunderstandings or misconceptions which learners may make.

The ability to observe develops over time, with practice and experience, as understanding of the importance of observation, why it is taking place, what is being observed and how it is being observed develops. Further, developing skills to observe effectively *for* learning is complex.

Observation is a skill that, in our view, may be overlooked. One reason for this might be that a teacher not only assumes they can see what is happening in their lessons and whether or not learners are progressing, but also that they do this well. However, in our view, this is not always the case. For example, a teacher may;

- set a learning activity and then fail to observe progress, for example, looking but not observing, seeing what they expect to see (and not see what they don't expect to see) or being more concerned with organising the next learning activity
- look but is not focused. Trying to focus on observing too many things at the same time, rather than having a single focus for the observation in relation to the success criteria for the learning outcomes, results in the teacher becoming overwhelmed by too much visual information

- not stand back and scan the whole class to observe any general points about learning, establish if all learners have understood the learning activity that has been set/what they are being asked to do and are engaged in the learning activity; rather, immediately circulate around groups or individual learners
- observe something other than learning. For example, observation may be of behaviour, or of performance rather than the progress that is taking place (although, of course, poor behaviour could be a sign that a learner is not progressing).

Thus, it is important that teachers do not take for granted their ability to observe but reflect on how effectively they observe *for* learning and, where appropriate, develop their ability to observe effectively *for* learning. Although we do not cover developing skills of observation in this book, there are other resources to which reference might be made. Killingbeck and Whitehead (2021a) might be a good place to start. Further, it might be useful to refer to the chapter on observation in previous editions of *Learning to Teach Physical Education* (e.g. Marsden, 2010).

As stated above, observation is also an important skill for learners to develop as they take increasing responsibility for their own learning. Therefore, a teacher should consider how they can support learners to develop their skills of observation. Here the use of technology can help. For example, a learner can record and then observe their own learning over time, identifying what that can do now that they could not do before and then identifying what the next steps in their learning might be (see also Supporting learners to develop their ability to observe, assess, provide feedback and to chart their own progress, below).

Observation *for* learning is essential for effective assessment *for* learning, which is considered next.

10.5 Assessment *for* learning

The Association Internationale des Écoles Supérieures d'Éducation Physique (International Association for Physical Education in Higher Education, AIESEP, (2020, p. 3) state that "Assessment is a process by which information on student learning is obtained, interpreted and communicated, relative to one or more predefined learning outcomes."

In order to obtain information to facilitate and enhance progress, below we consider assessment *for* learning in a bit more detail. Again, we do not cover how to assess. However, there are other sources to which reference can be made. As a start, it might be useful to look at (Lawrence, 2017; Newton and Bowler, 2021; Yong, 2022).

As teachers are all too aware, there are a variety of terms used in relation to assessment. These include, for example, summative and formative assessment, assessment *of* and *for* learning. Although these terms are not always used in the same way; broadly, summative assessment/ assessment *of* learning measures achievement, or performance, at a particular point in time. It is frequently used to give grades and to write a report at the end of a specific period of time.

On the other hand, broadly, formative assessment/assessment *for* learning informs the learner and teacher in the moment of current progress and the next steps needed to support learners to progress towards meeting the learning outcomes. Thus, without assessment *for* learning, it is questionable how progress can be facilitated and enhanced.

Such a premise is supported by the Assessment Reform Group (ARG, 2002). For them assessment *for* learning is a process of seeking and interpreting evidence to decide where learners are in their learning, where they need to go and how best to get there. Thus, assessment *for* learning provides information about what learning has already taken place and what progress has been made – whether or not the learner has learned and made progress – they can do what was intended and hence whether or not they are ready to move on – to progress.

As an integral part of effective teaching and learning, assessment *for* learning is an ongoing process, not a standalone event or an exercise that is introduced to a lesson at a specific time as a bolt on extra. Chappuis (2009) identifies assessment *for* learning as those processes used by teachers and learners to facilitate and enhance progress. It encompasses "all those activities undertaken by teachers and/or by their students which provide information to be used as feedback to modify the teaching and learning activities in which they are engaged" (Black and Wiliam, 1998, p. 8). These definitions highlight that assessment *for* learning may not involve learners doing anything different to what they are doing as part of the learning process. Likewise, it may not involve a teacher doing anything different than they normally do – observing, questioning and providing feedback to learners as they are working.

On the other hand, there could also be specific assessment task(s) designed to support learning. Where a specific assessment task is used it is important to remember that it is not the assessment task itself which is assessment *for* learning (rather than *of* learning); rather, this is determined by how, when and why a specific task is used for assessment. It is generally recognised (see, for example, Stiggins and Chappuis, 2005) that, if learners can answer the following three questions in relation to assessment, the assessment can be considered *for learning*:

- Where am I going?
- Where am I now?
- How can I close the gap?

In order for assessment to inform learning, there must be an alignment between what learners are supposed to be learning (the learning outcomes of the lesson), what is being taught (the content the learner is engaging with) and what is being assessed (the success criteria which provide evidence of progress towards the learning outcomes). Thus, once the learning outcomes learners are working to achieve have been identified, how achievement of the outcome might be demonstrated should be determined (the success criteria).

Further, an assessment task should be appropriate for the learners for whom it is set, and reflect learning and progress across the domains of learning (see Units, 5, 6 and 7).

Assessment *for* learning in physical education therefore highlights to learners what they are doing well, as well as what they need to develop in order to progress. It should also highlight any underlying misconceptions which need to be corrected before learners move on to learning more complex content (see, for example, Ofsted, 2022).

Assessment *for* learning also provides valuable information for the teacher. Information gained about past and current progress underpins planning for future progress. For example, does a whole class, some learners in the class or an individual learner need to spend more time on current learning or are they ready to progress to the next stage in their learning? Do they have the pre-requisites to move onto next learning? Is the learning activity appropriate? Are learning activities and/or teaching approaches effective?

New learning needs to be planned to build on the progress already made; therefore learners need the pre-requisite, underpinning learning. As an example, although learners are likely to remember and be able to repeat something taught in a lesson, this does not mean that it will be retained, converted into long-term memory and can be repeated, i.e. that it has been learned. Indeed, as stressed by Ofsted (2022), there may be evidence that a particular component of learning covered in a lesson can be demonstrated, but not that it has been learned. Hence, the learning needs to be reinforced, consolidated and applied through learners spending time practicing on appropriate learning activities and in appropriate contexts in the same and later lessons and through planned recall and review of the learning (see principles for facilitating and enhancing progress in Units 2, 3 and 9).

The concept of hinge points is relevant here (see, for example, Leahy, et al., 2005). These are points where a lesson can go in different directions, depending on learner progress. At such points checks are made (e.g. through observation or questioning) as to whether pre-requisite learning has been made and a learner is ready to progress further. Thus, hinge points help to determine the direction of any new learning and/or next steps in progress. By explicitly integrating these hinge points into lessons, teaching can be made more responsive to learners' needs at that specific time.

But what is assessed in assessment *for* learning?

10.5.1 *Focus of assessment for learning: Process versus product*

In order to facilitate and enhance progress (and to enable learners to take increasing responsibility for their own learning), assessing progress on the process of learning (including planning, performing and evaluating (see Unit 9)) is as, if not more, important than assessing the product of learning.

It is important to recognise that the underlying quality of learning is not always demonstrated through observations of physical performance at a particular point in time (Shea and Morgan, 1979). For example, when new learning is introduced, progress may be temporarily reversed until that new learning has been practised and integrated into previous learning. For example, as more complex movements such as a turn are introduced when learning to throw a discus, there may be a reduction in the distance the discus is thrown. As a result, it may appear that learning has regressed.

However, assessing the process of learning is difficult as performance is observable, but learning is not directly observable. Rather, learning is inferred from a person's behaviour or performance (Rink, 1985, p. 20). As a result, much assessment in physical education at present may focus on that which is easiest to observe and recognise; that is, the product of learning. Indeed, it has been suggested that in physical education, there is a high prevalence of product-oriented assessment practices, e.g. how high a learner jumped, how fast a learner swam a length, how well a learner performed a specific Movement Pattern. Further, in many cases this is detached from any consideration of where the movement is occurring or the context (Lorente-Catalán and Kirk 2016; Penney et al. 2009). This focus on the product of learning is linked to both observation *of* performance and assessment *of* learning rather than observation *for* learning and assessment *for* learning (see above). As well as being easier to observe and to assess, other reasons which might contribute to a focus on assessing the product of learning include, for example, the deep-rooted focus on sport culture in physical education in which high performance is accepted uncritically as a fundamental aim and is therefore the criteria for success.

10.5.2 Assessment for learning and motivation

According to AIESEP (2020, p. 3), assessment practices are "central to providing meaningful, relevant and worthwhile physical education." As a result, meaningful, relevant and worthwhile assessment *for* learning practices in physical education should motivate a learner to learn. For example, assessment *for* learning provides information to support teachers and learners in identifying their strengths and areas in which they can improve. Knowing about their strengths and areas in which they can improve enables the teacher and learners' to plan their learning in order to be more focused in their learning, which is more motivating (Deci and Ryan, 1985). It may also help them to identify changes learners could make to their learning strategies, which may be based on the kinds of challenges that hold the most educational value to them.

Active involvement by learners in the assessment *for* learning process can enable them to feel a greater sense of autonomy and ownership of their learning. This requires decisions about what and how to assess to be based on value and importance to the learners (Hay and Penney, 2013). This helps them to take responsibility for their own learning (see Unit 9) and can motivate them both in learning in physical education and in order to adopt a physically active lifestyle.

10.5.3 Sources of evidence of learning

In order to gain reliable information for assessment *for* learning, it is important to use a number of forms of assessment (Office for Standards in Education, Children's Services and Skills (Ofsted), 2022). Indeed, evidence of learning should come from multiple and varied sources (see for example, Black and Wiliam, 1998; Chappuis, 2009; Stiggins, Arter, Chappuis and Chappuis, 2004). As indicated above, these may not involve learners doing anything different to what they are doing as part of the learning process or may include specific assessment task(s). Common forms of assessment *for* learning include:

- Observation
- questioning, both of which may be accompanied by note taking
- self-assessment strategies
- Self-reflection

Whilst it is up to the teacher to consider the feasibility and appropriateness of various means of assessment *for* learning, depending on various factors, including the needs, abilities, previous learning experiences of the learners, and the context, they must also consider who is involved in the assessment process and thus how feedback is given to learners. Feedback is considered next.

10.6 Feedback *for* learning

Effective observation *for* learning underpins effective assessment *for* learning in physical education. In turn, this leads to effective feedback *for* learning, to facilitate and enhance progress. Indeed, " ... learning is more likely to occur when you use observation to give personalised feedback to reinforce, guide and advise learners" (Whitehead, 2015, p.174).

Whilst feedback *for* learning provides information to the learner, at the same time it also provides information to the teacher about what steps should be taken next to facilitate and enhance progress. It is helpful if progress is charted so that the learner, same teacher at a different time or a different teacher has the information to facilitate and enhance progress of learners in future.

Feedback can be direct or indirect:

- Direct feedback is that which is given on the learning itself. This requires consideration of what feedback should focus on, when it should occur, how much time is devoted to feedback, what role learners have in feedback and whether or not their voice is heard and how feedback is going to be followed up
- Indirect feedback refers to anything which provides information about what learning is valued in physical education. This relates to, for example, who the teacher chooses to give feedback to, about what, and equally, who and what is not a focus for feedback.

Although both types of feedback are important in facilitating and enhancing progress, in this Unit the focus is on direct feedback. However, it is also important that consideration is given to the indirect feedback which is being given.

We now consider briefly some aspects of feedback *for* learning to which consideration might be given in facilitating and enhancing progress.

10.6.1 Feedback for learning: some key points

As indicated above, information gathered through assessment *for* learning should provide an accurate picture of the current progress of each learner against the success criteria for the learning outcomes, so learners know what they need to be able to do to meet the learning outcomes. Likewise, to enable learners to progress, feedback should relate closely to the intended learning outcomes towards which learners are working in relation to all or some of the Physical, Cognitive and/or Affective Domains, as appropriate.

The more specific the focus of intended learning is, the more specific and focused feedback can be in order to bridge the gap between current progress and achievement of the learning outcomes.

Indeed, it is generally the case that learners find it easier to focus on one thing at a time (Whitehead, 2021b). Thus, for feedback to influence learning, it should be focused on a specific component of learning (Black *et al.*, 2003). This will provide learners with knowledge of progress specific to the learning focus, prevent them from becoming overloaded with too much information and potentially not focusing on the specific component that needs to be addressed). For example, if learners are working towards developing teamwork in a game, the feedback must focus directly on the key characteristics of effective teamwork they have been introduced to either during the lesson or previously. It is only through receiving feedback on the intended leaning that learners will know if they achieved the success criteria for a learning outcome. This means that the teacher (or the learner) needs to consider carefully which specific learning outcome or part of a learning outcome they are providing feedback on.

At times, some teachers may at some times be guilty of giving too much feedback, covering a range of aspects of the learning being carried out (e.g., about the Movement Patterns being used as well as the teamwork). On the other hand, some teachers may at some times give too little information to enable a learner to progress. For example, they just say 'well done.' without giving any specific information about what the learner could do to improve. Thus, feedback needs to be both precise and clear and provide specific, relevant information against the success criteria of the learning outcomes towards which learners are working.

As well as identifying components of the learning which can be improved and where progress is still needed, comment should also be made on positive aspects of progress (at least one positive comment should be given). Because motivation, confidence and growth in self-esteem are key to learning, feedback should exhibit optimism and a belief in learner potential.

In summarising feedback and its use in supporting progress, Hattie and Timperley (2007, updated by Hattie, Masters and Birch, 2016, p. 10), argue that feedback should follow three principles in gathering information to support progress. These relate to the focus of assessment *for* learning (see above). That is:

- Feed-up: where is the learner going? i.e., what is the learning outcome (and what are the success criteria) that needs to be accomplished?
- Feedback: how is the learner doing/where is the learner now? i.e. what is current progress against the success criteria for the learning outcomes and what information is this based on?
- Feed-forward: what should the next steps be/where to next? i.e. how to make progress/ what is the strategy for further progress against the learning outcomes?

Feedback is most effective when it is both understood and actively used to support progress. Thus, learners need to be given adequate time following feedback to take action; to practice and learn, taking on board the guidance given in the feedback (Ofsted, 2022). As with assessment *for* learning, this makes the learning meaningful (see above). When learners are clear about what they are learning, why and what they need to do in order to get there, and given time to practice, constructive feedback is meaningful and supports learning. In turn, this is motivating.

Giving individual feedback and spending quality time (re-)explaining key aspects of the learning is obviously the ideal in facilitating and enhancing progress. However, it takes considerable time. For a class of 30+ learners, one teacher is only able to give limited specific feedback to any learner in any one lesson. The teacher therefore needs to consider how best each learner can receive feedback as frequently as possible. For example, if a number of learners are making the same mistake or sharing the same misconception, whole class or group oral feedback, as appropriate, enables more learners to benefit from feedback. Where whole class or group feedback is given, learners who have made the required progress can be used as a learning resource to help other learners to address the mistake or clarify the misconception in question and what needs to be done to correct it.

Further, although much feedback in physical education is given by the teacher, in order to maximise feedback to individual learners, learners should be supported to develop their ability to give and receive feedback from another learner (peer feedback) and to give feedback to themselves (self-feedback) (for example, from video observation and analysis or from within (kinaesthetic feedback)). Not only does feedback by a learner to peer or self, enable more feedback to be given and received to aid learning, it also means that the recipient of feedback is doing more work than the giver. It also helps learners to take responsibility for their own learning. (See also Supporting learners to develop their ability to observe, assess provide feedback and to chart their own progress, below.)

However, it is important to note that observation of and feedback to a peer should generally precede observation of and feedback to self. This is because it is generally easier to observe and provide feedback to a peer than it is to self. Hence, peer observation is a stepping stone towards being able to observe and provide feedback to self. However, it may, on occasion, be most appropriate to observe and give feedback to self without first working with a peer. It is also generally easier for learners to observe a Movement Pattern rather than engagement in a Movement Activity. Hence, in developing their skills of observation, learners can start by observing a Movement Pattern.

In order to make use of feedback learners need to reflect on the information and what it means for their progress. Thus, the teacher can actively help learners to use feedback effectively by modelling reflection, through thinking aloud and encouraging learners to practice the same processes, initially together with the teacher. Learners can be directed to relevant information and helped to focus their attention on relevant components of learning and shown how to develop an analytical approach. This is important as part of learners developing their ability to take responsibility for their own learning.

To enable effective feedback to be given, as stated above, the teacher (or a learner giving feedback to a peer or to self) needs to be actively engaged in observing all the time learners are engaged in learning activities. By being alert to the learners' responses to a learning activity set, enables appropriate information to be gathered to enable feedback to be given to the learner as well as adapt/differentiate and redirect learning activities as appropriate.

So far, the Unit has focused on how information about the progress of each learner gained from observation *for* learning and assessment *for* learning informs the learner and the teacher in the moment and provides feedback *for* learning to each learner and to the teacher on any changes to teaching and learning activities to further facilitate and enhance progress. These, either on their own or together, are not necessarily sufficient to support learners to progress. Information about the progress of each learner needs to be charted.

10.7 Charting progress *for* learning

Information about the progress of each learner needs to be charted so that it is available to the same or other teachers, as well as to the learners. Such information is important for the same teacher teaching the same class a different unit of work in the same or a different academic year; a teacher taking over a class from another teacher in the same or a different academic year; and for the learner as they progress. We know that any break and/or change in content or the teacher may result in continuity in learning being lost. By charting the progress each learner is making, opportunities to build on prior learning to support progress can be identified and continuity enhanced. Below are some points of consideration in charting progress *for* learning.

10.7.1 *Charting progress for learning: Some key points*

10.7.1.1 *Charting progress of the process or the product of learning*

In line with what has been said above about observation *for* learning, assessment *for* learning and feedback *for* learning, charting the progress of that learning should focus on an individual learner's journey. Thus, for us, information about the process of learning through planning, performing and evaluating should be charted, rather than merely charting information about the end product of learning, i.e. achievement or performance at one point in time. This latter will not provide relevant information on the progress of each learner to inform the key steps the learner needs to take in order to make further progress and achieve the success criteria for the learning outcomes.

10.7.1.2 *Some considerations in relation to charting progress of individual learners*

What progress is charted creates and shapes learning. Thus, it is important to bear in mind that charting progress can undermine, as well as encourage, learning. For example, if the information charted is not useful, is too little (or too much), does not focus on the learning outcomes and success criteria, is not reliable and valid, it can undermine progress. It is therefore important to be clear about the purpose, validity, reliability and value (Kime et al, 2017) of what progress is being charted.

The progress of individual learners should be based on valid judgements of reliable information which should come from multiple sources. These include, for example, observation, questioning/verbal discussion, etc. Progress that is charted allows for reflection on the ongoing learning journey of each individual.

In the real world, there is no perfect, set method of charting progress. There is a need for flexibility. Whatever method is used, it is important that it is kept simple, uncomplicated and brief, whilst at the same time providing relevant information. This makes it both manageable and useful for the teacher and learner to inform future progress. Thus, progress should be charted by the best method that circumstances and resources allow, that is appropriate to the individual learner and to the focus of learning. Therefore, different types of learning may need to be charted in different ways.

Grades are not appropriate as they provide information about the product of learning, rather than the process of learning. Information charted to support progress should be descriptive. It should paint a 'picture' of where each learner is in relation to where they have come from it is this descriptive information that will enable the next steps in learning to be planned for an individual learner to make progress in a coherent way. Hence, our view is that notes might be a useful way of charting progress, as might pictorial and/or written descriptions at some times.

As with information provided in feedback *for* learning, the information charted needs to be understood and actively used to support progress. It is useful if there is some guidance as to what the learner needs to do next. Too frequently, information is charted in a way which is, for example, too complex which renders it hard to use, or which conflates information which results in it not being useful to inform future progress or does not give any indication of what the learners needs to do next.

As learning is an ongoing process, progress should be charted on a regular basis so that a picture of each learner's progress can be built up over time. This may be, for example, a note written during or at the end of a lesson rather than something more formal written at the end of a unit of work. This enables the teacher and the learner to know what progress is being made in the short, medium and long term. Further, it supports the same teacher and other teachers to plan learning activities and teaching approaches appropriate to each learner's current progress, their potential and capacity, and which are meaningful to and achievable by the learner. It enables the pace of learning to be set so that it is not so fast that the learner cannot keep up or that it is not too slow so that the learner gets bored. It enables learning to be adjusted so that each learner is stretched and challenged but also has the opportunity to consolidate learning. In summary, effectively charting the progress of each learner allows future learning activities to build on prior learning to facilitate and enhance future progress.

Although learners taking responsibility for their own learning has been mentioned at several points in this Unit, the last section of this Unit focuses on observation, assessment, feedback and charting progress in relation to this.

10.8 Supporting learners to develop their ability to observe, assess, provide feedback and to chart their own progress

If learners are going to take responsibility for their own learning (see also Unit 9), they need to be actively involved in observation, assessment, feedback and charting progress.

As stated above, one teacher to a class of 30+ learners means that each individual learner can only receive a limited amount of attention from the teacher in each lesson. Hence, by teaching learners some skills of observation, peer and self-assessment and feedback and being able to chart their progress over time, learners become better prepared to take responsibility for their own learning and drive their own progress forward. Additionally, developing declarative knowledge that underpins the learning of Movement Patterns and Movement Activities (e.g. Knowing how to move efficiently and effectively and recognising the effects of physical activity) and recognising the importance of and being able to plan for participation in physical activity should help learners to recognise and chart their own progress. This requires the teacher to work *with* learners so that learners know their current progress, where they need to be and how they are going to get there. Active involvement in the process can enable learners to feel a greater sense of responsibility for and ownership of their learning and hence to take responsibility for their own learning.

To achieve this, the teacher can initially consult with learners, where appropriate, then gradually increase learner involvement by, for example, over time enabling learners to:

- determine their learning priorities and set their own learning outcomes
- Determine the success criteria for meeting the learning outcomes
- Choose when and how to demonstrate their progress
- Have a part in the construction of their own assessment *for* learning
- Observe and engage in peer and then self-assessment of progress towards meeting the learning outcomes
- Identify strengths and areas needing improvement of peer and then self – initially in relation to a previously considered starting point, but then in relation to own personal goals
- provide feedback to peer and then to self
- Engage in dialogue with the teacher and peers about assessment and its outcomes
- Take action in response to feedback to learn and progress further
- Chart their own progress.

To enable learners to develop skills to recognise and chart their own progress, time needs to be built into lessons for them to fully reflect on their progress and what they still need to develop at key points during the lesson, i.e. how they are going to address the areas for development.

Finally, a brief note about observation as an integral part of learners taking responsibility for their own learning. As it is a key skill for teachers (see above), observation is also a key skill for learners to develop to enable them to take responsibility for their own learning. In physical education, learners observe in a range of contexts, for example:

- demonstrations by the teacher or peer(s)
- analysing a Movement Pattern or engagement in a Movement Activity, e.g. a swimming stroke, a group dance or gymnastics sequence, a tactic in a game, and
- via use of video recording of their own Movement Pattern or engagement in a Movement Activity.

With well-developed observation skills, the teacher is able to support learners to acquire and develop their skills of observation. Learners can be introduced to skills involved in observing effectively when they observe one specific aspect of a Movement Pattern or Movement Activity being demonstrated by the teacher or a peer(s). In turn, supporting learners to develop their observation skills enables them to receive a greater amount of feedback on their learning than one teacher can give to an individual learner (see above).

Initially, learners may be introduced to observation of a peer, for example, as part of peer assessment or in the reciprocal teaching style (Mosston and Ashworth, 2002; see summary of styles in Table 9.3, Unit 9) in which one learner, acting as the 'teacher,' observes and provides feedback to their partner. In the reciprocal teaching style, the 'teacher' can be asked to focus on a specific part of a Movement Pattern using specific criteria, for example, how far their partner attains a symmetrical position in jumping in gymnastics or whether the fingers are close together in a breaststroke arm action. What is being observed and the criteria to be used for the observation and feedback to their partner, can be written on, for example, wall posters or work cards. Guidance about positions from which to observe are also likely to be needed. Over time, as they practice observing, the 'teacher' can decide the key learning points they are going to observe, perhaps in collaboration with the learner themself. As they develop their observation skills, combined with developing their ability to analyse movement and identify strengths and areas for development, the 'teacher' is able to identify how learning is progressing and how to progress learning. They can also increasingly focus on engagement in a Movement Activity as well as a Movement Pattern.

However, it must be remembered that observation is a complex skill, even for teachers, and is particularly complex and challenging for learners. One reason for this is that learners, unlike the teacher, do not have a thorough grasp of the content which is the focus of the observation. Thus, learners are unlikely to be able to observe the teacher, each other or themselves effectively the first few times they attempt this – even with support. They need considerable guidance as to what to look for as well as considerable time and practice and carefully scaffolded learning opportunities before they can observe effectively. Hence, as with other components of learning, observation should not be introduced once and then not used again (maybe because it was not successful the first time).

10.9 Summary and key points

This Unit has focused on recognising and charting progress. It has considered observation *for* learning, assessment *for* learning, feedback *for* learning and charting progress *for* learning. The Unit has largely focused on the teacher in this enterprise, but the final section has focused on the importance of a learner being involved in observation *for* learning, assessment *for* learning, feedback *for* learning and charting progress *for* learning in order for them to take responsibility for their own learning.

Recognising and charting progress is highly challenging for the teacher, yet alone a learner. It needs to be done regularly to be able to facilitate and enhance the progress of each and every learner. There is no perfect method to being able to recognise and chart progress to facilitate and enhance progress. In order to identify the best method in a particular context, the teacher (and learner) need:

1. Knowledge about, and focus on, individual learners as both holistic and unique
2. Clear knowledge of learning outcomes, and the associated success criteria
3. Prioritisation of the process rather than the product of learning
4. Careful observation to be able to gather relevant information about the progress of each learner. It is the day-to-day observations and ongoing learning conversations which are essential to progress
5. Mastery of different ways to recognise and chart progress to capture the progress in respect of each individual learner
6. To be able to analyse reflectively the observed information
7. To create a system of charting the information which is quick and uncomplicated
8. To trust in the teacher's professional judgement on the evidence that each learner presents to be able to say, with confidence, what progress has occurred.

We finish by reinforcing the importance of recognising and charting progress; by reiterating that teaching does not necessarily result in learning. Therefore, it is no good teaching without checking whether or not learning is occurring and progress is being made. This requires that recognising and charting progress – including effective observation *for* learning, assessment *for* learning, feedback *for* learning and charting progress *for* learning – are integral to teaching, not add-ons.

Unit 11 focuses on the curriculum as another condition to enable the process of learners moving from one state or stage to another to occur, i.e. in facilitating and enhancing progress in the subject.

Unit 11 A Progressive Curriculum in Facilitating and Enhancing Progress

11.1 Introduction

This Unit focuses on the curriculum as an enabling condition to facilitate and enhance progress. To achieve this we view the curriculum as providing an optimal context and broad guidelines for progress rather than a document to be followed exactly. Indeed, it is important to remember that, as argued in Unit 2, a pre-planned curriculum does not replace the need to monitor progress by individual learners. This monitoring will require both the content of the curriculum (as well as of units of work and lessons) and teaching approaches to be adjusted to enable the needs of individual learners to be met. Individual learners and their needs must always supersede a pre-planned curriculum.

Throughout this book progress has been considered from three perspectives, being the physical, the cognitive and the affective. All three domains are important in enabling learners to develop their movement competence, to thrive in physical education lessons and to adopt a physically active lifestyle. Thus, it is argued that, broadly, in order to meet the aims of physical education, the curriculum must provide opportunities for learners to progress in the:

- Physical Domain, to facilitate and enhance progress in relation to Movement Patterns and Movement Activities (see Unit 5 and below)
- Cognitive Domain, to facilitate and enhance progress in relation to declarative knowledge about constituents and principles of movement and adopting a physically active lifestyle to underpin progress in the Physical Domain
- Affective Domain, to facilitate and enhance the development of a positive attitude towards learning in the subject, including motivation, confidence and autonomy.

The curriculum must also be flexible to cater for the range of individual learners.

What is taught within the curriculum (the content and outcomes – sometimes referred to as the product) is particularly relevant to progress in the Physical and Cognitive Domains, whereas how it is taught (sometimes referred to as the process) is particularly relevant to progress in the Affective Domain, as well as the Cognitive Domain in relation to, for example, the development of thinking skills and learning to learn.

However, it is accepted that any curriculum has to accommodate the nature of the context within which is 'delivered,' including, for example:

DOI: 10.4324/9781003172826-12

- School policies about allocation of time and length of lessons
- Staff available
- Nature of the school and local facilities for Movement Activities
- Equipment available.

Hence, the ideal might not become reality because of the nature/culture of the school (see also Unit 12). For example, what it is feasible to teach in a school may be linked to its location, e.g. a school with limited facilities in a city may have access to offsite facilities which can be reached easily and in a short time scale. A school near a river or coast may have access to facilities for water-based activities. Likewise, this may be linked to the extent to which the curriculum is centralised (for example, in England some schools working within Multi-Academy Trusts (see Glossary) are required to teach the same curriculum as the other schools in the Trust). However, regardless of constraints, a curriculum should ensure the best use of the time, staff, facilities and equipment available to enable every learner to make real progress in physical education.

The Unit starts by looking at some definitions of curriculum and approaches to curriculum planning, before briefly looking at the physical education curriculum in primary and secondary schools. The Unit then identifies some key considerations we deem relevant in relation to the curriculum as an enabling condition to facilitate and enhance progress to enable the aims of physical education to be realised.

11.2 Definitions of curriculum and approaches to curriculum planning

Kerr (1968, p. 16) defined a curriculum as "all learning which is planned and guided by the school, whether it is carried out in groups or individually, inside or outside of school." For Stenhouse (1976, p. 4), a curriculum is "an attempt to communicate the essential principles and features of an educational proposal in such a form that it is open to critical scrutiny and capable of effective translation into practice." More recently, Priestley (2019) described a curriculum as the totality of the learning experience (what, how and why). The view taken in this Unit is that a curriculum is a planning tool which identifies the broad intentions of learning to enable all learners to progress towards achieving the aims of the curriculum.

To consider how this might manifest itself in teaching (either in a school or subject), Kelly (2009) identified three approaches to curriculum planning;

- Curriculum as content – where the focus is on the transmission of knowledge
- Curriculum as product – where the focus is on the outcome of learning
- Curriculum as process – where the focus is on the development of the learner.

In our view, many curricula are 'product-based curriculum,' focusing on the content to be taught. This may result in the transmission of content through a teacher-centred approach, with limited acknowledgment made to the learner or the learning context. However, the approach we are advocating in this book is that learning is more than a product; the process of learning is equally important. This reflects a formative approach to learning, where it is progress that is facilitated and recognised (see Unit 10) and greater opportunities are provided for learners to develop responsibility for their own learning (see Unit 9). Thus, in our view, an education proposal or a curriculum, should reflect both the content to be taught, and how the curriculum is delivered to facilitate and enhance progress and positive attitudes to learning in order to develop appropriate learning behaviours. Thus, the product and the process should both be in evidence in the aims of the curriculum. It should also focus on the learner (thereby is learner-centred), able to respond to the needs of individual learners, and may involve learners in planning the curriculum.

In practice, a curriculum can cover a significant period of time, such as the throughout the whole of compulsory schooling, or the primary or secondary phase of schooling. Alternatively, it may provide a scaffold for a key stage or year of learning.

Notwithstanding a logically planned and sequenced curriculum to achieve specific aims, it must be viewed as provisional, thus building from the assertion that each learner is unique and each progresses differently in the Physical, Cognitive and Affective Domains. As a result, the curriculum (as well as schemes and units of work and lessons which stem from the curriculum) need to be flexible so that appropriate inclusive and differentiated/adapted lessons can be taught in which learning is appropriately scaffolded for each learner.

If learning progressions are well sequenced in the curriculum, teachers are able to focus on what learners will learn to enable them to progress towards meeting the aims of the curriculum. This focuses attention on the objectives of units of work and the learning outcomes of each lesson, rather than what the learner will do (i.e., the learning activity). This avoids the all too common practice of learning being driven by the Movement Activity being taught, rather than driven by the desired learning. Thus, teachers should be able to describe what learners should learn and hence what progress they should make by following the curriculum, with the activities selected for the curriculum to enable learners to achieve this learning and make progress. They should then be able to identify what was actually learned by following the curriculum (what the Office for Standards in Education, Children's Services and Skills (Ofsted) refer to as intent, implementation and impact (Ofsted, 2018) and, more recently, pillars of progress (Motor Competence, Rules, Strategies and Tactics, Health Participation) (Ofsted, 2023a).

11.3 The physical education curriculum

A fundamental question to be asked is, what priorities should there be in planning a physical education curriculum that can facilitate and enhance progress in Movement Patterns and Movement Activities across a range of Movement Forms with the aim of learners adopting a physically active lifestyle? In addition, what opportunities for learners to become confident in taking increasing responsibility for their own learning, allowing them to engage effectively in the learning process and developing positive attitudes.

Before focusing in more detail on factors that need to be considered in constructing a curriculum for progress during the years of compulsory schooling, it is useful to be reminded that new learning should always build on previous learning and be working towards an aim. Thus, young children's learning in the pre-school years (both through exploration and free and semi-structured play as well as the provision of learning opportunities through explicit teaching (see Unit 5)) should underpin curriculum planning in the early years of compulsory schooling. During the pre-school years, children should have explored, 'mastered,' and be confident in using, a range of general Movement Patterns (see, Pickard and Maude, 2021; Unit 5 (the Physical Domain)), including, for example, balance, flight, locomotion, manipulation and projection.

At the end of schooling, it must be clear what learners should be able to do, i.e. what progress they should have made by the time they leave compulsory schooling (see Unit 5; the Physical Domain).

11.3.1 The curriculum in the primary years (ages 5-10/11 years)

In the early years of compulsory schooling, the nature of the curriculum is best conceived as a learning journey which builds on the general Movement Patterns developed as a result of learning through early movement experiences. Although not covered in this book, it should also provide opportunities for learners who have not yet developed a range of general Movement Patterns to develop these to facilitate and enhance their progress during compulsory schooling (see for example Department for Education (DfE), 2021; Early Movers, n.d.). Thus, even from the time learners enter compulsory schooling, there should be some flexibility in the curriculum.

General Movement Patterns underpin the development of refined Movement Patterns. Therefore throughout primary schooling Movement Patterns become ever more refined and specific as they begin to be applied to simplified/modified forms of recognised Movement Activities (see also Unit 5 (appendix 5.1 and 5.2)).

While the exploratory, play approach largely adopted in the pre-school years should not be curtailed once learners move into compulsory schooling, it would be expected that learning will become more structured in enabling learners to build on the general Movement Patterns they have developed in the early years.

This period of schooling is an important learning bridge between a learner's involvement in physical play as an inherent urge to find out 'how to engage' with the world and learning specific Movement Patterns which facilitate and enhance learners to participate effectively in recognised forms of Movement Activity, which is largely the focus in secondary schools.

11.3.2 The curriculum in the secondary years (ages 11-end of compulsory schooling at 16 years)

The generally better facilities and resources available in secondary school (for example access to larger facilities and a wider range of equipment and opportunities) enables learners to progress from a focus on learning Movement Patterns and simplified/modified Movement Activities which were the focus in the primary school to applying these Movement Patterns to learning the full recognised version of a range of Movement Activities in different Movement Forms.

Some schools focus on a learning journey where learners progress their learning around 'big questions', specific to the subject they are being taught (for example 'How do you improve your performance?' 'How does physical activity affect you?)', which learners return to as they progress through their education. This creates a spiral curriculum (see Bruner, 1966 and Kelly, 2009 for more information) where Movement Patterns and Movement Activities are revisited across the learning journey to develop a deeper understanding of core concepts and ideas. This allows the learner to build on prior learning, but also to see how their learning supports what is coming in the learning journey. This learning journey incorporates both the product and process of learning and provides opportunities for the learner to take increasing levels of responsibility for their own learning.

As learners move through their secondary education, opportunities for them to choose Movement Activities to pursue in more depth become apparent through, for example, flexibility in curriculum choice, opportunities to study physical education to formal qualification and/or engagement in extra-curricular activities. These Movement Activities may be those a learner might wish to continue to engage with once they leave school.

11.4 Some key considerations in relation to curriculum planning

We now identify some key considerations in relation to the curriculum, irrespective of whether the curriculum is operating within a national curriculum, is a set curriculum or there is flexibility in how the curriculum is constructed. These considerations are in relation to the content and how it is taught to facilitate and enhance progress towards meeting the aims of the curriculum. Briefly, within this Unit we stress that, in order for learners to progress and achieve the aims of the curriculum, the curriculum needs, for example to:

- Be appropriate to enable the aims of the curriculum to be achieved
- Be progressive throughout compulsory schooling, leading learners towards the aims of the curriculum
- Exhibit logical continuity (to provide a coherent learning experience)
- Be broad (with a wide range of learning opportunities in relation to Movement Patterns and Movement Activities to cater for all), but balanced, but also
- Provide depth (sufficient time on each Movement Activity in different Movement Form to facilitate meaningful learning)
- Be taught using a range of appropriate teaching, learning and assessment strategies that reflect the individual needs of learners and enable them to take increasing responsibility for their own learning
- Be learner-centred, with the teacher facilitating learning opportunities and engaging learners in self-reflection with aim of developing positive attitudes
- Link appropriately to extra-curricular opportunities (note, consideration should also be given to opportunities outside school. This is covered in Unit 12).

Some of these points are now considered briefly. Unit 9 focuses on two of these points: how content is taught using a range of appropriate teaching, learning and assessment strategies that reflect the individual needs of learners and enable them to take increasing responsibility for their own learning;) and be learner-centred, with the teacher facilitating learning opportunities and engaging learners in self-reflection with aim of developing positive attitudes. Hence, reference should be made to Unit 9 for further consideration of these points.

11.4.1 *Be appropriate to enable the aims of the curriculum to be achieved*

Any curriculum is likely to have more than one aim. The aims should reflect the three domains of learning - the Physical, Cognitive and Affective and also both the product and process of learning. We acknowledge that by identifying aims we are in some respects arguing for the product model, but we are also encouraging teachers to think about how to develop learners ability to learn and therefore this is more process driven.

Whatever the aims of the curriculum are, they must be clear. If a school is working within a national curriculum, the aims of the school curriculum must enable the aims of the national curriculum to be met. Without a clear understanding of the aims of the curriculum, learning will not be planned effectively for these to be achieved. Therefore, in some respects, teachers must 'buy into' the aims of the curriculum.

However, although it may be clear to both learners and teachers what learners are trying to achieve in a lesson; for example, for learners to be able to do a forehand in tennis, the overall aims of the subject may get lost in the immediacy of the lesson. Therefore it is important that a teacher keeps the aims of physical education towards which learners are working at the forefront of their mind and thinks carefully how to best facilitate and enhance progress toward achieving these aims, paying specific attention to how the curriculum is taught. This will impact how the subject is taught and maintain the integrity of the physical education that is offered in the school.

11.4.2 *Be progressive throughout compulsory schooling, leading learners towards the aims of the curriculum*

To reiterate, progression has been defined as "the sequence built into children's learning through curriculum policies and schemes of work so that later learning builds on knowledge, skills, understandings and attitudes learned previously" (Department of Education and Science and the Welsh Office (DES/WO), 1990, p.1; see also Unit 2). Further, Ofsted (2022, p. 5) described progression simply when they said "the PE curriculum [in any one school] will benefit from a clear and coherent sense of what it means to 'get better' at the subject" (bracket added). Ofsted (2022) also made clear the importance of a focus on progression when they said that by carefully selecting and sequencing curriculum content learners are able to develop competence. This will enable more learners to believe that physical education is for them and hence inequalities can be reduced.

To be progressive, providing steps along the way to achieving the long term aims, content should be planned in a logical order, in a sequence of clear, coherent, continuous and progressive steps over time and across contexts. Learning at any one time should build logically on, and be assimilated into, previous learning. It also needs to anticipate and feed forward into more challenging learning that will follow, i.e. what will be taught next. The importance of this is stressed in this being one of the principles for facilitating and enhancing progress (see Units 2, 3 and 9). As regards curriculum planning, it is important to remember that the learning process breaks down if there is too much difference between current and next learning, if learning is repeated or if there are illogical link. To achieve this, units of work need to be planned so that there is a sequence to the learning within a unit (as well as between units) so that one component of learning both develops from the previous component and prepares learners for the next component. This would avoid a fragmented and disconnected approach to learning and replace what Newton (2023, p. 22) called the 'one-thing-after-another syndrome,' i.e. one component of a unit of work is chosen for one lesson, planned and taught, then a new component is chosen for the next lesson.

At a minimum this requires teachers to know what each learner has learned before and what they are going to learn afterwards. However, it may also involve teachers within and across schools working collaboratively in their planning (for example primary schools working with the secondary schools to which their learners transfer).

In summary, not all content can be taught at once; learning should take place over an extended period in steady stages. The curriculum should be designed (and learning activities planned) such that explicit connections are made to enable learners to progress steadily towards learning more comprehensive and increasingly complex Movement Patterns and a range of Movement Activities in different Movement Forms, as well as underpinning declarative knowledge and the development of positive attitudes, as well as taking increasing responsibility for their own learning. Although the same Movement Activity may be included in the curriculum at different levels/ages/in different years, the objectives and learning outcomes, the focus of learning, the context of the practices, the complexity of the learning activities and expectations of learners should be different. By adopting a **spiral curriculum**, teachers can add more complexity, and build up layers to the learning over time. To reiterate, the focus should be on the desired learning, not what the learner will do (i.e. the learning activity).

11.4.3 *Exhibit logical continuity (to provide a coherent learning experience)*

Continuity has been defined as "the nature of the curriculum experienced by children as they transfer from one setting to another" (DES/WO, 1990, p.13). Continuity involves learning being in a consistent line, without any logical contradictions (see principles of facilitating and enhancing progress, Unit 2).

The transfer from one setting to another could involve a change of teacher within a school or change of school. Whilst it is feasible to suggest that as learners move through a school, continuity in the curriculum will be evidence, this is not always the case (e.g. where a different teacher teaches a class). However, where there is a change of school there is less likely to be continuity. For there to be continuity in the curriculum, teachers in the same and different schools need to liaise with each other so that, for example, there is coherence of learning, e.g. between years or key stages within a school, between pre-school learning and learning in the early years of compulsory schooling, between infant and junior schools, between primary and secondary schools. The challenge here is therefore to look at ways in which approaches to learning are not significantly altered so that the possibility of learning, progress and the development of confidence and motivation in respect of physical educa-tion is not diminished. Further, consideration needs to be made regarding content which learners have already learned. Working with others is the focus of Unit 12.

11.4.4 *Breadth and depth*

Here we are looking at the two points: Be broad (with a wide range of learning opportunities in relation to Movement Patterns and Movement Activities to cater for all), but balanced; and Provide depth (sufficient time on each Movement Activity in each Movement Form to facilitate meaningful learning).

Before looking at the implications of breadth and depth in relation to the curriculum, what do we mean by the terms? In addition to breadth and depth we also describe balance - important in considerations about breadth and depth.

Breadth refers to the range of learning within a subject. In physical education this refers to the curriculum including learning a wide range of Movement Patterns which can be applied to an appropriate mix of Movement Activities in different Movement Forms.

Balance refers to the amount of time learners are engaged in learning different Movement Patterns and Movement Activities in different Movement Forms to facilitate and enhance progress to the extent that learners are able to identify those Movement Activities they prefer to participate in outside of physical education.

Depth refers to the extent to which Movement Patterns and Movement Activities are explored and revisited to embed learning. The more time spent on appropriate practice on a Movement Pattern or in a Movement Activity, the greater progress a learner should be able to make.

A curriculum which has breadth, is balanced and has depth should enable learners to progress in a range of Movement Activities in different Movement Forms for a number of reasons, including, for example:

1. Movement Patterns are developed within different contexts and so involvement in a wide range of contexts will foster progress in physical competence in its broadest sense
2. Movement Activities across the Movement Forms have very different characteristics.

Physical, cognitive and affective benefits of a curriculum that includes breadth, balance and depth include:

*   *Supporting/Developing*
    *   Awareness of options outside school
    *   A positive attitude to changing Movement Activities as a individual gets older
    *   Awareness of options to cater for the wide range of motivations/needs that will change throughout life
    *   A bank of meaningful experiences to equip an individual for life
    *   Confidence to try other activities throughout life

*   *Catering for a wide range of interests/needs/strengths*
    Motivation to take part in Movement Activity (Whitehead, 2010 p. 186) inter alia:

    *   The pure enjoyment of successful participation
    *   The excitement of competitive situations
    *   An appetite to experience and master challenges
    *   The enjoyment and satisfaction of moving in an aesthetic context

- The exhilaration of beating personal goals in respect of, for example, strength or speed
- The determination to match up to and beat others
- Social needs to be with others
- A personal need to relax away from the stress of a job
- A strong desire to become fitter or lose weight
- A love of the countryside.

- *Providing for meaningful learning experiences, i.e. that are:*
  - Purposeful, engaging, relevant and rewarding
  - involve learning and result in enhanced confidence and a positive attitude to participation in the future.

Prior to, and in the early years of, primary schooling learners should acquire and become more secure in a range of general Movement Patterns (see Unit 5 and above). In the primary school, breadth and balance refers to learning a wide range of Movement Patterns which learners can apply to simplified and/or simplified/modified forms of recognised Movement Activities (see Unit 5). This learning gives learners the grounding to learn and progress in developing a range of specific Movement Patterns for a range of Movement Activities in different Movement Forms, which becomes more a focus in the secondary school.

In the secondary school, there are a great many Movement Activities that could be included in a physical education curriculum and a great deal of knowledge that could support learning the Movement Activities. This presents a problem in that there is not time in the curriculum to allocate adequate time to every Movement Activity to enable learners to have meaningful learning experiences and to make progress. As a result, teachers have to make choices.

It is disappointing to us that one solution to this dilemma adopted in some secondary schools, has been to create very short teaching units/blocks or 'taster' courses to introduce learners to as many Movement Activities as possible. Guy (quoted in Kirk, 2010, p. 7) referred to curricula in which there are short blocks of learning across multiple activities as being 'a mile wide and an inch deep.' Siedentop (2002, p. 372) referred to the teaching of the same introductory units 'again, and again, and again.' The danger of feeling the need to introduce learners to as many Movement Activities as possible, is based, at least in part, on an assumption that this enables learners to select those Movement Activities they want to continue outside and after they leave school. However, the unfortunate outcome of such a curriculum is that so little time is dedicated to any particular Movement Activity that a learner is unlikely to have enough time to engage in challenging practices that enable them to develop their competence and confidence and then have the opportunity to establish, revisit, refine and develop their learning. As a result, any real depth of learning which allows really rewarding and meaningful experiences to facilitate and enhance progress in one Movement Activity before they move onto another Movement Activity is seldom available. In some senses, it may be the case that this 'taster' approach might well not be the most productive use of time.

In order to overcome the limitations of such an approach, we believe that while a range of Movement Activities should be selected, attention should be given not only to the number of Movement Activities per se but also that these exemplify the different Movement Forms. Each of these Movement Activities should be allocated enough time for learners to progress. Learning one one Movement Activity can then be transferred to other Movement Activities in the same Movement Form.

Thus, teachers need to make hard and rational decisions about the content of the curriculum, including how many and what Movement Patterns and Movement Activities should be taught to facilitate and enhance progress towards meeting the aims of the curriculum. This presents a real challenge. In the context of the aim of physical education being highlighted throughout this book, what should learners learn – and when, to make it more likely that they will adopt a physically active lifestyle?

One way of addressing this challenge of providing breadth, balance and depth is to group Movement Activities by considering their fundamental characteristics. A number of different ways of grouping Movement Activities have been identified in order that learners can be engaged in Movement Activities that provide them with a range of learning contexts. Some examples of different ways of organising Movement Activities are considered in Unit 5; the Physical Domain. However, we have chosen to group Movement Activities into five Movement Forms, comprising Adventure, Aesthetic and Expressive, Athletic, Competitive and Fitness and Health. These are shown in Table 11.1.

Table 11.1 Movement Forms

Movement Form	The particular nature of the Movement Form and examples of Movement Activities in the Movement Form
Adventure	focus on meeting risk and managing challenge, often in the outdoors in natural and often unpredictable environments. Activities can be carried out alone or as a group co-operative activity. *Activity examples include climbing, kayaking, orienteering*
Aesthetic and Expressive	focus on movement as an expressive medium within a creative, aesthetic or artistic context. *Activity examples include dance, artistic gymnastics, synchronised swimming*
Athletic	focus on reaching a personal best in respect of speed, distance, power or accuracy, within the context of competition in a controlled environment. *Activity examples include events in gymnastics, athletics (e.g. long jump, throwing a javelin)*
Competitive	focus on achieving pre-determined goals through outwitting opponents either individually or in teams, while (in some activities) managing a variety of implements and objects and coping with changing and challenging conditions and/or terrain. *Activity examples include tennis, hockey, basketball, volleyball*
Fitness and Health	concern to gradually improve functioning within the Physical Domain both qualitatively and quantitively through regular repetitive participation. *Activity examples include aerobics, circuits, Zumba*

Source: Adapted from Murdoch and Whitehead, 2010 and Murdoch and Whitehead, 2013; see also Murdoch and Whitehead, 2010, pp. 180–182, 2019; and Murdoch and Whitehead, 2013, pp. 60–61.

Note: the same Movement Activity can fit into a number of different Movement Forms, for example, swimming can be aesthetic and expressive (synchronised swimming), athletic and/or competitive (for speed) or for fitness and health.

By engaging in Movement Activities from all Movement Forms, learners will have the opportunity to progress inter alia:

- In a range of specific Movement Patterns, thereby enhancing movement competence
- In a range of environments
- By working alongside others in different ways to nurture interpersonal understanding and empathy
- Using initiative and imagination in interacting with unpredictable environments thereby encouraging self-confidence and independence
- In using movement as an expressive medium
- In coming to appreciate embodied health.

It is important to remember that breadth must not counteract depth. Where the curriculum becomes diluted (for example if Movement Activities and Movement Forms change on a half termly basis), the opportunities for learners to develop depth of knowledge and understand their abilities to execute effectively what they are learning may become compromised. Further, if Movement Activities are repeated on a yearly basis, but learning is repeated without moving learning forward, learners' motivation to continuing to participate may also be compromised.

In order that learners experience breadth and balance, but also depth, careful consideration needs to be given to how the time allocated to physical education is used throughout the period of time in which a learner is in school. Depth of learning gives learners a rewarding and worthwhile experience and enables them to develop competence and confidence to meet the aims of the curriculum. It is suggested that, for a thorough grounding to enable learners to adopt a physically active lifestyle, it is highly desirable for learners to have depth of experience in Movement Activities in all the Movement Forms.

In relation to curriculum planning, it is suggested that:

- A focus on fewer Movement Activities, each given more time and hence enabling learners to achieve greater depth, can support more learners to develop competency, and
- As each Movement Form offers unique learning challenges, that an equal amount of time should be given to each form.

Giving time to a Movement Form is time given to Movement Activities that come under the description of that Form. It is quite clear that this will result in very difficult decisions. However, it is argued that such are the common features of Movement Activities within a Movement Form that transfer of learning is possible. It is also argued that it is often the common feature of Movement Activities in a particular Movement Form that the learners find engaging and that learning in, for example, a particular dance genre or competitive game will serve to give learners a real feel for the nature of the Movement Activities within a Movement Form.

In order to develop depth of learning, Murdoch and Whitehead (2013) suggest three Movement Forms are covered in each year in secondary schools. They also suggest term-long blocks or units of work. This would allow time for consistent and sustained learning, with time to practice to develop and establish a Movement Activity including the associated

Movement Patterns, declarative knowledge and the development of positive attitudes, with learners taking responsibility for own learning. The Movement Activity is not just learned but has been reflected on, polished and demonstrates quality. The learner is secure in the context and has made, and been recognised for demonstrating, progress. Learning of this nature endures, is readily picked up again and can be applied readily in a variety of contexts.

There are different ways of providing this time, but Murdoch and Whitehead (2013) suggest that

- Initially, learners should learn to participate effectively in one Movement Activity in each Movement Form viz **Adventure** e.g. Swimming; **Aesthetic and expressive** e.g. Creative Dance; **Athletic** e.g. Gymnastics; **Competitive** e.g. Hockey; **Fitness and Health** e.g. Circuits. Equal time should be given to each Movement Activity (and Movement Form), then
- Add one other Movement Activity in each Movement Form viz **Adventure** e.g. Orienteering; **Aesthetic and expressive** e.g. Synchronised Swimming; **Athletic** e.g. Jumping events; **Competitive** e.g. Rugby; **Fitness and Health** e.g. Aerobics. Again, equal time should be given to each Movement Activity (and Movement Form) and finally
- In three Movement Activities of choice – no more than one activity in any Movement Form.

Murdoch and Whitehead (2013) provide an example. This is adapted in Table 11.2.
The value of this coverage is threefold. Every learner has the opportunity to:

1. Take part in Movement Activities from each of the Movement Forms
2. Reach a competent standard in a Movement Activity from each Movement Form
3. Think about Movement Activities or Movement Forms they might like to continue outside lessons and beyond compulsory schooling (see Unit 12).

It is understood that adopting such an approach to the curriculum may cause some problems as it is different from the present organisation adopted by many physical education departments in many schools. Such an approach might involve radical change to the curriculum to focus on learning in fewer activities within any one Movement Form, but a broader range of Movement Forms.

Table 11.2 An example of coverage of all Movement Forms in years 7–11

Movement Form/Year	Adventure	Aesthetic and Expressive	Athletic	Competitive	Fitness and Health
Year 7		✓	✓	✓	
Year 8	✓			✓	✓
Year 9		✓	✓		✓
Year 10	✓		✓	✓	
Year 11	✓	✓			✓

Source: Adapted from Murdoch and Whitehead, 2013, p. 63.

However, in our view, such consideration is important. As Ofsted (2022) ask:

- How well is the time that is provided in the curriculum to teach physical education being divided and used?
- Is enough time being provided to practise and develop competence?

The introduction of choices and options at different stages of schooling and the use of extra-curricular time to add to learning are also possible strategies to provide more time for learners to make real progress.

11.4.5 Link appropriately to extra-curricular opportunities

(Note, consideration should also be given to opportunities outside school. This is covered in Unit 10.)

Currently in some schools, extra-curricular provision largely comprises inter-school competition in various team games and other competitive activities such as athletics. In some schools there is also intra-school competition which allows learners who may not be picked for school representative teams or represent the school in other competitive activities to participate in competitive sport. Such an approach does not reflect the broad and balanced curriculum we are advocating above. Indeed, if a school curriculum is determined by what is offered in extra-curricular time, the curriculum is likely to be narrowed, particularly to Movement Activities which form part of inter- or intra-school competitions (see, for example, Ofsted, 2022; Petrie, Penney and Fellows, 2014). We would strongly advocate against this. Further in this approach, opportunities are provided for some learners, many of whom are likely to also have opportunities to participate in physical activity outside school in the wider community setting (Evans and Bairner, 2013; Evans and Davies, 2010). There may be a number of reasons for this, including the implicit or explicit views of physical educators or the priorities of the headteacher and/or governors (see Unit 12). Thus, in at least some schools, the success of a school's physical education programme may be measured by the achievement of school teams in inter-school sports competitions, rather than by the progress of all learners in curriculum physical education. However, in order for all learners to progress, physical education in these schools must move beyond the subject enhancing school kudos or the demonstration of high level physical skill of a few learners as the benchmark for success. In light of this, as stressed by Ofsted (2022, p. 21), "the curriculum aims cannot be met by games alone, nor can they be met by competitive activities alone."

Extra-curricular provision cannot dictate or replace the careful selection and sequencing of content that is required to enable all learners to progress (Ofsted, 2022). On the other hand, it can and should complement and enrich the physical education curriculum. It can be argued that as extra-curricular provision occurs in school, it should be educational and provide opportunity for as many learners as possible to progress and to adopt a physically active lifestyle – not just the few who participate in school teams (see for example Sport England (2023) and Department for Education (DfE, 2023c)).

In line with the focus on progression to facilitate and enhance progress, the extra-curricular programme should be joined up to the curricular programme. The physical education curriculum should therefore be supplemented by opportunities for all learners to be active during the school day (e.g. before school, at break, lunch time and after school), and through extra-curricular activities to enable all learners to maximise opportunities for progress. To support this, opportunities locally should be explored for learners to engage in a range of Movement Activities, of which they should be aware (see Unit 12).

Extra-curricular activities also provide opportunities for learners to support the learning of others. For example through older learners organising or supervising Movement Activity experiences at different times in the school day. This would support their progress in the Cognitive and Affective Domains, through them planning learning activities for others.

11.5 Summary and key points

This Unit has focused on the curriculum as an enabling condition to facilitate and enhance progress. It has stressed the need to cover the three domains of learning: the Physical, Cognitive and Affective and focus on the process as well as the product of learning. It has also stressed the need for a curriculum to be flexible to take account of the needs of individual learners, highlighting how the curriculum is designed and delivered will impact on the progress of each learner across the three domains of learning. The Unit started by looking at some definitions of curriculum and approaches to curriculum planning, before briefly looking at the physical education curriculum in primary and secondary schools. It then identified some key considerations we deem relevant in relation to the curriculum as an enabling condition to facilitate and enhance progress to enable the aims of physical education to be realised. These considerations were:

- Be appropriate to enable the aims of the curriculum to be achieved
- Be progressive throughout compulsory schooling, leading learners towards the aims of the curriculum
- Exhibit logical continuity (to provide a coherent learning experience)
- Be broad (with a wide range of learning opportunities in relation to Movement Patterns and Movement Activities to cater for all), but balanced, but also
- Provide depth (sufficient time on each Movement Activity in different Movement Form to facilitate meaningful learning)
- Be delivered using a range of appropriate teaching, learning and assessment strategies that reflect the individual needs of learners and enable them to take increasing responsibility for their own learning
- Be learner-centred, with the teacher facilitating learning opportunities and engaging learners in self-reflection with aim of developing positive attitudes
- Link appropriately to extra-curricular opportunities.

Some of these points were considered briefly, while others are covered in other Units.

As if the points we have considered in this Unit are not enough to think about, it is also important to reflect that learners learn more in schools than just what is taught in the formal curriculum. The hidden curriculum is also important. Kelly (2009, p. 5) defines the hidden curriculum as "those things which pupils learn at school because of the way in which the work of the school is planned and organized, and through the materials provided, but which are not in themselves overtly included in the planning or even in the consciousness of those responsible for the school arrangements". These are the unplanned parts of the curriculum including for example, how the curriculum is delivered, what message learners receive through experiencing the curriculum, what is learned from other learners – both within and beyond physical education lessons, e.g. the wider school environment, the behaviours and values of all the adults working in the school. For example, there may be inconsistencies or contradictions between what is explicitly taught in lessons and what is learned through the values, behaviours and attitudes of staff, by the quality of the learning environment and rules and routines. As a consequence progression and progress may be compromised (see Unit 9).

We acknowledge that the key points made in this Unit will need careful consideration not only by individual teachers but also by a department as a whole. Further as far as is possible, there needs to be collaboration between teachers in secondary schools and their feeder primary schools and between teachers and providers of physical activity and sport in the local community (see Unit 12). Some questions which may help to start this consideration include, for example:

- How often is the curriculum discussed and reviewed or is it historically what has always been done? Is the curriculum up-to-date, does it address the needs of the learners? Does it offer a broad enough approach, which is balanced and with enough depth to enable all learners to progress?
- In order to achieve the aim for learners to adopt a physically active lifestyle outside lessons and beyond school, what should the curricular and extra-curricular programme comprise of to enable all learners to progress?
- What is needed for a joined-up approach between curriculum physical education and extra-curricular activities to enable all learners to maximise opportunities for progress?
- How can participation in the extra-curricular programme by all learners be facilitated within the constraints of time, facilities, staffing? For example, do extra-curricular activities need to be led by an adult? Could they be led by older learners organising or supervising Movement Activity experiences at different times in the school day? Could learners organise their own Movement Activities as they learn to take increasing responsibility for their own learning?

We want to finish with a reminder that a pre-planned curriculum does not replace the need to recognise progress by individual learners nor to adjust teaching to the needs of individual learners. Individual learners and their needs must always supersede a pre-planned curriculum. Likewise, a unit of work and lesson should take into account the needs of the learners and not be taught as written.

Unit 12 The Broader Context

12.1 Introduction

In this book so far two different perspectives have been highlighted. Initially, the focus was on the progress of holistic, individual learners. The involvement of a teacher in facilitating and enhancing the progress of individual learners was implied but was not central. Nor was there any direct application to the school context and/or to physical education lessons. The focus of concern then shifted squarely to enabling conditions to facilitate and enhance learner progress in physical education lessons through focusing on, respectively, teaching, recognising and charting progress and the curriculum.

Attention now turns to a brief consideration of another enabling condition: other people with whom an individual teacher works in order to facilitate and enhance progress. The first part of the Unit focuses on the importance of all those who support the delivery of physical education in a school (both members of staff in the school as well as people who are external to the school) working together as a team (Note, we use the word team to take into account the range of people involved in delivering physical education in a primary or secondary school; both those internal to a school and those external to the school. In secondary schools the team would frequently be recognised as a department, although others internal and external to the school may contribute to the teaching of physical education. In a primary school the team might include, for example, a physical education lead teacher, all class teachers as well as external providers who may deliver some of the physical education curriculum).

The second part of the Unit focuses on others in the school - particularly the headteacher and governors, with whom the subject lead for physical education might work. Finally, the third part of the Unit focuses on the range of people external to the school with whom physical education teachers work to facilitate and enhance progress both within and outside the physical education curriculum. Throughout, the importance of these relationships and their management to facilitate and enhance the progress of all learners is reviewed.

12.2 Working together as a team

Whilst it may seem obvious that all those who support the delivery of physical education in one school should communicate and work together as a team, because physical education teachers (and others supporting the delivery of physical education) are busy people, too frequently, communication and collaboration within a team (across a school (in the context of

DOI: 10.4324/9781003172826-13

a primary setting) or a department (within the context of a secondary school)) may not be effective in facilitating and enhancing the progress of all learners in the subject.

If staff do not communicate and work effectively together, individual teachers, as well as others who are supporting the delivery of physical education, may end up working largely in isolation, without knowing and being clear about what others working in the same context are doing and hence what learners are experiencing within the subject. This may result in a disjointed approach to teaching and learning for learners and consequently reduce the amount of progress they can make.

Communicating and working together can be both formal, for example through regular scheduled meetings, or informal, that is interactions that take place in a less structured way, for example via a casual, quick conversation, the use of messaging systems or communications outside of the school environment. Whilst such approaches are not necessarily inappropriate, they can result in some key messages not being communicated to all members of the team, team members becoming marginalised and, in extreme situations, a breakdown in the team structure. Therefore, whilst the Unit focuses specifically on formal communications, having an understanding of and considering informal approaches, is also important.

Formal communication and working together is usually coordinated through team meetings or continuing professional development (CPD) time scheduled by the school. However, to facilitate and enhance progress, this requires meetings/CPD to be held regularly and to focus on progress, rather than, for example, day-to-day practicalities and/or organisation (e.g. what arrangements are in place for use of facilities (in a primary school this might be when classes have access to the school hall or playground; in a secondary school this might be what arrangement are in place when examinations are taking place); what transport has been organised (in a primary school this might be to take learners for swimming lessons or for both primary and secondary school be to transport school teams to an extra-curricular activity), or a key school priority. Rather, meetings/CPD should allow review, reflection and robust discussion in order to make deliberate, rational decisions on issues that facilitate and enhance the progress of individual learners. For example:

- The shared beliefs of the team – in relation to, for example aims, learning outcomes, content, pedagogy, assessment
- The structure and delivery of the curriculum – for example progression, coherence and continuity in the curriculum
- The progress being made by individual learners across the domains of learning
- Approaches to teaching and learning to establish what is working well, what might need to be improved upon and what further steps can be taken by the team to better facilitate and enhance the progress of all learners in the school – for example, the creation and review of a subject action plan.

Whilst different models of CPD (see for example, Guskey, 2002; Kennedy, 2005) exist, we acknowledge that some schools now disaggregate their CPD days (for example in some schools CPD is held as frequently as every week) which provides opportunities for different sessions to each have a specific focus. However, it is important that this CPD is subject specific rather than focusing on a school priority.

In addition, discussion in and subsequent action from team meetings/CPD may occur on a 'one off' basis. However, issues cannot be addressed once and not again. They need to be considered on a continuous basis for a number of reasons, including for example:

- the team of staff – teachers and other adults who contribute to physical education change over time as people leave or join the team and new team members need to be integrated into all aspects of physical education within the school (in addition, new members of the team may have new ideas they can contribute)
- As staff become busy during the school year, they may not continue to work on the agreed aspects, reverting to previous ways of working. On the other hand, current teachers and other adults working in curriculum time may have some difficulty in changing their practice to that agreed within the team and/or may 'drift' from what has been agreed, so need ongoing reinforcement and support.

In relation to the second bullet point, a challenge faced by teams is how change is managed, monitored and sustained. Whilst ideas might be discussed in team meetings/CPD and key priorities identified, consideration needs to be given to how this might be implemented and then how any change might be monitored. In this regard, it is important to recognise that change is a challenge and to remain engaged and change their attitudes towards teaching and learning, staff need to see the impact on learner progress (see Guskey, 2002). For example if a team are looking at specific learning outcomes they will need to consider how to write these, what the success criteria are, how they will be shared, and some form of monitoring will need to be put into place so that a record is kept of how teachers are implementing them in their own teaching and what impact this might be having on the progress of learners. Here, it is the impact that any change is having on the progress of the learners that must be front and centre. As Guskey (2002) highlights, it is "the experience of successful implementation that changes teachers' attitudes and beliefs. They believe it works because they have seen it work, and that experience shapes their attitudes and beliefs" (p. 383).

Ongoing discussion and planning within a team about how to develop progressive, continuous and coherent learning experiences to facilitate and enhance the progress of all learners (including taking on board the principles for facilitating and enhancing progress so that individual learners are more likely to progress in Units 2, 3 and 9) include, for example:

- how policy documents, including curriculum documents (in which there is likely to be considerable leeway for interpretation), and any guidelines are translated into specific learning activities appropriate for the context (Wallace and Priestley, 2017)
- How continuity of learning and the progress of each individual learner is assured when a new teacher takes over a class
- How one teacher hands over to another teacher and what information is needed by the new teacher to facilitate and enhance the progress of learners
- How monitoring of implementation is undertaken.

We know that schools are busy places and the pressures placed on staff to facilitate, enhance and maximise progress are ever present. We also know that many physical education teachers have additional leadership roles which may on occasion restrict the time they have to concentrate on facilitating and enhancing learner progress. Further we know that in many primary schools in England physical education is delivered by external organisations (see for example Lawrence 2017; Office for Standards in Education, Children's Services and Skills (Ofsted), 2023a). Thus, it is important that working together as a team is not put to one side in the busy day-to-day life of schools and teachers. If those responsible for the delivery of physical education do not work together, this is likely to do a disservice to the progress of individual learners, as well as have implications for teachers.

For example, from a *learner's* perspective, progress may be stunted because some of the principles for facilitating and enhancing progress are not applied consistently, for example:

1. Teachers may not focus on each learner being holistic, not considering the Physical, Cognitive and Affective Domains
2. Teachers may not know learners very well and hence find it difficult to treat each learner as an individual in order to facilitate and enhance the progress of each individual
3. Learning may not be purposive, towards achieving an aim
4. Learning may not be an ongoing process that takes time, practice, application and effort
5. New learning may not build from where the learner is in respect of current learning and hence may not move the learner on
6. Learning may not be coherent, with a logical order, going step by step
7. Learning may not be presented in such a way that it motivates the learner to apply themself
8. Learning may not accommodate opportunities for feedback to the learner
9. Learning may not provide opportunities for the learner to take responsibility for their learning (see principles for facilitating and enhancing progress in Units 2, 3 and 9).

There are also implications for the teacher. From the *teacher's* perspective, it is, for example, less likely that they share information which will enable them to:

- agree on the aims towards which learners are working (rather the aims prioritised are based on each teacher's beliefs about the subject itself – its aims and content, learners, learning and teaching; see Unit 9)
- know learners very well and hence find it difficult to progress the learning of each individual
- provide progressive and continuous learning experiences towards achieving the aims of the curriculum
- provide coherent experiences, in a logical order, going step by step
- build new learning from current learning.

And more likely that they:

- do not identify differences in their beliefs and, as a result, interpret all aspects of physical education (e.g. aims, the curriculum, content, teaching approaches and assessment) in different ways and hence have a different focus in, and priorities for, their lessons, thereby providing different experiences for learners. This may result in learners being confused about and/or making differential progress towards the aims towards which they are working

- teach different classes without detailed information about the progress of the class as a whole and of individual learners within the class
- repeat learning which learners have already covered – or miss out key components of learning and hence are less likely to progress the learning of individual learners.

In order to address such issues, it is important that teachers in a school/department work together as a team, through the adoption of a 'joined-up' approach (Capel and Blair, 2020).

12.2.1 *Working together: A joined up approach*

Capel and Blair (2020) referred to a joined up or aligned approach to physical education; that is, the individual parts connect and work together. For example, there needs to be alignment between policy/guidelines and practice to enable learners to progress towards specific aims in a progressive, continuous and coherent way throughout compulsory schooling. This requires teachers (and others with a stake in physical education) to work together.

 Consideration is given next to aspects of a joined-up approach in relation to the progress of individual learners.

12.2.1.1 *A joined-up approach to the progress of individual learners*

Ofsted (2022) identified the need to actively engage teachers in finding out what has been taught before or what will be taught after the age group/class they are teaching. This also applies to a teacher taking over a class during or at the end of an academic year. This knowledge can then be used to inform the selection of content and its sequencing, as well as ambitious end points for all learners. Thus it would seem to be the responsibility of those teaching physical education within a school and, where appropriate, across schools (e.g. at the primary/secondary transition) to sit down together and work as a team to ensure they discuss, inter alia:

- The culture of the team which in turn influences what is taught and how it is taught
- Ensuring the progress of each learner is at the heart of the work of the team (not, for example, producing winning school teams)
- Ensuring all teachers are prioritising facilitating and enhancing the progress of each learner
- Whether all teachers are providing a consistent message to learners, parents/carers and others about the subject
- Whether the focus of all work is on learners working towards the agreed aims for physical education in the school, curriculum and schemes of work, e.g. by year 6 or 11 what do we want to see and hear all learners do in physical education, and agree on how to achieve this?
- Whether progressive, continuous and coherent learning experiences are provided:
  - in the whole physical education curriculum
  - between and within units of work
  - between and within lessons?

- Whether the curriculum is up-to-date, addresses the needs of the learners in the school, is broad enough but allows for depth of learning, and whether it is interpreted in the same way by all teachers
- The various approaches teachers adopt, for example, what works and what does not work, how consistent the approaches taken by teachers are and whether the expectations of how lessons are conducted are similar. This is not to say that each individual teacher should not have their own identity and teaching approaches, but that the teaching approach taken fits into an overall plan and focus within each year and across years so there is progression in, progression through and progression out of the curriculum as well as progress of individual learners in all three domains and in taking increasing responsibility for their own learning
- Parity of expectations of the progress of learners
- An efficient system of filing unit of work/lesson plans, evaluations and of recognising and charting progress over time. This needs to be kept up to date and accessible (both in terms of how information is charted and how it is used).

12.2.2 *Working together effectively to facilitate and enhance the progress of each learner*

In order to provide progressive, continuous and coherent learning experiences which best facilitate and enhance the progress of every individual learner in physical education, the team needs, among other things:

- A well-articulated policy on the overall aims of physical education in the school, the curriculum content and how it is progressed in units of work and lessons and expectations of how lessons are taught (but also recognising that a pre-planned curriculum, units of work and lessons does not replace the need to recognise progress by individual learners and adjust teaching to the needs of individual learners. Individual learners and their needs must always supersede a pre-planned curriculum, unit of work or lesson (see Unit 11)). This policy needs to be developed and agreed, collaboratively, by all those delivering physical education rather than top down by the subject lead
- Agreement on the aims of physical education and how aims and curriculum documents are interpreted and developed into meaningful and engaging units of work and lessons which allow for progression over the short, medium and long term (in primary schools this needs to take account of where the delivery of physical education may be by an external organisation)
- A whole team approach to teaching and learning in physical education, including
    - A good mechanism to chart the progress and needs of individual learners
    - Some consistency in the classes which teachers teach so that they are able to get to know the learners as individuals and provide progressive learning experiences over time. It is valuable for one teacher to teach a whole 12.2.3 and, where possible, fewer rather than more different teachers to have contact with a class (this

is particularly relevant/important in secondary schools where the teacher may change depending upon on the content of a unit of work)

- Adults other than teachers working in curriculum time need to be clear about their role in supporting learning and the progress of individual learners (for example, in order to maximise their effectiveness, learning support assistants need information relevant to individual learners, e.g., the previous achievement of learners with whom they are working as well as their expected achievement in the lesson).

This cannot be achieved by teachers and others working in physical education curriculum time working in isolation; rather, this requires all those working in a team to be clear about their roles and 'pull in the same direction' as part of a team.

To achieve this requires, for example:

- Ongoing communication in both spoken and written forms
- Formal meetings to discuss policy, guidelines and plan practice
- Regular discussion by teachers of learner progress (of a class as a whole, groups and individual learners) and how they can improve this
- Informal discussions to keep progression, continuity, coherence and consistency of approach at the forefront of teachers (and other adults) minds
- Observation by teachers and other adults of each other, focused on consistency of approach, the outcomes of which can provide evidence to form part of feedback to individual staff and also inform ongoing discussions
- An efficient mechanism to chart the progress of individual learners
- Communication with the headteacher (and other members of the senior leadership team), governors, parents/carers etc. about how the team can be supported in facilitating and enhancing progress (see below).

So far in this Unit the focus has been on curriculum physical education. It now turns to extra-curricular activities provided by many physical education teams.

12.2.3 *The team and extra-curricular activities*

Many physical education teachers in the UK and beyond are also tasked with the provision of extra-curricular physical activities for learners in their school. At present, as stressed in Unit 11, much extra-curricular provision in secondary schools focuses on school teams which participate in inter-school (between schools) matches and competitions in various team games and other competitive activities such as athletics. This may be supplemented in some schools by an intra-school (within school) programme which provides opportunities for learners who may not be picked for school teams to participate in competitive sport. In primary schools, whilst there is also a focus on extra-curricular competitions (which in England are largely organised by School Games Organisers (see https://www.yourschoolgames.com/; Department for Education (DfE), 2023c, 2023d), there is also a focus on learning opportunities outside the classroom for learners to be physically active, for example, before school or during break and lunchtimes. There are a number of reasons for this, including for example, beliefs of physical education teachers themselves, access to additional funding (in England Primary Schools receive a minimum of £16,000 funding to support the delivery and enhancement of physical education; see DfE, 2023a, 2023b) and pressure from the headteacher and governors (see below).

As the purpose of schools and teachers is the progress of all learners, it needs to be asked whether the current extra-curricular provision in many schools which is catering for a relatively small number of able learners (many of whom have opportunities to partici-pate in physical activity outside school in the wider community setting (see, for example, Evans and Bairner, 2013; Evans and Davies, 2013)) in a limited range of usually competitive sports, is appropriate. This approach to extra-curricular provision contradicts all that has been argued in this book and it would seem to us to be a missed opportunity to provide opportunities to facilitate and enhance the progress of all learners in a range of phys-ical activities beyond the curriculum. Indeed, the majority of learners may be excluded from participating – at least some of whom will not have other opportunities to partici-pate in physical activity outside school. In addition, learners (and their parents/carers) may receive mixed messages about both the importance of the progress of all learners in physical education and the importance of the aim prioritised in this book – adopting a phys-ically active lifestyle.

In order for extra-curricular activities to contribute to the progress of each learner con-sideration should be given to extra-curricular provision:

- being educational – as extra-curricular activities are part of school provision
- being an extension of curriculum physical education for all learners, with a shared pur-pose (to facilitate and enhance the progress of all learners) and shared aims (including for learners to adopt a physically active lifestyle)
- providing equal opportunities for all learners to participate and
- including a wider range of Movement Activities in different Movement Forms to appeal to as many learners as possible (the range of opportunities will change at different ages as learners have different priorities and different Movement Forms are included in the curriculum in any one year) (see Unit 11).

Thus, in our view, extra-curricular activities should be seen as opportunities for all learners to participate in physical activity outside timetabled physical education lessons. These oppor-tunities may be provided before school (some schools provide physical activity sessions prior to school to support learners to self-regulate in preparation for them to more effect-ively learn during the school day), during breaks in learning (for example during break or lunchtime) or after school.

To achieve this, it is important that the team (and others who may contribute to extra-curricular provision) take a systematic approach, communicate and work together on all aspects of this provision. Thus, the team needs to discuss, be clear about, and agree on, for example,

- the purpose of extra-curricular provision
- how the aims of the extra-curricular programme link to the aims of curriculum physical education
- the focus of extra-curricular provision and how it builds on curricular provision

- what Movement Activities should be included in extra-curricular provision so that it is broad enough to be appealing to a range of learners and support them in adopting a physically active lifestyle
- how consistency in the experience is provided for learners across Movement Activities, i.e. how all extra-curricular activities reflect the ethos of the team and are delivered in line with these expectations, such that all learners should arrive at extra-curricular activities and know what will be expected of them.

Indeed, Ofsted (2022) (citing the work of De Meester, et al, 2014; Williams, Wiltshire and Gibson, 2021) said that "a systematic approach to planning and delivering extra-curricular opportunities should enable pupils to participate beyond their physical education lessons, giving them more time to practice, extend and refine their knowledge."

Having considered some points in relation to how teachers (and other adults) in a team can work together in both curriculum physical education and extra-curricular activities, the focus now turns to working beyond the team. The next section focuses on working with others within the school.

12.3 Working with others in the school

Although working with other members of staff in a team to facilitate and enhance the progress of individual learners is very important, curriculum physical education and school extra-curricular activities do not operate in isolation. They are both influenced by a range of factors beyond individual physical education teachers and the team. These include both the wider school environment and a range of agencies and organisations external to the school which have an interest in physical activity/exercise/sport/the physical wellbeing of children and young people (for example, government agencies (e.g. DfE, Ofsted), sports bodies (e.g. Sport England, Youth Sport Trust), local community clubs). Thus, the team and individual teachers have a multi-faceted role in relation to working with other people, both within and outside the school, in order to maximise the opportunities for each and every learner to progress and for them to adopt a physically active lifestyle.

Physical education is influenced by the broader school environment in a number of ways. These include the priorities of the head teacher and governors and the culture of the school.

12.3.1 Influence of headteacher and governors

The priorities of the headteacher and governors influence the culture of, and priorities for, the school. In turn, these impact on physical education – and hence the progress of learners in the subject, in a number of ways. A couple of examples of priorities of the headteacher and governors are given below, along with their impact on learner progress in physical education.

For example, if the headteacher and governors prioritise the league table performance of the school and hence Standardised Assessment Tests (SATs)/examination results, this may result in a culture in which learners are seen as dualistic, with more academic subjects prioritised over the more practical subjects such as physical education (this is against our view of learners being holistic). In primary schools, this might result in physical educa-tion lessons becoming repurposed to focus on core subjects such as English and mathem-atics in preparation for SATs. In secondary schools, this might result in the amount of time allocated to physical education in the timetable being significantly reduced in key stage 4 (ages 14-16 year olds) in order to provide additional interventions or help learners in other subjects. It might also skew the priorities in physical education towards focusing on examinations in the subject - mainly at ages 16 and 18 years (Ofsted, 2023a). Further, some learners, in some instances, may be withdrawn from physical education lessons to focus on a Core Subject (for example English, mathematics or science, e.g. to practise reading in key stage 1 or complete work from other subjects in key stage 4) either routinely or for individual lessons. The inevitable result of this prioritisation is that learners make less pro-gress in physical education.

On the other hand, in some schools, physical education may be a priority for, and championed by, the headteacher and governors. For example, in schools in which health and well-being is a priority, the progress of individual learners in physical education is likely to be prioritised. Likewise, if the headteacher and governors champion physical education (and the complementary role of the wider extra-curricular offer) to facilitate and enhance the progress of all learners as a whole and help all learners to be their best, such a cul-ture can rewrite learners' futures in terms of them adopting a physically active lifestyle now and in the future (Ofsted, 2022). However, if physical education is a priority for, and championed by, the headteacher and governors because it is seen as a proxy for school teams and winning trophies - the progress of individual learners (except those in school teams) is unlikely to be a priority. Further, this may impact on what is taught in physical edu-cation and how. For example, this is likely to lead to a narrowing of the curriculum to focus on activities in which the school competes in various competitions.

A third view taken by the headteacher and governors may be that physical education is recreational, optional and not involving significant or 'serious' learning. A likely outcome of this is that the promise - and potential of the subject to make a lasting and very valuable contribution to learner progress in schools and provide the underpinning for adopting a physically active lifestyle throughout life, will never be realised.

Where progress of individual learners is not prioritised in physical education, it is unlikely that progress will be maximised. One reason for this is that it is likely that the subject will be treated differently to other subjects. As with all school subjects, progress in physical education is essentially incremental in its nature, complexity and challenge. This requires learning to be regular and to build up over time. If physical education is not prioritised there may be, for example, irregular occurrence of lessons for a number of reasons. For example, changes in staffing (e.g. because the regular teacher is accompanying a school team rather than teaching a class), changes in the facility to be used (e.g. because a facility is being used for another purpose, e.g. lunch, examinations, school play), which may necessitate a change of focus in the learning and hence a lack of continuity and progression. If the assured pre-dictability of lessons is not honoured - as they are timetabled, at a particular time, with a particular member of staff and in a particular facility, this significantly diminishes the possi-bility of progress and the development of confidence and motivation in respect of physical education.

Whatever the priorities of the headteacher and governors and the resulting culture of the school, it is important that physical education teachers, as individuals and as a team, commit to the progress of each individual learner. Further, they need to be able to argue the case for the importance of physical education in facilitating and enhancing progress. They also need to work with the headteacher, governors and others to educate (where needed) and to gain support for a focus on the progress of each individual learner. Working with the headteacher and governors is considered next.

12.3.2 The importance of physical educators working with the headteacher and governors

In order for the progress of all learners to be prioritised in physical education, it is important that the headteacher (other members of the senior leadership team) and governors, are educated that physical education is not about examination results or winning school teams; neither is physical education an optional, recreational pursuit. Rather, it has a valuable role to play in facilitating and enhancing the progress of all learners and helping all learners to be their best. This may, at least in part, be the responsibility of the subject lead, but it is imperative that all teachers are clear about, and agree with, the purpose of physical education in the school and can make the arguments whenever the opportunity arises (see working together as a team, above).

As well as educating the headteacher and governors about what physical education is not, physical education teachers must also educate them as to what physical education is – emphasising the progress of each and every learner and the role of the subject in encouraging learners to adopt a physically active lifestyle now and in the future. This education should involve working with the headteacher (senior leadership and other teachers in the school) and governors so that they:

- view learners as holistic with the physical being as important as the cognitive
- view physical education in the same light as other subjects – recognising and respecting the focus of the team on enhancing the progress of all learners rather than prioritising, for example, examinations or winning school teams
- recognise what progress in physical education can provide for all learners
- provide enough time in the curriculum for a range of learning activities to occur
- respect physical education lessons as of value and therefore ensure they are not all too readily disrupted to cater for whole school issues such as use of physical education spaces for other events (e.g. lunch, examinations, school plays)
- assure the regularity of work in physical education so that the predictability of lessons is honoured – as per the timetable, at a particular time, with a particular member of staff and in a particular facility.

Physical educators must also work with the headteacher, the senior leadership team and governors to turn the support into practical reality, in order to provide the best environment to support their efforts to facilitate and enhance the progress of all learners in physical education. For example, they may work with the headteacher to identify and implement strong transition policies that support learners as they move from primary to secondary school, or in looking for opportunities for collaboration, for example through secondary schools providing support for the delivery of physical education in primary schools.

The third part of this Unit focuses on the external context in which physical education operates.

12.4 The external context

As physical education does not work in isolation within the school, it does not work in isolation from the external context. It is important that each physical education teacher individually and as part of the team is cognisant of the external context in which the subject is operating.

There are a range of agencies and organisations outside the school context which impact on physical education in a number of different ways and with whom physical education teachers need, or might wish, to work. These include, for example:

- Government and its various agencies (including, in England, the Department for Education and Ofsted) – which largely set the framework within which physical education operates. This includes, for example, the structure of schooling, external examinations and the national curriculum (both the whole curriculum and the National Curriculum for Physical Education)
- Physical activity and/or sports bodies – for example, the Association for Physical Education (AfPE), Governing Bodies of Sport, Sport England, Youth Sport Trust and External Providers which try to promote their particular activity/sport, by offering coaching/teaching both with curriculum and extra-curricular time, recognition of quality awards, CPD opportunities.
- Local community provision – for example local sport clubs, who might offer use of facilities, or provide opportunities and coaching for those learners who want to participate in a specific activity outside school.

It is important that physical education teachers work within the external context and with various agencies, organisations, bodies and local providers, rather than physical education being dictated by the external context and the priorities of these other providers. Likewise, it is important that in working within the external context and with various agencies, organisations, bodies and local providers, the focus is firmly on the progress of all learners in the subject. For example, in the context of primary schools in England, the availability of the Primary Physical Education and School Sport premium (DfE, 2023a, 2023b), whilst providing valuable resources to schools, has sometimes been seen as an opportunity to 'buy in' coaches to teach physical education. This has resulted in physical education in some schools being delivered solely by an external organisation(s). In other instances, schools buy 'schemes of learning,' which offer resources and planned lessons, but do not necessarily reflect the context in which the lessons are being taught. As highlighted by Ofsted (2023a), both of these raise questions around the continuity, coherence and progression of the curriculum offered to learners, and hence learner progress.

12.4.1 *Working with different agencies and organisations*

In working with a range of different agencies and organisations, physical education teachers need to, for example:

- Consider how best they can work within Government requirements to best facilitate and enhance the progress of learners in their particular context
- Work with physical activity and/or sports bodies and providers of physical activity and/ or sport in the local community to provide opportunities for all learners to progress within and outside curriculum time and outside school
- Consider whether, and how, it is appropriate to invite people from the various bodies to contribute to curricular and/or extra-curricular provision in the school
- Ensure involvement with external organisations provides opportunities for all learners, not just the able
- Ensure there is a focus on progress by any external providers.

However, working with physical activity and/or sports bodies and community organisations/ clubs is not as simple and straightforward as it might at first appear if the needs, and progress, of all learners are going to be taken into account. For example, to enable all learners to progress, partnerships may need to be developed with physical activity and/or sporting bodies and community organisations which work in different ways. For example,

- To offer a range of opportunities to both learners who are already participating outside school and for whom curriculum physical education (and extra-curricular provision in school) is only one part of a wider range of physical activity and/or sporting experiences in which they participate, as well as other learners for whom physical education is their only opportunity for learning in the Physical Domain
- Bring appropriate personnel (e.g. coaches, sports development officers, sports leaders, volunteers, parents/carers) into the school to highlight the opportunities available and to ease access into the relevant opportunity outside school for those learners for whom school-based provision is currently their only opportunity to learn, progress, participate and develop positive attitudes towards the subject and physical activity but who would like to participate outside school but do not know how to access opportunities
- Bring appropriate personnel into the school to provide a wider range of opportunities that are attractive to learners who do not currently want, or are unable, to participate in physical activity and/or sport outside school. Indeed, Blair (2018) suggested that bringing people into school to broaden the range of opportunities available to learners as extra-curricular activities on the school premises and within the school day, may help to bridge the current gap between some learners who are able to access a variety of opportunities and other learners for whom access to other opportunities is very limited. This could range from, for example, pilates, yoga or dance to aquatic based activities such as stand up paddle boarding, kayaking or swimming.

A number of questions are raised in working with external agencies and organisations to extend opportunities for all learners to participate in physical activity and/or sport beyond physical education lessons. For example:

- How can wider opportunities be developed and managed for the benefit of all learners within time constraints, without additional funding and with limited budgets?
- what should be the role of those supporting physical education in coordinating a broader range of learning experiences to facilitate and enhance progress for all learners?
- How can physical educators work with local providers of physical activity and/or sport outside school to support learners to learn about the importance of being physically active now and in the future?

See Blair, 2018; Blair and Capel 2013 for further discussion on this issue.

12.5 Summary and key points

This Unit has focused on teachers working together with others to facilitate and enhance the progress of individual learners. We recognise the scale of the issues and the complexities involved in working closely together as a team to facilitate and enhance the progress of individual learners. However, this is important. In addition, physical education and extra-curricular provision does not operate in isolation from the rest of the school. Particularly influential are the headteacher and governors who set the priorities of, and culture in, the school, therefore it is important to engage with the headteacher, governors and others in the school. In addition, school-based physical education and extra-curricular provision does not work in isolation from the external context. Thus, working with others outside school is also important.

Working together is complex and takes some time. It may require difficult choices to be made in relation to teaching the subject to facilitate and enhance the progress of all learners. However, it is necessary if learners are going to have progressive, continuous and coherent learning experiences in school and opportunities to participate outside school that enable them to progress as individuals. The time spent as a team working on this is therefore important and well worthwhile.

GLOSSARY

Word	Definition
Accountability for own learning	Taking responsibility for what doing to enhance learning and being able to give a satisfactory reason for it. Accountability may be evaluated or measured against specific criteria
Active learning	Engagement of the learner in construction of their own knowledge
Adaptive teaching	Actions taken by the teacher to modify planned activities to ensure that learners can make progress. Also known as differentiation
Agency	Control felt by the learner in relation to their own learning
Aims	What the learner is expected to learn in the longer term, i.e. the overall intent or goal of a curriculum or scheme of work. The achievement of learning outcomes and objectives build towards achievement of aims. See also learning outcomes, objectives
Aspect of a domain	A key feature of learning in each of the domains of learning (Physical, Cognitive and Affective) (it is the highest level of analysis, followed by Foci and Ladders of Progress). See also Domain: Affective, Domain: Cognitive, Domain: Physical, domain of learning, Foci, Ladder of Progress
Assessment	The collection and use of information to provide evidence about learners learning and progress; see also assessment for learning, assessment of learning, criterion-referenced assessment, formative assessment, ipsative assessment, norm-referenced assessment, summative assessment
Assessment for learning	Assessment in which the first priority is to facilitate and enhance progress. It allows teachers and learners to understand where learners are in their learning currently and where they need to go next. It encourages learners to take responsibility for their own learning. Also frequently referred to as formative assessment. See also assessment, assessment *of* learning, criterion-referenced assessment, formative assessment, ipsative assessment, norm-referenced assessment, summative assessment
Assessment of learning	The periodic, summative assessment of learners' attainment in a variety of ways and for a variety of purposes, e.g. to record a grade, to report to parents/carers. Also frequently referred to as summative assessment. See also assessment, assessment *for* learning, criterion-referenced assessment, formative assessment, ipsative assessment, norm-referenced assessment, summative assessment
Assessment: criterion referenced	See criterion-referenced assessment
Assessment: ipsative	See ipsative assessment

Word	Definition
Assessment: norm referenced	See norm-referenced assessment
Balance	An even distribution of movement experiences in the curriculum, i.e. Movement Activities from different Movement Forms. Movement Activities from different Movement Forms are given equal amounts of time
Belief	Something that is accepted, considered to be true, or held as an opinion. See also values
Breadth	Learning a range of Movement Activities from different Movement Forms. This enables learners to understand differences between them
Capability	"The expression of a human dimension by an individual. A capability is a desirable human expression of being, the development of which should be available to every individual" (Whitehead, 2021b, p. 202)
Choreographic principles	Those compositional elements or factors to be considered to attain an aesthetically satisfying dance or gymnastics sequence
Coherent	Learning which occurs or progresses in the short, medium and longer term in a logical order or sequence of clear, continuous steps, following an expected path or sequence, each of which builds from the previous one
Collaboration	Working with others to facilitate and enhance progress
Complexity	The level of challenge embedded within an activity; many different parts are related or inter-connected making learning more intricate and complicated
Consistency	The extent to which a learner is able to repeat a movement or behave in a similar way
Continuity	A feature of a curriculum and within and between units of work and lessons that ensures that learning builds on what has already been learned and prepares learners for what is to come. See also progression
Conventions of a Movement Activity	The rules, principles and protocols for participating in a specific Movement Activity. See also principles of a Movement Activity, protocols of a Movement Activity, rules of a Movement Activity
Criterion referenced assessment	A process in which learning is measured by relating a learner's responses to pre-determined criteria. See also assessment, assessment for learning, assessment of learning, formative assessment, ipsative assessment, norm-referenced assessment and summative assessment.
Curriculum: physical education	A planning tool which identifies the broad intentions of learning (including declarative and procedural knowledge and positive attitudes) to enable all learners to progress towards achieving the aims of the subject. It should be provisional, adapted according to the needs of learners
Curriculum: school	The full range of learning experiences in a learners time in a school or education as a whole, planned so that knowledge is developed in sequence. It is usually organised into subjects
Declarative knowledge	See knowledge: declarative
Deliberate decision	A conscious, intentional, careful decision
Depth	Sufficient time on each Movement Activity in different Movement Forms to facilitate meaningful learning
Differentiation	Matching work to the differing capabilities and learning needs of individuals or groups of learners in order to enhance their learning. Also known as adaptive teaching. See also adaptive teaching

Word	Definition
Domain: Affective	The manner in which people deal with things emotionally, such as appreciation, attitudes, enthusiasms, feelings, motivations and values (Krathwohl, Bloom and Masia, 1964) See also domain of learning holistic
Domain: Cognitive	Declarative knowledge and understanding, which (in relation to physical education) underpins learning procedural knowledge in the Physical Domain. See also Domain: Physical, domain of learning
Domain: Physical	Capabilities of an individual in relation to movement. See also domain of learning
Domain of learning	A particular interest, activity or type of knowledge which is a distinctive, but functionally integrated aspect of human potential (in this book Physical, Cognitive and Affective Domains). See also Aspect of a domain, Domain: Affective, Domain: Cognitive, Domain: Physical holistic
Endowment	A quality or ability possessed or inherited by someone. Something that a person has from birth
Evidence	Information which is used to provide confirmation of what learning has taken place
Extra-curricular activities	Although extra-curricular activities go beyond physical activity and sport (e.g. extra-curricular activities in, for example, drama or music) in this book they refer to physical activity or sport-related activities and clubs in which learners can participate in addition to timetabled physical education lessons. These might include, but are not limited to, before-school clubs, lunchtime clubs and after-school clubs, representing the school in inter-school competitions and sport-related leadership opportunities
Foci	Different components of learning in an Aspect in a domain (it is a more detailed level of analysis than Aspect and leads into the identification of Ladders of Progress). See also Aspect, domain of learning, Ladder of Progress
Formative assessment	Assessment in which the first priority is to facilitate and enhance progress. It allows teachers and learners to understand where learners are in their learning currently and where they need to go next. It encourages learners to take responsibility for their own learning. Also frequently referred to as assessment for learning. See also assessment, assessment for learning, assessment of learning, criterion-referenced assessment, ipsative assessment, norm-referenced assessment, summative assessment.
General Movement Pattern	Direct developments from a young learner's early movements. They include, for example, balancing, climbing, gesturing, inverting, jumping, receiving, rotating, running, sending, striking, travelling. The acquisition of general Movement Patterns is the prerequisite to developing refined Movement Patterns (see Murdoch and Whitehead, 2010, p. 179). See also Movement Pattern, refined Movement Pattern, specific Movement Pattern
Goal	See aim, learning outcomes, objectives
Holistic	Recognition of the individual as a whole rather than individual components
Individual journey	Acknowledgement that each learner is unique and therefore their learning will differ to those around them

Word	Definition
Ipsative assessment	A process in which performance is measured against previous performance by the same person in order to track their progress. See also assessment, assessment for learning, assessment of learning, criterion-referenced assessment, formative assessment, norm-referenced assessment, and summative assessment.
Key Stage	The periods in each learner's education to which the elements of the National Curriculum for England apply. There are four Key Stages, normally related to the age of the majority of learners in a teaching group. They are: Key Stage 1, beginning of compulsory education to age 7 (Years R (Reception), 1 and 2); Key Stage 2, ages 7–11 (Years 3–6); Key Stage 3, ages 11–14 (years 7–9); Key Stage 4, age 14 to end of compulsory education (Years 10 and 11). Post-16 is a further Key Stage.
Knowledge	Facts, information, understanding learners are expected to gain through the subject; see also knowledge: declarative, knowledge: procedural
Knowledge: declarative	Facts and information about a topic (knowing what)
Knowledge: pedagogical	Knowledge by the teacher of approaches to support effective teaching and learning
Knowledge: procedural	Knowledge about how to do something/knowledge exercised in the performance of a task (knowing how)
Knowledge: subject content	Knowledge by the teacher of the subject content being taught
Ladder of Progress	An instrument designed to identify what progress might look like in the key components of learning (in Aspects and Foci). Progress is identified as baseline, growing, establishing, consolidating in each Ladder. See also Aspects; Foci
Learner-centred teaching	All teaching, and all decisions made by a teacher, has learner progress at its heart. Careful attention is paid to the knowledge, attitudes and beliefs that learners bring to their learning. Learners are encouraged to take an active role in learning and to take responsibility for their own learning, for example, choosing the purpose of the learning and identifying the learning outcomes and success criteria, selecting the content and appropriate learning activities and how they might engage with these, determining the timing and method of learning, assessing and evaluating the learning and providing own feedback
Learning	A change, development, general improvement or progress in a human capacity not due to growth, that lasts over a period of time
Learning activities	Activities in which learners engage designed to facilitate and enhance progress
Learning outcome	The learning which it is intended will take place; specifically, the short term goals of an individual lesson. See also success criteria
Learning: process	The means by which a learner makes sense of learning to acquire new knowledge
Learning: product	An increase in knowledge which is the outcome (or product) of learning
Lesson	A defined period in which teaching takes place
Lesson plan	A plan which guides the learning in the lesson, normally including the learning outcomes (with associated success criteria) which learners are to work towards, the learning and assessment activities and teaching approaches that will be used, the resources and materials required

Word	Definition
Movement Activity	Purposeful, more or less structured, named events which are carried out in larger or smaller groups, in pairs or by individuals, have specific rules, principles and protocols and operate within a defined area. Movement Activities are many and varied and in this text are grouped into different Movement Forms. See also Movement Forms
Movement Capacity	The constituent abilities of an articulate, robust and secure Movement Pattern. These include, for example, accurate placement of parts of the body, agility, balance, control, coordination, flexibility. See also Movement Pattern
Movement Form	Recognised and named groups of the many and varied Movement Activities which share some common features or characteristics. In this book, five Movement Forms are identified, that is the Adventure Form, the Aesthetic and Expressive Form, the Athletic form, the Competitive Form and the Fitness and Health Form. See also Movement Activity
Movement Pattern	Co-ordinated actions comprised of a number of components and body parts, designed to achieve a particular outcome. Movement Patterns progress from general Movement Patterns to refined Movement Patterns to specific Movement Patterns. See also general Movement Pattern, refined Movement Pattern, specific Movement Pattern
Movement Phrase	A number of Movement Patterns linked together to form a distinctive pattern. A longer phrase is often called a movement sequence. See also Movement Pattern
Movement Vocabulary	A language to describe movement
Multi Academy Trust (MAT)	An academy chain or trust that operates more than one academy school in England, primary and/or secondary
Norm-referenced assessment	A process in which performance is measured by comparing learners responses. Individual success is relative to the performance of all other learners. See also assessment, assessment for learning, assessment of learning, criterion-referenced assessment, formative assessment, ipsative assessment, summative assessment
Objective	The medium term goals of a unit of work. The achievement of learning outcomes build towards the achievement of objectives and the achievement of objectives build towards achievement of aims. See also aims, learning outcomes
Physical activity	Physical activity is a broad term that covers any bodily movement produced by skeletal muscles that requires energy expenditure for various purposes, including movement as part of work, during leisure time or for transport (see, for example, World Health Organisation (WHO, 2022)). Physical activity can range from lifestyle activities to sports. Examples include recreational cycling, walking, dancing, team games, swimming and yoga.
Physical education	The term used to describe any structured/organised/purposeful physical activity within the curriculum in compulsory schooling (Whitehead, 2010, p. 204)
Principles of a Movement Activity	Encompass, for example, choreographic principles (those compositional elements or factors to be considered to attain an aesthetically satisfying dance or gymnastics sequence) as well as principles of fair play and etiquette. See also conventions of a Movement Activity, procedures of a Movement Activity, rules of a Movement Activity

Word	Definition
Procedural knowledge	See knowledge: procedural
Procedures of a Movement Activity	An established or official way of doing something in a Movement Activity. See also conventions of a Movement Activity, principles of a Movement Activity, rules of a Movement Activity
Progress	The process of moving (improving or developing) from one state or stage to another over a period of time. See also progression
Progress: charting	An approach to noting progress which is designed to facilitate and enhance future progress
Progress: Ladder of	See Ladder of Progress
Progress: recognising	Activities undertaken to identify the learning which has taken place, including observation, assessment and the feedback given to learners
Progression	The conditions which allow the process of moving (improving or developing) from one state or stage to another over a period of time to occur (i.e. for progress to occur). See also progress
Rational decision	Having a reason or understanding for making a decision
Refined Movement Pattern	Developments from general Movement Patterns such that a range of distinct Movement Patterns are identified, for example, the general Movement Pattern of sending is refined into bowling, shooting, throwing or striking is refined into batting, dribbling and driving. In turn refined Movement Patterns lead into specific Movement Patterns. See also Movement Pattern, general Movement Pattern, specific Movement Pattern
Reflection	A systematic process of thinking about or reflecting on learning in order to facilitate and enhance progress
Responsive	A person who reacts quickly and positively
Rules of a Movement Activity	A set of specific, explicit and understood requirements governing conduct for participating in a particular Movement Activity (e.g. rules in a game or for a change over in a relay in athletics or swimming). In turn these impact on how learners enact a Movement Activity (e.g. the strategies and tactics that can be adopted in a game within the rules). See also conventions of a Movement Activity, principles of a Movement Activity, procedures of a Movement Activity
Scheme of work	A planned course of study over a period of time (e.g. a Key Stage or a Year)
Sequence of learning	A smooth, continuous, incrementally progressive learning journey in which each small step is designed for learners to succeed before moving onto the next step
Special educational needs and disabilities (SEND)	A learner of compulsory school age or a young person has a learning difficulty or disability if he or she: • has significantly greater difficulty in learning than the majority of others of the same age, or • has a disability which prevents or hinders him or her from making use of facilities of a kind generally provided for others of the same age in mainstream schools or mainstream post-16 institutions (DfE, January 2015). Learners with SEND are not a homogenous group. Physical education might present different barriers to participation and learning from other subjects for some learners with SEND. Any references to learners groups, such as high or low attainers, will include learners with SEND unless specifically stated.

Word	Definition
Specific Movement Pattern	Further developments of refined Movement Patterns in the context of the demands and rules of specific Movement Activities. For example batting in cricket. In turn this is broken down into various types of batting stroke (e.g. cut shots, defensive shots, drives, glance shots, pulls and hooks and sweep shots), each of which can be further broken down (e.g. cover drive, off drive, on drive, square drive, straight drive, etc.). See also Movement Pattern, general Movement Pattern, refined Movement Pattern
Sport	A range of activities performed within a set of rules and undertaken as part of leisure or competition whether carried out by teams or individuals. See also physical activity
Success criteria	The means to measure learners progress towards the learning outcomes of a lesson. See also learning outcome
Summative assessment	Assessment linked to the end of a course of study. It sums up achievement in aggregate terms and is used to rank, grade or compare learners, groups or schools. It uses a narrow range of methods which are efficient and reliable. See also assessment, assessment for learning, assessment of learning, formative assessment, ipsative assessment, norm-referenced assessment
Unit of work	Medium-term planning of work for learners over a number of weeks. The number of lessons in a unit of work may vary according to each school's organisation. It usually introduces a new component of learning. Units of work derive from the curriculum and schemes of work and are the basis for lesson plans. See also curriculum, lesson plan, scheme of work
Values	What the teacher or learner believes is important and how meaningful an activity is viewed. Values impact on behaviour of the teacher or learner. See also beliefs

REFERENCES

AfPE (Association for Physical Education) (2018a) 'A simple guide to National Curriculum progression in physical education,' *Physical Education Matters*, Summer 8, p. 49, available at: www.afpe.org.uk/page/PublicationsandResources (accessed 27 March 2024).

AfPE (Association for Physical Education) (2018b) *End of Key Stage One and Two Expectations in Physical Education*, available at: https://cdn.ymaws.com/www.afpe.org.uk/resource/resmgr/images/posters/head-hands-heart-web.pdf (accessed 22 April 2024).

AIESEP (Association Internationale des Écoles Supérieures d'Éducation Physique/International Association for Physical Education in Higher Education) (2020) *Position Statement on Physical Education Assessment*, available at: https://aiesep.org/wp-content/uploads/2020/06/AIESEP-Position-Statement-on-PE-Assessment-FINAL1.pdf (accessed 24 April 2024).

Ambrose, S.A., Bridges, M.W., DiPietro, M., Lovett, M.C., and Norman, M.K. (2010) *How Learning Works: Seven Research-based Principles for Smart Teaching*, San Francisco, CA: Jossey-Bass.

Ames, C. (1992a) 'Achievement goals and the classroom motivational climate,' in D.H. Schunk and J.L. Meece (eds.) *Student Perception in the Classroom*, Hillsdale, NJ: Erlbaum, pp. 327–348.

Ames, C. (1992b) 'Classrooms: Goals, structures and student motivation,' *Journal of Educational Psychology*, 84 (3), 261–271.

Anderson, J.R. (1976) *Language, Memory and Thought*, Mahwah, NJ: Lawrence Erlbaum.

Anderson, J.R. (1993) *Rules of the Mind*, Mahwah, NJ: Lawrence Erlbaum.

Anderson, J.R. (1995) *Cognitive Psychology and Its Implications* (4th edition), New York: W.H. Freeman and Company.

Anderson, J.R. (2007) *How Can the Human Mind Occur in the Physical Universe?* Oxford: Oxford University Press.

Anderson, L.W. and Krathwohl, D.R. (eds.) (2001) *A Taxonomy for Learning, Teaching, and Assessing: A Revision of Bloom's Taxonomy of Educational Objectives*, Boston, MA: Allyn and Bacon (Pearson Education Group).

ARG (Assessment Reform Group) (2002) *Assessment for Learning: 10 Principles*, Cambridge: University of Cambridge Assessment Reform Group.

Atkinson, J.W. (1964) *An Introduction to Motivation*, Princeton, NJ: Van Nostrand.

Ausubel, D. (1968) *Educational Psychology: A Cognitive View*, New York: Holt, Rinehart and Winston.

Aynsley, S., Brown, C. and Sebba, J. (2012) *Opening Minds: An Evaluative Literature Review*, London: RSA, available at: www.thersa.org/globalassets/rsa-om-literature-review.pdf (accessed 12 January 2024).

Balasundaram, P. and Avulakunta, I.D. (2022) *Human Growth and Development*, Bethesda, MD: National Library of Medicine, available at: www.ncbi.nlm.nih.gov/books/NBK567767/ (accessed 1 March 2023).

Bandura, A. (1977) 'Self-efficacy: toward a unifying theory of behavioral change,' *Psychological Review*, 84:191–215.

Barić, R., Vlašić, J. and Saša, E. (2014) 'Goal orientation and intrinsic motivation for physical education: Does perceived competence matter?' *Kinesiology*, 46, 117–126.

Bernstein, E., Phillips, S. and Silverman, S. (2011) 'Attitudes and perceptions of middle school students toward competitive activities in physical education,' *Journal of Teaching in Physical Education*, 30, 69–83.

Bin Mizzy, N. (2022) 'Being a reflective teacher: Using narrative enquiry as professional development in physical education,' in S. Capel, J. Lawrence, M. Martens and H. Abdul Rahman (eds.) *CPD for Teaching and Learning in Physical Education: Global Lessons from Singapore*, Abingdon: Routledge, pp. 209–231.

Black, P. and Wiliam, D. (1998) *Inside the Black Box: Raising Standards through Classroom Assessment*, London: Kings College.

Black, P. and Wiliam, D. (2009) 'Developing the theory of formative assessment,' *Educational Assessment, Evaluation and Accountability*, 21 (1), 5–31, https://doi.org/10.1007/s11092-008-9068-5.

Black, P., Harrison, C., Lee, C., Marshall, B. and Wiliam, D. (2003) *Assessment for Learning: Putting it into Practice*, Buckingham: Open University Press.

Blair, R. (2018) 'The deliverers debate,' in C. Griggs and K. Petrie (eds.) *The Routledge Handbook of Primary Physical Education*, Abingdon: Routledge, pp. 61–74.

Blair, R. and Capel, S. (2013) 'Who should teach physical education in curriculum and extra-curricular time?,' in S. Capel and M. Whitehead (eds.) *Debates in Physical Education*, Abingdon: Routledge, pp. 171–187.

Bloom, B.S., Engelhart, M.D., Furst, E.J., Hill, W.H. and Krathwohl, D.R. (eds.) (1956) *Taxonomy of Educational Objectives, Handbook I: Cognitive Domain*, New York: David McKay.

Borghouts, L.B., Slingerland, M. and Haerens, L. (2017) 'Assessment quality and practices in secondary PE in the Netherlands,' *Physical Education and Sport Pedagogy*, 22, 473–489.

Bowler, M. and Salmon, P. (2020) 'Health-based physical education (part 1),' *Physical Education Matters*, 15, 60–63.

Brian, A. and Taunton, S. (2018) 'Effectiveness of motor skill intervention varies based on implementation strategy,' *Physical Education and Sport Pedagogy*, 23, 222–233.

Brookhart, S.M. and McMillan, J. (2020) *Classroom Assessment and Educational Measurement*, New York and Abingdon: Routledge.

Bruner, J.S. (1960) *The Process of Education*, New York: Vantage.

Bruner, J.S. (1966) *Towards a Theory of Instruction*, New York: W.W. Norton.

Bureau, J., Howard, J., Chong, J. and Guay, F. (2022) 'Pathways to student motivation: A meta-analysis of antecedents of autonomous and controlled motivations,' *Review of Educational Research*, 92 (1), 46–72.

Cambridge Advanced Learners Dictionary and Thesaurus (n.d.) *Progress*, available at: https://dictionary.cambridge.org/dictionary/english/progress (accessed 16 March 2023).

Cambridge Advanced Learners Dictionary and Thesaurus (n.d.) *Progression*, available at: https://dictionary.cambridge.org/dictionary/english/progression (accessed 16 March 2023).

Cambridge Dictionary (n.d.) *Knowledge*, available at: https://dictionary.cambridge.org/dictionary/english/knowledge (accessed 3 April 2024).

Cambridge Dictionary (n.d.) *Thinking*, available at: https://dictionary.cambridge.org/dictionary/english/thinking (accessed 3 April 2024).

Capel, S. and Blair, R. (2020) 'Physical education – a joined up approach,' in S. Capel and R. Blair (eds.) *Debates in Physical Education* (2nd edition), Abingdon: Routledge, pp. 55–68.

Capel, S., Cliffe, J. and Lawrence, J. (2021a) *A Practical Guide to Teaching Physical Education in the Secondary School* (3rd edition), Abingdon: Routledge.

Capel, S., Cliffe, J. and Lawrence, J. (2021b) *Learning to Teach Physical Education in the Secondary School: A Companion to School Experience* (5th edition), Abingdon: Routledge.

Carey, M.P. and Forsyth, A.D. (2009) *Teaching Tip Sheet: Self-Efficacy*, APA (American Psychological Association), available at: www.apa.org/pi/aids/resources/education/self-efficacy#:~:text=Self%2Defficacy%20refers%20to%20an,%2C%20behavior%2C%20and%20social%20environment (accessed 6 February 2024).

Chappuis, J. (2009) *Seven Strategies of Assessment for Learning*, Portland, OR: ETS Assessment Training Institute.

Chatzipanteli, A., Digelidis, N., Karatzoglidis, C. and Dean, R.A. (2016) 'A tactical-game approach and enhancement of metacognitive behaviour in elementary school students,' *Physical Education Sport and Pedagogy*, 21, 169–184.

Collins Dictionary (n.d.) *Thinking Definition and Meaning*, available at: www.collinsdictionary.com/dictionary/english/thinking (accessed 3 April 2024).

Coppens, E., De Meester, A., Deconinck, F.J.A., De Martelaer, K., Haerens, L., Bardid, F., Lenoir, M. and D'Hondt, E. (2021) 'Differences in weight status and autonomous motivation towards sports among children with various profiles of motor competence and organized sports participation,' *Children*, 8 (2), 156, https://doi.org/10.3390/children8020156, available at: www.mdpi.com/2227-9067/8/2/156 (accessed 24 April 2024).

De Meester, A., Aelterman, N., Cardon, G., De Bourdeaudhuij, I. and Haerens, L. (2014) 'Extra-curricular school-based sports motivating vehicle for sports participation in youth: A cross sectional study,' *International Journal of Behavioural Nutrition and Physical Activity*, 11, article no. 48, available at: https://ijbnpa.biomedcentral.com/articles/10.1186/1479-5868-11-48 (accessed 27 August 2024).

Deci, E.L. (1971) 'Effects of externally mediated rewards on intrinsic motivation', *Journal of Personality and Social Psychology*, 18 (1), 105–115.

Deci, E.L. and Ryan, R.M. (1985) *Intrinsic Motivation and Self-Determination in Human Behavior*, New York: Plenum.

Deci, E.L. and Ryan, R.M. (2000) 'The 'what' and 'why' of goals pursuits. Human needs and the self-determination of behaviour,' *Psychological Inquiry*, 11, 227–268.

Demos (2005) *About Learning: Report of the Learning Group*, London: Demos, available at: https://dera.ioe.ac.uk/id/eprint/23216/1/About_learning.pdf (accessed 12 January 2024).

DES (Department of Education and Science) (1989) *Physical Education from 5 to 16, Curriculum Matters 16: An HMI Series*, London: HMSO.

DES/WO (Department of Education and Science and the Welsh Office) (1990) *Physical Education National Curriculum Working Group: Interim Report*, London: HMSO.

DES/WO (Department of Education and Science and the Welsh Office) (1991) *Physical Education for Ages 5 to 16, Proposals of the Secretary of State for Education and Science and the Secretary of State for Wales*, London: HMSO.

DES/WO (Department of Education and Science and the Welsh Office) (1992) *Physical Education in the National Curriculum*, London: HMSO.

Descartes, R. (1970) *Philosophical Letters* (trans A. Kenny), Oxford: Clarendon Press.

Dewey, J. (1938) *Experience and Education*, New York: Macmillan Company.

DfE (Department for Education (2013) *National Curriculum in England Physical Education Programmes of Study*, available at: www.gov.uk/government/publications/national-curriculum-in-england-physical-education-programmes-of-study/national-curriculum-in-england-physical-education-programmes-of-study (accessed 1 April 2023).

DfE (Department for Education) (2014) *The National Curriculum in England Framework Document, December 2014*, available at: https://assets.publishing.service.gov.uk/government/uploads/system/uploads/attachment_data/file/381344/Master_final_national_curriculum_28_Nov.pdf (accessed 30 March 2023).

DfE (Department for Education) (2021) *Development Matters: Non-statutory Curriculum Guidance for the Early Years Foundation Stage*, London: Crown Copyright, available at: https://assets.publishing.service.gov.uk/media/64e6002a20ae890014f26cbc/DfE_Development_Matters_Report_Sep2023.pdf (accessed 26 August 2024).

DfE (Department for Education) (2022) *Working Definition of trauma-informed practice*, available at: www.gov.uk/government/publications/working-definition-of-trauma-informed-practice/working-definition-of-trauma-informed-practice (accessed 11 March 2024).

DfE (Department for Education) (2023a) *Guidance PE and Sport Premium for Primary Schools* (Published 19 September 2014, Last updated 6 October 2023), available at: www.gov.uk/guidance/pe-and-sport-premium-for-primary-schools (accessed 22 April 2024).

DfE (Department for Education) (2023b) *Pupil Premium: Overview, updated 14 April 2023*, available at: www.gov.uk/government/publications/pupil-premium/pupil-premium (accessed 16 August 2023).

DfE (Department for Education (2023c) *School Sport and Activity Action Plan, July 2023*, available at: https://assets.publishing.service.gov.uk/government/uploads/system/uploads/attachment_data/file/1172036/School_Sport_and_Activity_Action_Plan.pdf (accessed 4 March 2024).

DfE (Department for Education) (2023d) *School Sport and Activity Plan*, available at: https://assets.publishing.service.gov.uk/media/64b7c813ef5371000d7aee6c/School_Sport_and_Activity_Action_Plan.pdf (accessed 22 April 2024).

DfEE/QCA (Department for Education and Employment and Qualifications and Curriculum Authority) (1999) *The National Curriculum for England, Physical Education Key Stages 1–4,* London: HMSO.

DfE/DoH (Department for Education/Department of Health and Social Care) (2015) *Special Educational Needs and Disability Code of Practice: 0 to 25 years (Statutory guidance for organisations which work with and support children and young people who have special educational needs or disabilities),* available at: https://assets.publishing.service.gov.uk/media/5a7dc b85ed915d2ac884d995/SEND_Code_of_Practice_January_2015.pdf (accessed 28 July 2024).

Donnelly, F.C., Mueller, S.S. and Gallahue, D.L. (2016) *Developmental Physical Education for all Children: Theory into Practice* (5th edition), Champaign, IL: Human Kinetics.

Duda, J. (2004) 'Goal setting and achievement motivation in sport,' *Encyclopedia of Applied Psychology,* 2, 109–119

Duggan, M. (2022) 'Instilling positive attitudes to physical activity in childhood – challenges and opportunities for non-specialist PE teachers,' *Education 3-13,* 50 (1), 129–143, DOI: 10.1080/ 03004279.2020.1833958, available at: www-tandfonline-com.ezproxy.brunel.ac.uk/doi/pdf/ 10.1080/03004279.2020.1833958?needAccess=true (accessed 28 October 2022).

Dweck, C.S. (1986) 'Motivational processes affecting learning,' *American Psychologist,* 41 (10), 1040–1048.

Dweck, C.S. and Leggett, E.L. (1988) 'A social-cognitive approach to motivation and personality,' *Psychological Review,* 95 (2), 256–273.

Early Movers (n.d.) *What is Physical Development?* available at: www.earlymovers.org.uk/about-pd (accessed 28 April 2024).

Education Scotland (2017) *Physical Education, Physical Activity and Sport,* available at: https:// education.gov.scot/parentzone/learning-at-home/supporting-health-and-wellbeing/physical-education-physical-activity-and-sport/ (accessed 1 April 2023).

EEF (Education Endowment Foundation) (2018a) *Metacognition and Self-regulated Learning: Applying Metacognitive Strategies in the Classroom,* available at: https://educationendo wmentfoundation.org.uk/education-evidence/guidance-reports/metacognition (accessed 11 March 2024).

EEF (Education Endowment Foundation) (2018b) *Metacognition and Self-Regulated Learning: Guidance Report,* London: EEF.

EEF (Education Endowment Foundation) (2021) *Teacher Feedback to Improve Pupil Learning: Guidance Report,* available at: https://d2tic4wvo1iusb.cloudfront.net/production/eef-guida nce-reports/feedback/Teacher_Feedback_to_Improve_Pupil_Learning.pdf?v=1699427026 (accessed 7 March 2024).

Encyclopaedia.com (n.d.) *Attitude,* available at: www.encyclopedia.com/social-sciences-and-law/ political-science-and-government/military-affairs-nonnaval/attitude (accessed 5 April 2024).

Ennis, C.D. (2015) 'Knowledge, transfer, and innovation in physical literacy curricula,' *Journal of Sport and Health* Science, 4, 119–124.

ETI (The Education and Training Inspectorate) (2022) *A Thematic Evaluation of Physical Education in Primary Schools,* Bangor, NI: ETI.

Evans, J. and Bairner, A. (2013) 'Physical education and social class,' in G. Stidder and S. Hayes (eds.) *Equity and Inclusion in Physical Education and Sport,* Abingdon: Routledge, pp. 141–159.

Evans, J. and Davies, B. (2006) 'Social class and physical education,' in D. Kirk, D. Macdonald and M. O'Sullivan (eds.) *The Handbook of Physical Education,* London: SAGE, pp. 796–808.

Evans, J. and Davies, B. (2010) 'Family, class and embodiment: Why school physical education makes so little difference to post-school participation patterns in physical activity,' *International Journal of Qualitative Studies in Education,* 23 (7), 765–784.

Evidence Based Education (2020) *Great Teaching Toolkit: Evidence Review,* available at: https:// f.hubspotusercontent30.net/hubfs/2366135/Great%20Teaching%20Toolkit%20Evide nce%20Review.pdf (accessed 20 April 2024).

Evidence Based Education (2022) *A Model for Great Teaching,* available at: https://evidencebased. education/a-model-for-great-teaching/ (accessed 20 April 2024).

Feedback for Learning (n.d.) *Feedback for Learning: Closing the Assessment Loop,* available at: https://feedbackforlearning.org/ (accessed 20 April 2024).

Fitts, P.M. and Posner, M.I. (1967) *Human Performance,* Oxford: Brooks/Cole.

Ford, P., De Ste Croix, M., Lloyd, R., Meyers, R., Moosavi, M., Oliver, J., Till, K. and Williams, C. (2011) 'The long-term athlete development model: Physiological evidence and application,' *Journal of Sports Sciences*, 29 (4), 389–402, https://doi.org/10.1080/02640414.2010.536849.

Gage, N.L. (1997) *The Scientific Basis of the Art of Teaching*, New York: Teachers' College Press.

Gagné, R.M. (1971) *Domains of Learning, Presidents Address at the AERA Conference*, New York, 7 February 1971.

Gagné, R.M. (1985) *The Conditions of Learning* (4th edition), New York: Holt, Rinehart and Winston.

Garn, A.C., Cothran, D.J. and Jenkins, J.M. (2011) 'A qualitative analysis of individual interest in middle school physical education: Perspectives of early-adolescents,' *Physical Education and Sport Pedagogy*, 16, 223–236.

Graham, G. (2008) *Teaching Children in Physical Education: Becoming a Master Teacher*, Champaign, IL: Human Kinetics.

Green, K. (2008) *Understanding Physical Education*, London: Sage.

Guskey, T.R. (2002) 'Professional development and teacher change,' *Teachers and Teaching: Theory and Practice*, 8 (3/4), 381–391.

Hanna, R. and Maiese, M. (2009) *Embodied Minds in Action*, Oxford: Oxford University Press.

Harris, C. (2019) 'Active learning,' in S. Capel, M. Leask, S. Younie, E. Hidson and J. Lawrence (eds.) *Learning to Teach in the Secondary School: A Companion to School Experience* (9th edition), Abingdon: Routledge, pp. 309–326.

Hastie, P. and Mesquita, I. (2017) 'Sport-based physical education,' in C.D. Ennis (ed.) *Routledge Handbook of Physical Education Pedagogies*, Abingdon and New York: Routledge, pp. 68–84.

Hattie, J. (2012) *Visible Learning for Teachers – Maximizing Impact on Learning*, Abingdon: Routledge.

Hattie, J. and Timperley, H. (2007) 'The power of feedback,' *Review of Educational Research*, 77, (1, March), 81–112.

Hattie, J., Masters, D. and Birch, K. (2016) *Visible Learning into Action: International Case Studies of Impact*, Abingdon: Routledge.

Hay, P. and Penney, D. (2013) *Assessment in Physical Education: A Socio-cultural Perspective*, Abingdon: Routledge.

Haydn, T. (2016) 'Assessing pupil progress: What do we know about good practice, in S. Capel, M. Leask and S. Younie (eds.) *Learning to Teach in the Secondary School: A Companion to School Experience* (7th edition), Abingdon: Routledge, pp. 447–470.

Heritage, M. (2008) *Learning Progressions: Supporting Instruction and Formative Assessment*, Paper prepared for the Formative Assessment for Teachers and Students (FAST) State Collaborative on Assessment and Student Standards (SCASS) of the Council of Chief State School Officers (CCSSO), Washington DC: Council of Chief State School Officers.

ICCSPE (International Council of Sport Science and Physical Education) (2010) *International Position Statement on Physical Education and Sport November 2010*, available at: www.icsspe.org/sites/default/files/International%20Position%20Statement%20on%20Physical%20Education.pdf (accessed 1 April 2023).

Johnson, M. (1987) *The Body in the Mind*, Chicago, IL: The University of Chicago Press.

Kapfer, P.G. (1970) 'Behavioural objectives and the curriculum processor,' *Educational Technology*, 10 (May) 14–17.

Kelly, A.V. (2009) *The Curriculum: Theory and Process*, New York, London, New Delhi: SAGE.

Kennedy, A. (2005) 'Models of continuing professional development: a framework for analysis,' *Journal of In-service Education*, 31 (2), 235–250.

Kerr, J.F. (1968) 'The problem of curriculum reform,' in J.F. Kerr (ed.) *Changing the Curriculum*, (13–18), London: University of London Press.

Killingbeck, M. and Whitehead, M. (2020) 'Observation in physical education,' in S. Capel, J. Cliffe and J. Lawrence (eds.) *Learning to Teach Physical Education in the Secondary School: A Companion to School Experience* (5th edition), Abingdon: Routledge, pp. 241–261.

Kime, S., Christodoulou, D., Coe, R., Lee, S., Oates, T., Peacock, A. and Weston, D. (2017) *What Makes Great Assessment?* Durham: Evidence Based Education, available at: https://s3.amazonaws.com/thinkific/file_uploads/133755/attachments/6fc/2ea/f33/WMGA_ebook.pdf (accessed 7 March 2024).

Kirk, D. (2010) *Physical Education Futures*, Abingdon: Routledge.

Krathwohl, D.R. (2002) 'A revision of Bloom's taxonomy: An overview,' *Theory into Practice*, 41 (4), 212–218.

Krathwohl, D.R., Bloom, B.S. and Masia, B.B. (1964) *Taxonomy of Educational Objectives: The Classification of Educational Goals. Handbook II: Affective Domain*, New York: David McKay.

Laban, R. (1974) *The Language of Movement*, Boston, MA: Plays.

Lawrence, J. (2017) *Teaching Primary Physical Education* (2nd edition), London: SAGE.

Lawson, H.A. (ed.) (2018) *Redesigning Physical Education: An Equity Agenda in which Every Child Matters*, Abingdon and New York: Routledge.

Leahy, S., Lyon, C., Thompson, M. and Wiliam, D. (2005) 'Classroom assessment: Minute by minute, day by day,' *Educational Leadership*, 63 (3), 18–24.

Leask, M., Liversidge, T. and Lewis, H. (2022) 'Improving your teaching: An introduction to practitioner research, reflective practice and evidence-informed practice,' in S. Capel, M. Leask, S. Younie, E. Hidson and J. Lawrence (eds.) *Learning to Teach in the Secondary School: A Companion to School Experience* (9th edition), Abingdon: Routledge.

Legislation.gov.uk (2002) *Education Act 2002*, available at: www.legislation.gov.uk/ukpga/2002/32/part/6/crossheading/general-duties-in-respect-of-the-curriculum?view=plain (accessed 14 October 2022).

Lloyd, R.S., Oliver, J.L., Faigenbaum, A.D., Howard, R., De Ste Croix, M.B.A., Williams, C.A., Best, T.A., Alvar, B.A., Micheli, L.J., Thomas, D.P., Hatfield, D.L., Cronin, J.B. and Myer, G.D. (2015a) 'Long-term athletic development, Part 1: A pathway for all youth,' *The Journal of Strength and Conditioning Research*, 29, 1439–1450.

Lloyd, R.S., Oliver, J.L., Faigenbaum, A.D., Howard, R., De Ste Croix, M.B.A., Williams, C.A., Best, T.A., Alvar, B.A., Micheli, L.J., Thomas, D.P., Hatfield, D.L., Cronin, J.B. and Myer, G.D (2015b) 'Long-term athletic development, part 2: Barriers to success and potential solutions,' *The Journal of Strength and Conditioning Research*, 29, 1451–1464.

López-Pastor, V.M., Kirk, D., Lorente-Catalán, E., MacPhail, A. and Macdonald, D. (2013) 'Alternative assessment in physical education: A review of international literature,' *Sport, Education and Society*, 18 (1), 57–76.

Lorente-Catalán, E. and Kirk, D. (2016) 'Student teachers' understanding and application of assessment for learning during a physical education teacher education course,' *European Physical Education Review*, 22 (1), 65–81.

Maiese, M. (2015) *Embodied Selves and Divided Minds* (International Perspectives in Philosophy and Psychology), Oxford: Oxford University Press.

Maiese, M. and Hanna, R. (2020) *The Mind-Body Politic*, Cham, Switzerland: Palgrave Macmillan.

Marsden, E. (2010) 'Observation of pupils in PE,' in S. Capel and M. Whitehead (eds.) *Learning to Teach Physical Education in the Secondary School: A Companion to School Experience* (3rd edition), Abingdon: Routledge, pp. 46–60.

Marshall, S.J. and Welk, G.J. (2008) 'Definitions and measurement,' in A.L. Smith and S.J.H. Biddle (eds.) *Youth Physical Activity and Sedentary Behavior*, Champaign, Il.: Human Kinetics, pp. 3–29.

Maslow, A.H. (1943) 'Theory of human motivation,' *Psychological Review*, 50, 370–396.

Maslow, A.H. (1970) *Motivation and Personality* (2nd edition), New York: Harper and Row.

McClelland, D.C. (1961) *The Achieving Society*, Princeton, NJ: Van Norstrand.

McLellan, R. (2022) 'Motivating pupils,' in S. Capel, M. Leask, S. Younie, E. Hidson and J. Lawrence (eds.) *Learning to Teach in the Secondary School: A Companion to School Experience* (9th edition), Abingdon: Routledge, pp. 152–170.

Merleau-Ponty, M. (1962) *Phenomenology of Perception* (trans by C. Smith), New York: Routledge.

Ministry of Education Singapore (2016) *Physical Education Teaching & Learning Syllabus Primary, Secondary & Pre-University*, available at: www.moe.gov.sg/-/media/files/post-secondary/syllabuses/pe/physical_education_syllabus_2014.ashx (accessed 1 April 2023).

Mosston, M. and Ashworth, S. (2002) *Teaching Physical Education* (5th edition), Boston, MA: Benjamin Cummings.

Moura, A., Graça, A., MacPhail, A. and Batista, P. (2021) 'Aligning the principles of assessment for learning to learning in physical education: A review of literature,' *Physical Education and Sport Pedagogy*, 26, 388–401.

Muller, J. and Young, M. (2019) 'Knowledge, power and powerful knowledge re-visited,' *The Curriculum Journal*, 30, 196–214.

Murdoch, E. (2004) 'NCPE 2000 – where are we so far?' in S. Capel (ed.) *Learning to Teach Physical Education in the Secondary School: A Companion to School Experience* (2nd edition), Abingdon: Routledge, pp. 280–300.

Murdoch, E. and Whitehead, M. (2010) 'Physical literacy, fostering the attributes and curriculum planning,' in M. Whitehead (ed.) *Physical Literacy Through the Lifecourse*, Abingdon: Routledge, pp. 175–188.

Murdoch, E. and Whitehead, M. (2013) 'What should pupils learn in physical education?' in S. Capel and M. Whitehead (eds.) *Debates in Physical Education*, Abingdon: Routledge, pp. 55–73.

Newton, A. and Bowler, M. (2021) 'Assessment for and of learning in physical education' in S. Capel, J. Cliffe and J. Lawrence (eds.) *Learning to Teach Physical Education in the Secondary School: A Companion to School Experience* (5th edition), Abingdon: Routledge, pp. 144–160.

Newton, D.P. (2023) *A Practical Guide to Teaching Science in the Secondary School* (2nd edition), Abingdon: Routledge.

Nicholls, J.G. (1984) 'Achievement motivation: Conceptions of ability, subjective experience, task choice and performance,' *Psychological Review*, 91 (3), 328–346.

Nicholls, J.G. (1989) *The Competitive Ethos and Democratic Education*, Cambridge, MA: Harvard University Press.

Nixon, J., Martin, J., McKeown, P. and Ranson, S. (1996) *Encouraging Learning: Towards a Theory of the Learning School*, Buckingham: Open University Press.

Ntoumanis, N. (2001) 'A self-determination approach to the understanding of motivation in physical education,' *The British Journal of Educational Psychology*, 71, 225–242.

Nussbaum, M.C. (2000) *Women and Human Development: The Capabilities Approach*, Cambridge: Cambridge University Press.

Ofsted (Office for Standards in Education, Children's Services and Skills) (2018) *An Investigation into how to Assess the Quality of Education through Curriculum Intent, Implementation and Impac*t, London: Crown Copyright, available at: https://assets.publishing.service.gov.uk/media/5fb3e55fe90e07208fd2cb85/Curriculum_research_How_to_assess_intent_and_ implementation_of_curriculum_191218.pdf (accessed 26 August 2024).

Ofsted (Office for Standards in Education, Children's Services and Skills) (2022) *Research and Analysis Research Review Series: PE*, published 18 March 2022, available at: www.gov.uk/government/publications/research-review-series-pe/research-review-series-pe#fn:1 (accessed 9 February 2024).

Ofsted (Office for Standards in Education, Children's Services and Skills) (2023) *Levelling the Playing Field: The Physical Education Subject Report Published 20 September 2023*, available at: www.gov.uk/government/publications/subject-report-series-pe/levelling-the-playing-field-the-physical-education-subject-report (accessed 22 March 2024).

Oxford Advanced Learners Dictionary (n.d.) *Progress*, available at: https://www.oxfordlearnersdictionaries.com/definition/english/progress_1 (accessed 27 July 2024).

Oxford Advanced Learners Dictionary (n.d.) *Progression*, available at: www.oxfordlearnersdictionaries.com/definition/english/progression (accessed 16 March 2023).

Oxford Learners Dictionary (n.d.) *Attitudes*, available at: www.oxfordlearnersdictionaries.com/definition/english/attitude?q=attitude (accessed 3 April 2024).

Oxford Learners Dictionary (n.d.) *Emotions*, available at: www.oxfordlearnersdictionaries.com/definition/english/emotion?q=Emotions (accessed 3 April 2024).

Oxford Learners Dictionary (n.d.) *Feelings*, available at: www.oxfordlearnersdictionaries.com/definition/english/feeling (accessed 3 April 2024).

Pavlov, I.P. (1927) *Conditioned Reflexes: An Investigation of the Physiological Activity of the Vertebral Cortex*, London: Oxford University Press.

Penney, D., Brooker, R., Hay, P. and Gillespie, L. (2009) 'Curriculum, pedagogy and assessment: Three message systems of schooling and dimensions of quality physical education,' *Sport, Education and Society*, 14 (4), 421–442.

Petrie, K., Penney, D. and Fellows, S. (2014) 'Health and physical education in Aotearoa New Zealand: An open market and open doors?' *Asia-Pacific Journal of Health, Sport and Physical Education*, 5, 19–38.

Piaget, J. (1962) *Judgement and Reasoning in the Child*, London: Routledge and Kegan Paul.

Pickard, A. and Maude, P. (2021) *Teaching Physical Education Creatively* (2nd edition), Abingdon: Routledge.

Placek, J.H. (1983) 'Conceptions of success in teaching: Busy, happy and good?' in T.J. Templin and J.K. Olson (eds.) *Teaching in Physical Education*, Champaign, IL: Human Kinetics, pp. 46–56.

Priestley, M. (2019) 'Curriculum: Concepts and approaches,' *Impact*, 6 (summer), 5–8.

Public Health England (2022) *Physical Activity: Applying all our Health,* available at: www.gov.uk/ government/publications/physical-activity-applying-all-our-health/physical-activity-apply ing-all-our-health#why-promote-physical-activity-in-your-professional-practice (accessed 1 April 2023).

QCA (Qualifications and Curriculum Authority) (2007) *Physical Education Programme of Study,* London: QCA.

Quennerstedt, M. (2019) 'Healthying physical education – on the possibility of learning health,' *Physical Education and Sport Pedagogy,* 24, 1–15.

Richards, K.A.R. and Gaudreault, K.L. (2017) (eds.) *Teacher Socialization in Physical Education: New Perspectives,* New York: Routledge.

Richards, K.A.R., Iannucci, C., McEvoy, E. and Simonton, A. (2020) 'The professional socialization challenge: Teacher education for a preferable future for physical education,' in A. MacPhail and H.A. Lawson (eds.) *School Physical Education and Teacher Education: Redesign for the 21st Century,* New York: Routledge, pp. 70–81.

Rink, J.E. (1985) *Teaching Physical Education for Learning,* St Louis, MO: Times Mirror/Mosby College Publishing.

Rink, J.E. (2009) *Teaching Physical Education for Learning* (6th edition), New York: McGraw-Hill Education.

Rosenshine, B. (2012) 'Principles of instruction: Research based strategies that all teachers should know,' *American Educator,* 36 (1, Spring), 12–19, 39.

Rosenthal, R. and Jacobson, L. (1968) *Pygmalion in the Classroom,* New York: MSS Modular Publications.

Ryan, R.M. and Deci, E.L. (2000) 'Self-determination theory and the facilitation of intrinsic motivation, self-development, and well-being,' *American Psychologist,* 55 (1), 68–78

Sartre, J.P. (1957) *Being and Nothingness* (Trans H. Barnes), London: Methuen.

Shea, J.B. and Morgan, R.L. (1979) 'Contextual interference effects on the acquisition, retention, and transfer of a motor skill,' *Journal of Experimental Psychology: Human Learning and Memory,* 5, 179–187.

Siedentop, D. (2002) 'Content knowledge for physical education,' *Journal of Teaching in Physical Education,* 21, 368–377.

Simón-Chico, L., González-Peño, A., Hernández-Cuadrado, E., and Franco, E. (2023) 'The impact of a challenge-based learning experience in physical education on students' motivation and engagement,' *European Journal Investigating Health, Psychology and Education,* 13, 684–700, doi: 10.3390/ejihpe13040052, available at: https://pubmed.ncbi.nlm.nih.gov/37185905/ (accessed 24 April 2024).

Simonson, M. and Maushak, N. (2001) 'Instructional technology and attitude change,' in D. Jonassen (ed.) *Handbook of Research for Educational Communications and Technology,* Mahway, NJ: Lawrence Erlbaum Associates, pp. 984–1016.

Simpson, E.J. (1972) *The Classification of Educational Objectives: The Psychomotor Domain* (Volume 3), Washington, DC: Gryphon House.

Skinner, B.F. (1938) *The Behavior of Organisms: An Experimental Analysis,* New York: Appleton-Century.

Skinner, B.F. (1953) *Science and Human Behaviour,* New York: Macmillan.

Smith, P.L. and Ragan, T.J. (1999) *Instructional Design,* New York: John Wiley & Sons.

Sport England (2015) *This Girl Can,* available at: www.sportengland.org/funds-and-campaigns/this-girl-can (accessed 1 April 2023).

Sport England (2019) *We are Undefeatable,* available at: www.sportengland.org/funds-and-campai gns/we-are-undefeatable (accessed 1 April 2023).

Sport England (2020) *Join the Movement,* available at: www.sportengland.org/news/join-movement (accessed 1 April 2023).

Sport England (2022a) *Active Lives Adult Survey November 2020–21 Report,* available at: https:// sportengland-production-files.s3.eu-west-2.amazonaws.com/s3fs-public/2022-04/Act ive%20Lives%20Adult%20Survey%20November%2020-21%20Report.pdf?VersionId=nPU_ v3jFjwG8o_xnv62FcKOdEiVmRWCb (accessed 1 April 2023).

Sport England (2022b) *Active Lives Children and Young People Survey Academic Year 2020-21 Report*, available at: https://sportengland-production-files.s3.eu-west-2.amazonaws.com/s3fs-public/2022-12/Active%20Lives%20Children%20and%20Young%20People%20Survey%20Academic%20Year%202021-22%20Report.pdf?VersionId=R5_hmJHw5M4yKFsewm2vGDMRGHWW7q3E (accessed 1 April 2023).

Sport England (2023) *Secondary Teacher Training Programme: Support for Teachers in Secondary Schools to Access Professional Development Opportunities and Put Pupils' Enjoyment at the Heart of PE and School Sport*, available at: https://www.sportengland.org/guidance-and-support/secondary-teacher-training-programme (accessed 20 April 2024).

Stenhouse, L. (1976) *An Introduction to Curriculum Research and Development*, London: Heinemann Educational Books.

Stiggins, R. and Chappuis, J. (2005) 'Using student-involved classroom assessment to close achievement gaps,' *Theory into Practice*, 44 (1), 11-18.

Stiggins, R., Arter, J., Chappuis, J. and Chappuis, S. (2004) *Classroom Assessment for Student Learning: Doing It Right - Using It Well*, Portland, OR: Assessment Training Institute.

Sun, H., Li, W. and Shen, B. (2017) 'Learning in physical education: A self-determination theory perspective,' *Journal of Teaching in Physical Education*, 26, 277-291.

Thorndike, E.L. (1905) *The Elements of Psychology*, New York: A.G. Seiler.

Topping, K. (2005) 'Trends in peer learning,' *Educational Psychology*, 25, 631-645.

Tse Sheng, T (2022) 'You as the teacher: Teacher identify and how it relates to your philosophy of teaching,' in S. Capel, J. Lawrence, M. Martens and H. Abdul Rahman (eds.) *CPD for Teaching and Learning in Physical Education: Global Lessons from Singapore*, Abingdon: Routledge, pp. 149-168.

UNESCO (United Nations Educational, Scientific and Cultural Organisation) (2013) *Declaration of Berlin of the Fifth International Conference of Ministers and Senior Officials Responsible for Physical Education and Sport (MINEPS V)*, Berlin, Germany, 28-30 May 2013, p. 3, available at: https://unesdoc.unesco.org/ark:/48223/pf0000221114#:~:text=It%20focuses%20on%20developing%20physical,lifelong%20participation%20in%20physical%20activity (accessed 1 April 2023).

Utesch, T., Bardid, F., Büsch, D. and Strauss, B. (2019) 'The relationship between motor competence and physical fitness from early childhood to early adulthood: A meta-analysis,' *Sports Medicine*, 49, 541-551.

Vygotsky, L. (1978) *Mind in Society: The Development of Higher Psychological Processes*, (translated and edited by M. Cole, V. John-Steiner, S. Scribner and E. Souberman), Cambridge, MA: Harvard University Press.

Vygotsky, L.S. (1962) *Thought and Language*, Cambridge, MA: MIT Press.

Wallace, C. and Priestley, M. (2017) 'Secondary science teachers as curriculum makers: Mapping and designing Scotland's new Curriculum for Excellence,' *Journal of Research in Science Teaching*, 54 (3), 324-349.

Washburn, R. and Kolen, A. (2018) 'Children's self-perceived and actual motor competence in relation to their peers,' *Children*, June, 5 (6), 72, https://doi.org/10.3390/children5060072, available at: https://pubmed.ncbi.nlm.nih.gov/29890698/ (accessed 24 April 2024).

Weiner, B. (1972) *Theories of Motivation: From Mechanism to Cognition*, Chicago, IL: Markham.

Whitehead, M. (2010) *Physical Literacy Throughout the Lifecourse*, Abingdon: Routledge.

Whitehead, M. (2015) 'Learner-centred teaching: A physical literacy perspective,' in S. Capel and M. Whitehead (eds.) *Learning to Teach Physical Education in the Secondary School: A Companion to School Experience* (4th edition), Abingdon: Routledge, pp. 171-183.

Whitehead, M. (ed.) (2019) *Physical Literacy across the World*, Abingdon: Routledge.

Whitehead, M. (2021a) 'Aims of physical education,' in S. Capel, J. Cliffe and J. Lawrence (eds.) *Learning to Teach Physical Education in the Secondary School* (5th edition), Abingdon: Routledge, pp. 20-35.

Whitehead, M. (2021b) 'Learner-centred teaching: A physical literacy perspective,' in S. Capel, J. Cliffe and J. Lawrence (eds.) *Learning to Teach Physical Education in the Secondary School: A Companion to School Experience* (5th edition), Abingdon: Routledge, pp. 227-240.

WHO (World Health Organisation) (2022) *Physical Activity*, available at: www.who.int/news-room/fact-sheets/detail/physical-activity (accessed 11 May 2024).

Wiliam, D. (2015) 'Designing great hinge questions,' *Educational Leadership: Journal of the Department of Supervision and Curriculum Development*, 73, 40–44.

Williams, H., Pfeiffer, K., O'Neill, J., Dowda, M., McIver, K., Brown, W. and Pate, R. (2008) 'Motor skill performance and physical activity in preschool children,' *Obesity*, 16, 1421–1426.

Williams, O., Wiltshire, G. and Gibson, K. (2021) 'Health inequalities: How and why physical education can help and hinder the equity agenda,' in J. Stirrup and O. Hooper (eds.) *Critical Pedagogies in Physical Education Physical Activity and Health*, Abingdon: Routledge, pp. 170–183.

Wilson, V. (2014) 'Examining teacher education through cultural historical activity theory,' *Teacher Education Advancement Network (TEAN) Journal*, 6 (1), 20–29.

Wood, D., Bruner, J.S. and Ross, G. (1976) 'The role of tutoring in problem solving,' *Journal of Child Psychology, Psychiatry, and Applied Disciplines*, 17, 89–100.

Wright, S., McNeill, M., Fry, J. and Wang, J. (2005) 'Teaching teachers to play and teach games,' *Physical Education and Sport Pedagogy*, 10, 61–82.

Yong, M. (2022) 'Assessing student's progress formatively,' in S. Capel, J. Lawrence, M. Martens and H. Abdul Rahman (eds.) *CPD for Teaching and Learning in Physical Education: Global Lessons from Singapore*, Abingdon: Routledge, pp. 110–129.

YST (Youth Sport Trust) (2023a) *Girls Active National Report*, Loughborough: Youth Sport Trust, available at: www.youthsporttrust.org/research-listings/research/girls-active-national-reports (accessed 14 March 2024).

YST (Youth Sport Trust) (2023b) *PE and School Sport. The Annual Report 2023,* Loughborough: YST, available at: www.youthsporttrust.org/media/5bcgx4kh/yst_pe_school_sport_report_2023_final_revd.pdf (accessed 14 March 2024).

YST (Youth Sport Trust) (2024) *Improving Children and Young People's Wellbeing and Achievement: A Manifesto for Action Shaped by Leading Voices from Education, Sport, Physical Activity and Health and Wellbeing*, available at: www.youthsporttrust.org/media/qyupy4vo/yst_manifesto_2024_final_revb_digital.pdf (accessed 22 April 2024).

AUTHOR INDEX

SUBJECT INDEX